JACKAROO

Following his years as a jackaroo, Michael Thornton began writing for *The Terang Express* and *The Pastoral Review*, and later for *The Weekly Times*. He was also published in *The Bulletin* and more recently wrote a regular column in a local country paper, *The Alexandra Standard*, on the vicissitudes of small-acre farming. Michael has also published a book on fundraising in the education sector, and is Director of Advancement at the Melbourne Business School.

www.michaelthorntonbooks.com

JACKAROO

A Memoir

MICHAEL THORNTON

VIKING
an imprint of
PENGUIN BOOKS

VIKING

Published by the Penguin Group
Penguin Group (Australia)
250 Camberwell Road, Camberwell, Victoria 3124, Australia
(a division of Pearson Australia Group Pty Ltd)
Penguin Group (USA) Inc.
375 Hudson Street, New York, New York 10014, USA
Penguin Group (Canada)
90 Eglinton Avenue East, Suite 700, Toronto, Canada ON M4P 2Y3
(a division of Pearson Penguin Canada Inc.)
Penguin Books Ltd
80 Strand, London WC2R 0RL England
Penguin Ireland
25 St Stephen's Green, Dublin 2, Ireland
(a division of Penguin Books Ltd)
Penguin Books India Pvt Ltd
11 Community Centre, Panchsheel Park, New Delhi – 110 017, India
Penguin Group (NZ)
67 Apollo Drive, Rosedale, North Shore 0632, New Zealand
(a division of Pearson New Zealand Ltd)
Penguin Books (South Africa) (Pty) Ltd
24 Sturdee Avenue, Rosebank, Johannesburg 2196, South Africa

Penguin Books Ltd, Registered Offices: 80 Strand, London, WC2R 0RL, England

First published by Penguin Group (Australia), 2011

10 9 8 7 6 5 4 3 2 1

Cover and Text Design by Cathy Larsen © Penguin Group (Australia)
Cover images: 'The Catcher' by Stephen Permezel, Landscape by The Right Image/Wildlight,
Cattle Grazing by Rob Cleary/Wildlight
Typeset in 11/16pt Sabon Roman by Sunset Publishing Services, Brisbane, Queensland
Printed and bound in Australia by McPherson's Printing Group, Maryborough, Victoria

National Library of Australia
Cataloguing-in-Publication data:

Thornton, Michael.
Jackaroo : a memoir / Michael Thornton.
ISBN: 9780670075782 (pbk.)
Thornton, Michael.
Jackeroos–Australia–Biography.
Country life–Australia.
Ranches–Australia.

338.10994

penguin.com.au

To Richard and Mel,
and in loving memory of Jamie

Contents

Prologue

I haven't a clue what to expect when I shake hands with the future Prime Minister. But I'm experienced now – so different to how I was four years ago, when I started as a jackaroo – and I'm sure I can withstand whatever grilling Mr Fraser gives me.

It's Christmas Eve 1970. I've arrived at Nareen via Birregurra – a minor town south of Colac, on the edge of Victoria's lush Western District – where two hours ago I sat wedged in a lumpy chair opposite a pair of ancient twin sisters, sipping tea in an equally ancient farmhouse full of damp and old-people smells. The sisters had made one of three replies to a 'Position Wanted: Senior Jackaroo' advertisement I ran in *Stock & Land* before I escaped Queensland's depressing drought, which was followed by even more devastating floods. The first reply to the ad, so Mum said when I phoned from Brisbane to ask if I'd had any bites, was from a pastoral company in the Riverina, but it's one of those huge outfits with a dozen testosterone-charged boys at a time. At twenty-one, I can't be bothered competing in another teenage hothouse, with unhappy memories of boarding school still fresh. Yesterday, on my way down the Hume Highway I phoned the manager at Jerilderie to say thanks-but-no-thanks.

The old ladies had sat in matching rockers and, well, rocked. Sporting matching outfits and hairdos, they spun me matching stories. The women didn't want a jackaroo, they quickly confessed;

they wanted me to manage what they promised was still a thriving soldier settlement farm. Repeating each other's story of woes word for word in case I missed it the first time, they explained that their brother – the soldier – had died two years ago, and last month the chap they replaced him with to keep the fat lambs churning out had been carted off to a nursing home. As healthy as Birregurra's lambs appeared, it seemed the human flock was on its last legs.

Even though I know nothing about raising fat lambs – my experience is with beef cattle and wool growing Merinos – at such a young age I concede I'm chuffed by the old ladies' offer of manager. Especially when the sweet things have said they'll pay me whatever I want, within reason of course.

Yet the thought of working for the famous Malcolm Fraser MHR, and the doors which that might open, appeals more. Call it what you like – ego, pretentiousness, snobbery – but I want Mr Fraser, a politician-farmer admired by millions of Australians, to offer me the job. Indeed, since Mum told me he'd rung about the ad, I've begun to crave his endorsement. What an opportunity it would be to learn from a man who has accomplished so much in life – and still only forty years of age.

To find Nareen, I bear right off the Glenelg Highway at Coleraine and climb north over never-ending rolling hills, each swank farm entrance indicating another Western District dynasty – all thanks to great-grandpa, who got off a boat from England, scattered a few surveyors' pegs, and only later under pressure paid a pittance for what today is worth millions.

Thirty kilometres on, I come to the hamlet of Nareen, no more than a community hall and a tennis court with thistles serving off the baselines. Finally, on the next hill I find the nameplate that whispers to me that I've reached my destination – NAREEN – home to easily Australia's most famous farmer. Peering in, yet pausing to let it soak in, I'm struck by the twin rows of pine trees that stretch along a driveway leading to goodness-knows-where, possibly heaven itself.

It beckons a game jackaroo to try his luck.

The boy in me wonders what protection the Minister for Defence gets. Snipers? Either there aren't any, or they're well-concealed.

Ignorant on matters of national security, I focus on what I do know: agriculture.

Paddocks either side of me boast metre-high, browned-off pasture that sways in the hot northerly breeze. Then I catch sight of a porcelain insulator fixed to a solid fence post, indicating a modern farming practice I've not experienced – yet the kind of thing to impress any boy still to suffer the indignant and painful sting that comes from inadvertently touching a live electric fence wire and getting 2000 volts up his bony arse.

In the paddock on my left, lanky Corriedale ewes graze a strip of green pasture, cut again since the recent haymaking, and for a moment I wonder why the second cut, until I see the telltale windsock. Even a perfectly maintained airstrip for planes to come and go. Wow! We get to fly, I think, excitedly, naively, but again typical for a boy. On my right, under shade of overhanging cypress branches, a clutch of Hereford bulls laze, each with his impressive manhood flopped immodestly over his lower leg down to the dirt below.

Still with minutes to go before my midday appointment with Mr Fraser, I slow my treasured ute. A good ute is a badge of honour for any self-respecting jackaroo. I bought mine, a 1964 HR series Holden, at Mortlake a year ago – light blue, tinted upper windscreen, wide tyres, the body lowered to tell anyone it passes (including the occasional eager cop) that its driver definitely isn't someone to be messed with.

I pass a house, its size and the assortment of upturned kids' toys littering the lawn telling me it probably belongs to a farmhand. I'm not far off – it turns out to be the overseer's home.

Moving on – as my nerve ends begin to swell – the drive gives way to a clearing, clearly the working hub of Nareen, with three more workmen's cottages and in the foreground a stand-alone bungalow, which I later learn is the jackaroos' quarters. How many jackaroos the Frasers cram in there I have no idea.

On my right I spy the obligatory woolshed and sheep yards, while on my left, slightly down the hill sits an unusually shaped, imposing building with a corrugated-iron roof that begins at ground level on one side and curves all the way over the top and down to the ground on the other. Once an army Quonset, I'll discover it houses the mechanic's workshop plus an assortment of tractors and motorbikes, most in working order, some kept for parts.

With seconds to go, my adrenalin fairly pumping given I'm about to shake hands with a man more famous than anyone I've ever seen, let alone met face-to-face – and for a formal job inter-view at that – I crawl across a cattle grid onto a perfectly kept, yet narrow, scoria driveway, little wider than a garden path. I don't know if I should be driving on it or out raking it. Maybe I should have parked my ute back at the sheds . . . Ah, what the heck – better to feign a look of daring than come across as a total wimp. Like the bulls loitering along the driveway, a jackaroo needs to show a prospective employer he has balls.

Nareen's overflowing garden is in full summer bloom. Abundant camellias spew bulk colour, even if their woody stems do scratch the sides of my precious ute as I inch my way past. The garden then opens to a clearing with a four-door garage at the rear. And here, with wash cloth in one hand and garden hose in the other, wearing white moleskin trousers tucked neatly into tall black gumboots, stands the Honourable Member for Wannon beside a gleaming BMW.

Hang on. Don't VIPs have staff to do crap chores like this? But then, maybe Mr Fraser's reason for wanting a new jackaroo is staring me in the face, menial tasks being part of the deal for someone like me on farming's bottom rung. And where's the government car, the big, black Ford LTD that ministers have on call, and the peak-capped driver dressed in black who comes with it? Where are they? That's what a boy has come all this way to see, isn't it? Yet, finding the VIP washing his car gives me heart – as if my potential employer is no different to me after all. Except he has a high-number Beemer and all I've got is a cheap Holden ute. I guess a jackaroo needs to know his place.

I park in front of one of two closed garage doors, grab my jacket off the seat next to me and take a deep breath before climbing out. Showtime!

'Good morning,' says Mr Fraser, authoritatively, tossing the chamois in the bucket. Huge fear instantly envelops me. Suddenly, I feel totally and completely out of my depth. Me, a scrawny 21-year-old jackaroo; the man I'm facing up to, so successful, accomplished . . . powerful.

I hear Mum's voice telling me to stand up straight, look Mr Fraser in the eye, and speak slowly.

'Good – morning – Mr – Fraser,' I reply as I approach, but only after I force a cough so my still unreliable voice doesn't crack and have me look like a girl. I think I just did okay separating the words. Somehow, I force myself to brush aside my incredible nervousness and set about getting the eye thing right. I notice we're the same height, something over six-foot-four, except Mr Fraser is shorter than me in the legs and longer in the body. Plus, I'm stuck with the build of a garden rake.

'Have a good drive?' Mr Fraser asks, casting one last eye over his shiny vehicle.

'Yes – thank – you,' I reply. My mind jumps to the old dears at

Birregurra who right now are hoping this interview, which I was finally forced to declare as an excuse to escape their claws, is a disaster. I've been thinking how I might weave their offer of manager into this discussion. Isn't that how one's supposed to play it at an interview – use whatever it takes to land the job?

'So,' Mr Fraser asks as we shake hands, 'for whom have you worked previously?'

Yes! The perfect question.

'Dick Webb at Habbies Howe,' I reply.

These are five words guaranteed to get me a job on any farm of note. Indeed, they've already earned me two positions. I see no need to tell Mr Fraser how on my third day at Habbies Howe I resigned, wrecked and terrified, yet because no one would drive me into town, I stayed the year. The fact that I've just left a corporate Merino stud in south-west Queensland pales compared to having been a jackaroo for Dick Webb. Over five decades the grazier trained no less than eighty boys, three at a time. Almost all, we were told, went on to become top graziers. Two became diplomats. One larrikin, so people whispered with a hand half covering their mouth, became a full-on renegade; no one dared speak his name in public. One loser lasted just one day.

Habbies Howe's reputation as a tough school for jackaroos is legendary.

Without another word Mr Fraser turns and begins to stride along the garden path towards the homestead. Not knowing what I'm meant to do, I follow.

At the veranda he turns right into what appears to be an office and closes the door behind him, leaving me standing on the porch. With no one else around, I peek around the corner. I see a massive front lawn and for a second wonder whose job it is to mow the thing. Derr.

Moments later, Mr Fraser emerges from the office. 'Mr Webb's in Adelaide,' he says, closing the door after him. That'd be right; my mentor is never home when I need him. Mr Fraser certainly executed the reference check quickly. Did the Minister for Defence do a Maxwell Smart and dial a secret number, look both ways, then whisper down the line, 'Get me Dick Webb at Habbies Howe. Immediately!'? Maybe *I'll* get to use the secret phone.

Then he does something weird. After saying, 'I'll call him later and let you know', he enters the house proper and closes the door, again leaving me on the veranda. Alone.

What do I do? I mean, I've just driven four-and-a-half hours from Melbourne for an interview for which I've carefully rehearsed all the way from Queensland, and within seconds it's over. Was that the interview? Also, it's stinking hot standing on the airless porch.

The door re-opens. 'Would you like to join us for lunch?' Mrs Fraser asks, with her famous smile.

'Thank you, Mrs Fraser.' I bet she scolded the Cabinet Minister good and proper for leaving the boy standing at the door. Or did she? What if I'd walked away? But maybe this is how it works in Establishment circles, with interviews being more about testing common sense than answering boring questions about past experience. A far better way to do things, I promptly decide. But not for very long.

I'm ushered down the hallway and into the dining room. Mr Fraser stands at the sideboard.

'Would you like a beer?' he asks, holding forth a tempting, ice-cold can of Foster's.

It's a hot day. 'Thank you,' I answer, before realising how it must be part of the test, in this case to see if I'm an alcoholic like my dead father. Has ASIO already told him I'm from a broken home, that my father toppled to his death over the balcony of a St Kilda hotel when I was thirteen? Does the Minister know everything there is to know about our family's dark side? Or am I indulging myself far too much?

The can comes without a glass, and the fact that Mr Fraser doesn't get himself a drink makes me feel even more out of sorts. Yes, it definitely seems part of the test, and one which right now I'm failing very badly.

Four junior Frasers enter the room, like official judges filing into an Olympic swimming pool. The eighth place at the table is taken by Mr Fraser's mother, who sits on my left. What to do with the stupid beer can? The polished table looks far too posh for it. Damn it, I put it down anyway. Surely a D-minus for that. Hey, I only want to work on the man's farm – I'm not applying to be Minister for Etiquette.

And have a guess what they serve for lunch, with the four children scrutinising my every action – spaghetti, the most impossible-to-gather-up food known to mankind. (Jackaroo Employment Manual, Step 4: Food To Test Them With.) As I struggle to capture slippery strands on my fork, eight young eyes rise and fall with my every forkful. Any moment I quite expect the smallest Fraser to hold up a score card and give me a miserable one out of ten. The elder son grins at me, and I'm tempted to fling a forkful of spaghetti fair at him, like the more daring boys at boarding school did.

'Michael,' says Mrs Fraser, grabbing everyone's attention. 'You do know Mr Fraser went to Melbourne Grammar?'

Stupid, stupid, stupid me. If ever there is a day not to wear my old school tie, today is it. It's Mum's fault. We argued about it before I left home this morning, but snob that she is, she made me put it on, along with a dark blue shirt, moleskin trousers so heavily starched they could run Nareen on their own, and a brown sports jacket. She is oblivious to the fierce rivalry that exists between my school and Mr Fraser's. How does the chant at the Head of the River go? *If you can't get a girl / Get a Melbourne Grammar boy.*

This doesn't seem quite the moment to repeat the verse, especially when the opposition is a prospective employer – and a pretty powerful one at that. Besides, his wife mightn't be too impressed with the tone of it.

I want to crawl under the table. Wearing my school tie is my second mistake after accepting the stupid can of beer and being the lone drinker in the dining room. At times like this, I decide, big white linen serviettes are more for hiding a blushing face than wiping away recalcitrant spaghetti sauce.

For the remainder of the meal I sit silently, feeling utterly alone, wishing it will end or that I'll just drop dead. Yet, despite my woeful performance over lunch I know it will be Dick Webb's reference that will decide my fate. I drive back to Melbourne praying my old boss will say nice things about me, now that becoming a jackaroo at Nareen is my life's foremost goal.

Mr Fraser phones on Boxing Day and asks me to start on Monday week – 4 January 1971.

For Mum, all the kerfuffle about my having quit the family wool-buying firm – and thus having spat the silver spoon from my mouth – is suddenly history. All is forgiven. Having a son who works for none less than Australia's Minister for Defence has to be the best thing to have happened to her since getting past the first round at Wimbledon in 1938.

Boy, does Mum have something to brag about when the bridge fours resume in the New Year.

PART ONE

Habbies Howe

1

School

It's the period before recess – Year Nine double English – and a master comes and drags me out of class to take a phone call, which never happens at boarding school unless someone has died.

It's Mum's voice on the line. 'Your father died yesterday,' she announces without further ado. 'Fell over the balcony of the George Hotel in St Kilda.'

I stand with the phone to my ear, but I don't say anything. I couldn't care less. I'm reading the names of boys on the lists on the office wall next to the phone.

Mum persists. 'Once an alcoholic, always an alcoholic,' she says.

This means nothing to me. I don't even know what being an alcoholic means.

'He only had one kidney,' she continues. I don't understand what that means either, so I let it go too. A kidney's a kidney, isn't it?

'So?' I reply, eventually. She could have saved this up for the holidays for all it interests me.

'I also ought to tell you that after your father left us, he re-married – and had another son.'

Well, there's some news. So, he started a new family? I go back to class wondering why he'd do that when he'd had such little interest in doing it the first time. Maybe he hated having a son who's called 'Unco' all the time. Thought he'd try again.

I'm not looking forward to recess because I know boys will tease me. Because I'm a weakling. And because when I came back from answering the phone, I wasn't crying, like someone is meant to if their father has just died. They wouldn't understand that my father means nothing to me.

I'm thirteen, and boarding school and I don't click. Yet I'm told I'm privileged.

'Privilege' is a word that gets used a lot here by masters and the headmaster. We're privileged, we're told, because we go to the best school in Australia, and because our families pay a lot of money for us to come here. We're privileged, we're told, because we get to do lots of stuff, like sport and PE, and because we get to use the library. But I'm useless at sport and pathetic at schoolwork, so the privilege thing doesn't apply to me.

Nothing important at boarding school applies to me.

The masters also say I'm privileged because I'm in the choir, even though the other boys bash me for it and call me a poofter. Chapel here is formal: we dress up in a red cassock, which looks like a dress because it goes right to the floor. If you're not careful you can trip yourself up in it. Over the red cassock we wear a white surplice, which on short kids looks really stupid because it stops at their ankles. We process down the aisle while we sing the first hymn. I hate processing because the scabs in the pews call out nasty things as I pass by. Even though I sing really loudly I still hear them call out names like 'fairy' and 'loser' and 'poofter', and I can't wait to get to the safety of the choir stalls up the front. But I like singing, especially last year when we did Haydn's *Creation*. It starts really softly, with us choristers whispering, '*And God said, Let there be light*'. And then comes, '*And there was LIGHT*', where we yell the second 'light'. During rehearsal, the boy in the orchestra on the cymbals was meant to clang them hard enough to wake up Ballarat. But the kid was far too timid for the choir-master Mr Barlow's liking. He climbed down from his organ seat and stormed over, his black gown swirling behind him. He grabbed the cymbals from the kid and said, 'Not like that, silly boy. Like *this* . . .' And he clapped them together so hard the Air Force sent jets.

While the choir stalls might be my safe haven, the sports oval certainly is not. I keep asking myself why I am so different to other boys, who love to catch balls and are good at it. I'm not; I'm hope-less with balls. Which is strange, given my mother was captain of every ball sport at her school, and even played at Wimbledon, an achievement I get bashed up about at home all the time. (She got rubbed out in the second round in 1938.) But the teasing I get at home is nothing compared to the treatment I get here at school. The teasing I get here twists my stomach into a knot so tight. Like in the mornings when we have to line up naked for our cold shower. The bullies roll up their towels really tightly and use them to flick our bare bums, or worse, they aim for our dicks, which can really hurt if you've still got half a stiffy.

The masters have a way of remembering things that make us privileged, but I notice they never mention the food in this way. That's because the food here is a joke. Take the porridge, which comes with an island in the bowl. The island rises out from the centre, like an iceberg comes out of the sea. It's made of uncooked glug and whenever my bowl comes to me with an island, I dry retch. I can't help it. And the more I stare at my island the more I do it. I've seen boys do worse – they've spewed just from looking at theirs. But I don't spew; I just dry retch.

Some good things happen in the dining room, like when we won the rowing and to celebrate eighteen boys picked up their table and flipped it over with everything on it. They got caned for that. But mostly bad things happen. Like the other day at lunch when a boy sent his almost-untouched plate of silverside down to the slushies, because it was green and revolting and he couldn't bear to look at it. Frogley, his housemaster (not mine, thank God), saw the food being thrown out and made the slushies put it back on the boy's plate. It was sent back up to the kid and Frogley told him to eat it. The boy stared at his plate, which had his green silverside on it now as well as other boys' leftovers, and the poor kid spewed his guts across the entire table. It was gross and the whole dining room went quiet. Frogley was red-faced, but he stood his ground and made the boy put a piece of green silverside in his mouth, at which point the kid fainted. It's funny how some people, even masters, refuse to give in, even when it's clear to everyone that what they're doing is wrong.

It's funny, too, how no adult went up to Frogley and punched him. Lots of boys wanted to.

Sports days are the worst. Mum never comes, I think because she's ashamed I'm not in a team. I'm never in a team. I stand off to the side and watch as fathers and sons greet one another, shaking hands like grown men do. Or they have pretend fisticuffs, using open hands and hips. The fathers are strong men, tanned from working their farms. They wear tweed sports jackets with dark leather elbow pads and they have fresh stubble on their face by the time the chicken sandwiches come out for lunch. They all have big, broad shoulders and deep voices. Last sports day, I overheard one father, upon hearing about his son's achievement, say in a deep, approving voice, 'Well done, son.'

No one has ever said 'Well done, son' to me, chicken sandwiches or no chicken sandwiches. I've never shaken hands with a man who loves me. I've never touched a shaved face, or smelt aftershave close-up.

It's funny how God never makes boys who can sing *and* play football.

I know not all of my misery is caused by others. Once in Year Three I showed the art teacher what some awful boy did to another boy's drawing. The master went ape and kept everyone in after class. He waited two hours for the culprit to own up. But the boy didn't. He even thanked me twice in front of everyone for bringing it to his attention. I have to say whoever scribbled on the drawing did make it better, but I guess that wasn't the point. When finally I got home, I told Mum what had happened. She said it would have been far better for the boy to have owned up and taken his punishment like a man. It would have been the end of it, she said. At three o'clock the next morning, when I couldn't sleep any longer, I woke her and told her it was me. She said she'd thought as much all along. It must have been something I said. I certainly wasn't the most popular boy in class that day. But do you know what? It was the bit about 'like a man' that stuck.

Things just got worse. Four years ago, when I was in Year Five, I was sent on the Year Six end-of-year camp. The masters said I was being considered as a leader for our group the following year. Even now I don't understand why I got chosen. (I think they meant to take Thompson.) Me, a leader? They were so wrong and the camp was so bad. The Year Sixers hated me; they teased me and otherwise froze me out all week. I couldn't wait for it to end. Back home, I put on a brave face and told Mum the one good bit – the poem I learnt from the bigger boys. It went:

My bonnie lay over the ocean,
My bonnie lay over the sea,
My daddy lay over my mummy,
And that's how they had little me.

Well, did Mum go mental. I have no idea why. The next morning she stormed in to see Mr McMillan, the headmaster, and from that moment on everything about school turned bad for me. Camps were banned, and because of that, the treatment I got not only from the Year Six boys who were there with me, but the entire Fifth and Sixth Years, has continued to now.

By the time I got to Year Seven, my misery was pretty much permanent. It's like the bigger your body grows, the meaner people are to you. And now I'm in Year Nine it's still just as bad. I'm never included in anything, like when boys get together in a huddle and talk about nothing in particular, or ride their bike to the store for chocolate, I never get asked to go. Even when they decide to do something naughty, I'm never asked to join in.

The teacher who hates me most here is the PE master, Mr West. We call him 'Ikey'. Ikey labelled me a weakling the moment he set eyes on me. So what if I'm a puny waif? The man has enough muscles on him to make up for every waif who ever lived. He has bones behind his face that make his cheeks and jaw stick out further than God meant them to. He's what another boy's father calls a 'man's man', which I'm told means he's someone we should look up to. He's also what Mum calls a male role model, and she says the reason I've been sent to boarding school is to find male role models. Funny, but no one has ever explained to me exactly what a male role model is, or shown me, unless it has something to do with men hurting boys.

My worst moments with Ikey are in the gym, when he decides to punish us with his wooden horse. It's the same wooden horse as Steve McQueen used in *The Great Escape*. And here's something: Ikey always places the horse lengthways to make it harder for us weaklings to vault, regardless of how long he makes the run-up, or how fast we're going when we hit the springboard, or whether he grabs us and flings us beyond the stupid thing.

As bad as PE is for me, it is far, far worse for Jonathon Clifford, a short and chubby ginger-haired boy. Clifford breaks out in enough sweat to drown a dog whenever he hears the words 'gym', 'Ikey' or 'wooden horse'. It means the poor kid used to spend most of his days wringing wet and miserable. But he doesn't any more.

One cold winter's morning last year, Ikey lined us up at the far end of the gym while he stood beside his precious horse, about twenty yards away. Standing in line behind Clifford, both of us scared to death, I couldn't help but notice his shaking. He was petrified. To be honest, both of us were petrified, but Clifford was sweating and shaking.

At PE we wear regulation white shorts and sandshoes, while the colour of our tee-shirt is determined by the boarding house to which we belong. Clifford's house is brown, except on this day his shirt was a dark chocolate colour because of all his nervous sweat.

Shaking even more as his turn got closer, his neck glistened under the gym's bright lights. Sweat fell off him onto the floor, making it slippery for the rest of us in our rubber sandshoes.

I whispered 'Don't worry' over his shoulder. He turned and looked at me. It was then that I saw his eyes. They were white, and bulging like a King Charles spaniel's.

Clifford looked right through me, as if he was in a foreign country, or wishing he was.

Seconds later, it was his turn, and another dollop of his sweat hit the floor between us.

Down at the horse, Ikey stood with his feet firmly anchored a regulation twenty-two inches apart, his arms reaching high into the air ready to grab Clifford's flabby arm in his vice-like grip, to fling the poor kid across the horse, away to the far side. The power in Ikey's arms usually sees the likes of us weaklings land with a thump several yards past the horse, hopefully but never for sure on the ridiculously thin rubber mats. The routine serves no practical purpose for later life whatsoever – and to think our parents and grandparents pay for it through their noses.

I said a quiet prayer for my friend as he began his run-up, and soon Clifford was travelling faster than the train that takes us back to Melbourne for the holidays.

He hit the springboard with so much force that as high as Ikey tried to reach up and grab him, even making one of his pathetic little hops, he couldn't lay a finger on the boy. It was an amazing sight: Clifford was flying six feet above the wooden horse, sailing through the air like Superman but without the cape and studio sound effects. I so much wished he'd given Ikey a good drenching of sweat, or better still, wee, as he flew over him.

He landed on the third mat along – an amazing achievement when you think of it. But he didn't stop there. Clifford kept rolling and rolling until somehow he managed to roll onto his feet. He shot through the door at the far end of the gym and never came back to PE classes again.

Word got round that his father, a Qantas pilot, wrote a rude letter to the headmaster, and ever since Clifford has spent PE classes in the library, the lucky bastard.

'NEXT!' shouted Ikey, his face blank, apart from *Good riddance* smeared across his jaw. He'd just killed off another weakling. Like so many masters, Ikey seems far happier spending his time on able, sporty boys, and is happy to see – if not cause – the demise of us losers.

A few weeks after the Clifford incident, I had occasion to hand Ikey a note from the school doctor. The note asked that I be excused from PE due to a weak knee. I knew it wouldn't go down well. Ikey glared at me as he grabbed the paper from my hand. He read it while he made the rest of the class run laps of the gym. I stood in front of him, shivering, scared to death. It took him what seemed like forever, or maybe it just felt that way because the man is grizzly and at that moment my unimportant life was on hold.

'Weak knee, eh?' he roared. 'Like the rest of you.' He thrust the note at my chest, causing me to reel back and almost fall. Is this the man's man, the father-figure, the male role model I'm supposed to look up to, from whom I'm meant to learn manly ways?

Most masters hardly bother to write anything in my school reports. The ones who do, like my housemaster, get around my inadequacies by saying I'm a 'sensitive boy'. Something must stop them from writing what they really think.

And yet many years later I will come across my headmaster's autobiography, in which he writes: 'To be good at this school-mastering, you have to like the little swines.'

I'm sixteen, and in my final year at school. I'm over all the crap about privilege. My grandfather pays the school fees; I survive. It's as simple as that. I'm trying to get by in this jungle where only one thing counts: sporting ability.

Take rowing, which I tried last year. A big mistake as it turned out, even though I did have prior experience. My sister and I used to spend our summers rowing our small dinghy at Mt Eliza on Melbourne's Mornington Peninsula. And naturally, I believed I could row as well as, if not better than any other boy. Not so. I soon found full-on schoolboy rowing wasn't like mess-ing about in a dinghy at the seaside. But also – and I have to say this – I found the whole idea of being in a boat with seven other boys, plus another tiny one up the back to steer the thing, about as exciting as learning Latin verbs. So, I resigned from rowing. Of course, the coach's version of my leaving that sport differed to mine. He said I was a weakling and that I didn't 'pull a big enough puddle' (rowing speak), and that was why he threw me out of the top crew for our age group. (Masters never consider the psycho-logical scarring that comes from throwing a boy from a team for inadequacy.) It had nothing to do, he said, with me resigning. Well, bully for him.

So, at the end of last year, as soon as I got home for the holidays, I put plan B into effect.

I jumped on my bicycle, bathers and towel around my neck, and peddled to the local swimming pool. It would be my final chance before leaving school to prove myself good at a sport, any sport, to make my Wimbledon-playing mother treat me like a real boy.

So far in life, all I'd been, in terms of sport and just about everything else, was a loser.

After parking my bike at the door, I went inside, changed into my bathers and returned to the counter. I asked the lady if I could speak to a coach.

'That's Mr Donnet over there, with the whistle round his neck,' she said, pointing to a fit-looking older man in white shorts and white flannel shirt talking to a mother.

When my turn came, I took my chance. 'My name's Michael, sir. I want to learn breaststroke. Mum says she'll pay for the lessons if you'll teach me.'

Mr Donnet looked me up and down, and then said, 'Best get in the pool so we can see you swim.' He pointed to the water, although his eyes were supervising the whole pool.

For a moment, time froze. I stared at him. *You mean, you're letting me have a try?* is what I wanted to say. But I couldn't get the words out.

I threw my towel at a nearby chair and dived in, the water drowning my confusion. This, I told myself, was the most important moment of my life. I had to succeed, to impress. I was so sick of being called Unco, laughed at, told to go away, even told once to 'let a real boy do it'. I wanted so much to be equal with the sporty kids at school.

I swam with all my concentration. All I knew about

breaststroke was that you needed to stretch out your arms and get into a sweeping kind of rhythm using both arms and legs together, and get your body up and onto a plane without breaking the surface with your hands or feet, because if you broke the surface you got disqualified. It was something I loved to practise at the beach, but never in the school pool. In the sea I scooped up as much water as I could with my hands before pushing it behind me with my stick-like fingers locked tightly together, all the while getting right the pumping, frog-like action with my embarrassingly gangly legs.

After six laps, Mr Donnet called me from the water. I got out and went up to him, not concerned about fetching my towel. I stood in front of the man, shaking, not from cold or exhaustion but from nerves. Hoping against hope this adult wouldn't tell me to go away, I crossed my arms hard against my pathetic chest.

'Be here every day from seven 'til nine, and again from one to three,' he said. 'Every day. You can have Christmas Day off. Do you understand?'

'YES, SIR!' I shrieked, my heart pounding, tears welling. My shaking must have been obvious, probably the tears as well. But I didn't care. I'd never been happier in all my life.

And do you know what? Just as Mr Donnet finished speaking, he smiled at me. The man actually smiled at me. It was the first time any adult associated with any kind of sport had done so. My brain was frozen with shock – and excitement. I stared back at my new coach, not believing what he'd just said.

'Now get back in the water and do another thirty laps,' he said. Another smile.

He must have known how at that very moment he had made one skinny boy's life. He turned away only to look back at me over his shoulder as I was about to jump in the water again, and called out, 'Don't forget to be back here at one o'clock.'

For the next seven weeks all I did was swim–eat–sleep,

swim–eat–sleep. I went to bed each night at seven o'clock and got up at six. I dreamt swimming. I became like a machine and loved every moment of it. The one disappointment was Christmas Day, when I rode to the pool with my bathers and towel, but it was locked.

Arriving back at school, I have two problems. First, there are just two Open Breaststroke events in the inter-school competition – the 50 and 100 yards – and already there are two popular boys who've not only been members of the swimming team all through school, but any day now they're likely to be named school prefects. So the pair are natural favourites with the master in charge of the sport and almost unbeatable. Any chance I have of making the swimming team and representing my school at something – at last – lies with swimming faster than one, or better still, both boys.

The other problem – and I think you might have guessed it – is that the master in charge of swimming is . . . none other than Mr Ivan 'Ikey' West.

I've not told anyone about my secret training regime with Coach Donnet, basically because there's no one and nothing to tell. The only thing that will count at the trials is who comes first, not how you get there. I do, however, have another secret: 'Freckles'. His real name is Steven, another breaststroker under Mr Donnet's coaching at the Armadale pool. And here's the bit that really hurts: this freckly, baby-faced, cheeky kid, who's eighteen months younger than me and forty centimetres shorter, swims like there's no tomorrow. And each time we raced, which Mr Donnet made us do every day, Freckles beat me. I can tell you that being beaten by a snotty-nosed fourteen-year-old really hurt. Whatever I did to try to get an advantage over him – like arrive at the pool earlier and swim more laps than him – I couldn't touch the wall first. I even challenged him to a race the day he came to the pool looking deadly sick, but that didn't work because Mr Donnet saw how ill he was and sent him home.

Thank goodness Freckles doesn't go to my school.

I even thought of killing him. No, I didn't. Well, I did, kind of . . . You have to understand that grinding my way up and down a swimming pool lane, four hours a day, every day of the summer holidays, when other boys my age were making love to a delicious girl or in their bedroom pretending, did cause the mind and body to wander. Yet, Freckles was the best thing ever to have happened to me. After Mr Donnet, that was.

The day of the trials is hot, but overcast. On entering the pool precinct, straight away I can feel knives in my back. Every older boy is already a member of the swimming team from the previous year and not one of them is about to give me an inch. I'm an outsider in their territory, a fact they make plain by giving me the cold shoulder.

Such treatment isn't unusual at my school. If you're not good at sport, you're rat shit.

Oh, and there's another small yet embarrassing thing. Not having been a member of the swimming team previously means I'm the only boy at the pool, apart from the Year Seven babies new to the school, not wearing the school's official Speedos. Standing alone in my green bathers makes me look and feel totally out of place, which is not something a teenager likes to be. It's yet another of my dreadful alone moments.

My turn comes. Ikey calls out, 'One – Hundred – Yards – Open – Breaststroke,' projecting each word separately through his big red megaphone like he's auditioning for *Twelfth Night*.

Ikey knew in advance I'd be trying out, because last Monday he saw me put my name on the list outside his office. He came out to see what I was doing, unable to hide a smirk as I wrote my name in the column. Neither of us spoke, but oh, how he must have been overjoyed at the thought of me making a fool of myself in the pool.

Weak knee, eh? Like the rest of you.

Standing on the block, I can hear sniggering around the pool. I force it from my mind. Instead, I think of Freckles. I feel terrible that I even considered hurting him. The truth is in the end we became good friends, even if the little shit always did beat me. We learnt to respect each other, something surely missing here at the school pool. I just wish Freckles was here. He'd show them.

I'll show them.

Ikey stands a few metres up the side of the pool. He has me in the first lane, nearest him, I guess so that he can gloat close-up. He's put the two recognised breaststrokers in lanes four and five – no doubt to pace each other – and non-breaststrokers in the remaining three lanes. I know it's designed to put me off, but I don't care. I know everyone here is hoping I'll come a miserable, embarrassing last.

But Mr Donnet doesn't want me to come last. And I know Freckles wants me to win. This time.

I've not had a gun-start before and the noise of it sends me hurtling into the water. From there, I quickly get up onto the required plane and charge up the fifty-yard saltwater pool, with everything to lose. I force the word from my mind and focus instead on what Mr Donnet told me over and over again: 'stretch–rhythm–breathing'.

Plus, I focus on beating Freckles. I have to catch Freckles.

At the far end, I turn. As my head comes out of the water, to my amazement I see all five other swimmers coming towards me. Any excitement, however, is short-lived because as the breaststroker in lane four swims past me to finish his first lap I see a vision of another boy way out in front of me. It's Freckles. Bloody Freckles. I have to beat Freckles.

I swim like mad.

When I finally touch the wall to finish, I spin round to see where I've come. As I shake water from each ear, I'm struck by the eerie silence; no cheering, nothing. For a moment I think I've lost my hearing and I shake my head again in case there's water still in my ears. But then I hear the distant splashing of the other swimmers coming towards me, the two breaststrokers still several yards back, the other three boys a mile away. It isn't my hearing. This will be the only event swum all afternoon where there's no barracking, not a peep from a bunch of normally rowdy, out-of-control teenage boys yelling support for their school mates.

And to think, we're all supposed to be on the same team.

Blowing water gently in front of me, I twist my head ever so slightly to snatch a glance at Ikey, whose mouth is gaping at the stopwatch. He shakes it again, this time harder to make sure it's working properly. As if. He just doesn't want to believe what it's telling him.

Boy, how he must hate having to announce a new record.

In the months that follow, Mum doesn't come to watch me swim for my school. She says she's busy playing tennis.

Swimming meets come and go, and all too quickly the season ends. I win my share of races.

A week later, someone tells me I should look at the Colours list outside the headmaster's office. Ikey has awarded me Half Colours. Mum must be feeling guilty, because twenty-four hours after I phoned her with the news, I'm wearing the shiny white sweater she's rushed into Buckley & Nunn to buy and send to me.

It's amazing how a garment – a simple jumper – can make a boy walk ten feet tall.

On Tuesday I ask Mr Renney, coach of the First XVIII, if I can have the job of team manager again, like last year. It involves looking after footballs and being timekeeper, and means I get to spend Fridays or Saturdays on a bus going to other schools. It also includes a week-long interstate trip for a round of pre-season practice games.

Plus, it gets me out of having to play a winter ball sport.

'No way,' replies Mr Renney, going for his stern look. 'Last year you lost fifty footballs.'

I can't help it if boys steal them. My mind races far too fast. 'What if I get them back?' I say, without immediately thinking how I might achieve it.

'And how will you do that?'

Again my voice runs far faster than my brain. 'Trust me, sir. I'll get them back.'

'I'll believe that when I see it,' he replies dismissively, before walking away.

I take his words as permission to do whatever is needed to retrieve the footballs I lost, or which more to the point were stolen. So the next morning, while everyone is in class, I borrow the big wheelbarrow from maintenance, grab the school's electric brand-ing iron from the football shed behind the scoreboard, and set off for the boarding houses.

Now, I have to tell you that at our school, venturing into locker rooms other than the one in your own boarding house is exception-ally dangerous work. It's like trying to get into Fort Knox – only the bravest try. But I'm on a mission, and nothing, not even the prospect of being caught by a handful of senior boys and being held down, stripped naked and having my balls nuggeted, will deter me from my goal.

I want my cushy job of team manager back, interstate trip and all.

So, for the next ninety minutes, any football without a boy's name burnt into leather gets branded with the school's initials. A name inscribed with a marker pen doesn't get past me.

By recess, I've branded more than one hundred footballs and tucked them all safely away in the shed. Then I invite Mr Renney to inspect it.

Something inside must have shifted because when he opens the door, fifty footballs cascade over him. Of course, he knows straight away what I've done. More than half of them can't be school property – some have boys' names inscribed in texta on their brand new leather – and yet all of them now have the school's initials burnt into them, forever. What can he do? We're both in deep shit – together – and the man has no option but to give me back my job and keep quiet about what we've done.

Of course, all hell breaks loose in the boarding houses. Boys everywhere, some of them in tears, are screaming their wealthy heads off over their precious, missing footballs.

For my part, I don't care. I'll be on the bus heading to Adelaide for the pre-season trip.

A week later, we're returning to school at the end of the pre-season practice trip. The bus gets word we're to play an extra game against the local team from Dunkeld, a small yet rich squatters' town east of Hamilton in the wealthiest quarter of Victoria's Western District. The area is home to a number of the school's grazing families, some of whose bullish offspring are here on the bus.

I'm billeted to stay at Yarrum Park with the Baillieus, a family I've known all my life. Their son, Antony, and I have been together since kindergarten, while a century ago our mothers were girls together at St Catherine's. It almost makes us family, except they're rich and we're not.

I assume it's because I'm team management and because Mrs Baillieu is pals with my mother, but for dinner she puts me opposite her at the far end of their massive dining table, which is like the ones poor people pay good money to trudge past in roped-off areas in historic mansions. Mr Baillieu must be at his day job at the Melbourne Stock Exchange.

All goes swimmingly until dessert when, without warning, Mrs Baillieu looks past the sea of acne-ridden faces, and asks, 'So, Michael, what are your plans for next year?'

It's the kind of question you'd expect from a close family friend, one who still plays tennis regularly with Mum in Melbourne on weekdays.

The ten jocks lining the sides turn their heads a hundred and eighty degrees to face me. Some snigger, but shield their faces so Mrs Baillieu doesn't see.

Seizing my moment, I puff out my swimmer's chest, and with breathless confidence I reply, 'I'm to spend the year as a jackaroo for Dick Webb at Habbies Howe.'

Of course, I have absolutely no idea whatsoever what 'jackaroo for Dick Webb at Habbies Howe' means. They're just words I'm repeating, words I've been told at home a thousand times. My year at the famous sheep and cattle station has been arranged by my wool-buyer grandfather, who wants me to learn from his old friend Webb about wool from the lamb up before I join the family wool-buying business. At least that part makes sense.

As one, the jocks turn their heads and carry the volley back to Mrs Baillieu, eager to hear what she will make of my answer. Of course, I fully expect her to tell everyone at the table how awfully clever I am to have secured a place at the prestigious Habbies Howe, it being such an esteemed property and all. Again, I've been told so at home a thousand times.

I sit up straight, anticipating the thunderous praise I'm about to get from our host. Yet silence hangs in the air for what seems a touch too long.

Then, staring straight at me past the sea of revolting faces, and without a hint of motherly love, the woman says, ever so calmly, 'I'll be surprised if you last a year there.'

All eyes again revert to me, except this time every footballer's face has a smirk on it the size of a carnival clown's, while mine turns the most brilliant shade of dead=set scarlet.

My lonely, yet safe and predictable world is about to come crashing down around me.

2

Arrival

New Year's Day, 1967

Melbourne is turning into a real scorcher even before we leave home.

Four days ago, Mum took me shopping with a list of things Mrs Webb told her over the phone I'll need as a jackaroo at Habbies Howe.

First, we went to Myer, where we bought shiny white moleskin trousers that weigh a tonne, and size thirteen elastic-sided R. M. Williams riding boots that weigh another tonne. Mrs Webb said to get R. M. Williams boots because they're the best. On me, they look like small boats.

We then went, without Mum having a clue as to the pain it caused me, to the same army disposal store in Russell Street where, eight years ago when I was nine, the elderly shop assistant who led me to the change rooms and fitted me with shorts put his hand inside and began to play with my penis, saying he needed to make sure everything fitted properly. Children of later generations would be taught to tell someone if they got touched in wrong places. At that time I was too scared to say anything, and even now the memory haunts.

This time, the grubby shop assistant was gone – lucky for him – and we bought an oilskin jacket that weighs two tonnes, and a stockwhip. More than four tonnes of gear.

And now, with all but the new clothes I'm wearing safely packed in the car ready for our pleasant Sunday drive into the country, I stare out our living room window and again I ask myself why I'm being sent to be a jackaroo (whatever that means) for Dick Webb (whoever he is) at Habbies Howe (wherever that is), and recall Mrs Baillieu's chilling forecast nine months ago that I won't survive my year there. How will I meet my demise? Will it be quick?

I look out across the street at my friend David's place. All is quiet and I wonder if he is any happier about going back to his school in a few weeks' time for another year. But then, he doesn't have a frightening alternative that makes returning to school a safer and more attractive option. Since school finished weeks ago I've begun to wish I was going back. Despite its drawbacks, school not only makes for a comfortable existence, with lots of spare periods, but the prospect of an early death would be less likely.

Plus, I could swim again.

Seeing me stare out the front window, my sister Penny, eighteen months my senior, can't resist. 'You look like the Lone Ranger without his horse,' she says, in her usual mocking tone as she gets up from her piano stool.

I don't need to look down at myself. I know this time my mean sister is right. I look a complete dag in all this rural get-up. So not me.

'You're supposed to wear the shoes, not the boxes they came in,' she adds. I mouth *good riddance* as she leaves the room. My sister's world consists of studying for a music degree at Melbourne University and singing in the Melbourne Chorale, the latter so she can drool over a dull boy chorister while performing Verdi's *Requiem*. I know the boyfriend is dull – he grows flowers. Real men don't grow flowers.

With Penny's words hanging in the air, I check my watch. We're due at Habbies Howe at midday, in time for lunch. Mrs Webb told Mum to allow two hours, it being New Year's Day, Sunday, and a public holiday.

Suddenly, Mum is at the door. 'Michael . . .' she says.

I half turn to face her. 'What?'

'Promise me one thing. Promise me you won't drink at Habbies Howe. You know it killed your father.' She finally got out the words she must have been saving since the day he died.

I glare at her. 'I'm *not* my father,' I reply angrily, turning back to face the window.

The Holden is unusually bare for the trip. Normally, when Mum drove Penny and me to our respective boarding schools, the car was stacked to the gunnels with huge quantities of food, all of it contraband yet essential for survival in our stark lives. This time there's nothing but the oilskin jacket and stockwhip, and a small grey suitcase containing three pairs of jeans, various school shirts and jumpers, two extra windcheaters, and a bunch of socks and undies. Plus, there's an electric shaver, which is still on probation while I practise removing post-pubescent bumfluff from my angelic, choirboy face.

In the car, I run my fingers along the plaited stockwhip. I'll be ready for any molesters from now on, I tell myself, trying to think positive thoughts while quietly shitting myself in the back seat.

For the umpteenth time, I ask myself what I'm doing with all this rural stuff. I'm not a tough farm boy like the rurals at school, and in truth I don't have an aggressive bone in my puny body, unlike most of them. And Mum doesn't have an affected English accent like other boys' parents, who turned up at sports days in their Mercedes, brand-new if wool prices permitted or if they'd sold another back paddock to pay for it. The rurals were all sporty types. They had impressive muscles and they were popular. I know I'm not like them, yet here I am, about to be thrust into their world, a world I know nothing about.

'I'm sure Mrs Webb will feed you,' says Mum, as cheerfully as she can after I complain about there being nothing on board to eat, as we head towards the city's northern suburbs.

'I'm not so sure,' I reply, observing Melbourne for possibly the last time in my relatively short life. Maybe it's starvation that Mrs Baillieu was referring to. Who knows?

After Mrs Baillieu had made her frightening remark over dinner at the end of the football tour last year, as soon as the bus returned to school I ran to the phone and called Mum. Until then, what little thought I'd given to my future was mostly positive. The idea of being a jackaroo on a famous sheep and cattle station, located within relatively easy reach of Melbourne, verged on the romantic. It was probably the 'famous' bit I found appealing. All boys want to be famous, or to know someone who is. And given the senior management roles I had at school – which in truth amounted to nothing more than storing the footballs and keeping time during matches – I'd taken for granted that within moments of arriving at Habbies Howe, I'll be assuming a senior management position there too. Plus, it will be my chance to stick it up the rurals at school, many of whom will return to do another year as rowers and footballers (even though private schools supposedly have rules prohibiting nineteen-year-olds being enrolled just to play sport).

All Mum said on the phone was, 'Your grandparents are best friends with Dick and Molly Webb, and since you were twelve you've been booked in to be a jackaroo at Habbies Howe. It'll be your chance of a lifetime to learn about sheep and wool from the ground up, before you join the firm.'

The phrase 'chance of a lifetime' has been used many times as a weapon by my mother and her parents. I'm almost convinced this plan is part of a carefully orchestrated, family-wide conspiracy, because they've known all along that Mr Webb is the hardest of taskmasters, and that I'm about to be toughened up in ways that even boarding school couldn't do. I'm certain my family not only knows what I'm in for, but they welcome it.

'Yeah, yeah, yeah,' I interrupted her, 'you've told me that a thousand times. They were the Webbs' first house guests after Mr and Mrs Webb got married, blah, blah, blah. But what about Mrs Baillieu saying last night I won't survive my year there?'

There was silence down the line. I could tell Mum was hedging. 'Your grandfather says you need to learn about wool-growing. It will be your chance of a lifetime.'

There it was again, that phrase. And with that I'm supposed to feel chuffed about dying an honourable death in some remote paddock out the back of Seymour.

Mum was just doing what mothers are for – offering comfort, encouraging, basically lying to their children. Anything to get through another day with as little grief as possible. But it didn't work. I was the one standing at the phone that night with warm yellow fluid running down my inner leg.

At home, the issue of my departure wasn't discussed any further. It was banned as a topic of conversation, which left me with nothing to talk about. Bossy-boots Penny had said, 'Now listen to me. You will go to Habbies Howe. You will learn all about wool. And you will enjoy it. End of subject. Now *drop it.*' Mum agreed with her. Two against one.

We hit the Hume Highway and Mum plants her foot. I'm not sure if it's because she thinks we'll be late, or because she wants me to be put out of my misery sooner rather than later.

At Seymour we turn right off the Hume and head east along a flat stretch of road towards the high country. It's hot inside the car, damned hot, and I unwind my window in the back seat.

I notice how the paddocks along the flat land are bare. Whirl-winds of dust vacuum up remaining topsoil as they spin their way across blackened ground either side of the road. The few animals I can see look sick and starving; they hug what little shade there is, even though dead trees with sparse limbs don't offer much by way of comfort. There isn't a cloud in the hot summer sky, only a shimmering, burning haze that waves back at you from distant horizons.

We climb a winding road, past a sign that says THE HIGH-LANDS, and we enter an area of high country roughly equidistant from the towns of Seymour, Euroa and Yea. Suddenly the view changes. Gone are the bare, brown paddocks. In their place tall dry grass appears left and right; slender, brown stalks standing proud against the intense summer sun. The shimmering haze also is gone. What is it about this country? What is it that makes these paddocks appear so much more productive than those we just passed coming out of Seymour?

More animals appear: healthy-looking cattle, some black, some red, and sheep, lots of recently shorn sheep, lolling around in the grass under the shade of vast gum trees. The animals appear well fed and relaxed. Here, huge gums reach out and almost hug each other, like those I saw last year at Dunkeld on the football trip. Suddenly we've stumbled upon an oasis – rich and prosperous.

I begin to figure it out. I guess it has to be a case of choos-ing the right area to farm leading to good prices, and good prices to more money in the bank, which in turn allows the successful farmer or grazier to buy even more country. Or so my seventeen-year-old brain reasons, anyway.

Maybe, just maybe, where I'm heading won't be so terrifying after all.

For a moment I wonder if I'll be placed at the far end of the dining table here too.

'This looks a lot better,' says Mum, as we reach the top of the climb and begin a long, downward descent. Bless her heart. Mum has no more idea what she's talking about than I do.

As we drive down the winding road, the country opens to reveal an awesome valley, which stretches further than the eye can see. Big paddocks with occasional clusters of gums undulate their way up each side of the valley from meandering streams below. Pastures rise up to join outcrops of granite, each cluster drenched in sunlight, each big shiny white rock looking like it too is a thriving product of the hills. Despite the brownness of the dry summer grass, I notice green strips running downhill at intervals. Why do only parts of the hills get water? I wonder.

Further on, on our right side stands a row of cypress trees, defining an area set aside for human activity, and buildings which I take to be the headquarters of a substantial farming operation. A big, red Hereford bull sits in the shade of one of the trees, while a group of sheep on our left, disturbed by our car, jump to their feet and run beside us along the inside of their fence. Again, I ponder what makes this country so much more healthy looking.

And here, at the bottom of the hill after we cross a small culvert, a hundred metres further on, beneath the row of cypress trees and painted on a solid-looking wooden fence in big fat capital letters, are the two words I've been dreading: HABBIES HOWE.

'At last,' declares Penny, as if she can't wait to become an only child.

'Isn't it beautiful?' says Mum, hopelessly failing to put my mind at ease.

My eyes dart left and right, then ahead. A further hundred metres in front of us down the sloping driveway sits a wide, low-lying, single-storey old house with a grey roof, all of it dwarfed by a line of tall, leafy English trees out front. To the left of the house is a four-car garage, two doors to which are open. They reveal what

I can just make out to be a green utility and a grey four-wheel drive vehicle. The boy in me wonders which one will be mine to drive.

If I could drive.

To the left of the garage more buildings come into sight, including what I assume is a shearing shed and adjoining sheep yards. Beyond them under the shade of a huge cypress tree is a set of taller yards, which I assume must be for cattle. The farm buildings all are shiny white, with large, dark grey double doors and roofs. I guess the doors are shut because it's New Year's Day, Sunday, and a public holiday.

There isn't a sign of life anywhere, and for a moment I want to shout, *Quick, let's turn round and escape before anyone sees us!*

Too late. An old man emerges from the homestead and stumbles his way across the courtyard, waving his arms in the air like a madman.

Mum stops the car on the gravel next to the chest-high, blue-stone fence in front of the house, just out from the trees. What strikes me immediately about the old man – what I can see of him – is his big silver moustache, his bulky, short-sleeved blue shirt, and his soft-brimmed hat. The hat looks like it might have seen younger days. Indeed, most of what I'm looking at seems pretty ancient. As he makes his way towards us, still madly waving his arms in the air – which I assume is his way of greeting guests – he shoots us a quick glance, before again looking down at the lumpy cobblestones to prevent a stumble.

I'm moments away from shaking hands with the revered Richard Cappur Webb, of Habbies Howe, the famous property where some jackaroos apparently don't last long.

My mind flits back to my first day at boarding school, and the strange and scary new surroundings into which I was delivered, or some might say abandoned. To when I was removed from my mother's safe if not always loving arms into those of hard, unsympathetic men and cruel boys, who would kick me around for years until I learnt to fend for myself, learnt to avoid harm, learnt to play their game yet be one step ahead of them, always on guard, ready for ridicule, for the next bashing.

Is it all just about to start again?

3

Dougie

My mother and sister can't escape from Habbies Howe fast enough, although manners demand forty minutes of politeness over lunch with Mr and Mrs Webb. It's taken in the dining room. It will be the only time I set foot in the real part of the homestead, a house in which my family thinks I will live for a year. My mother and sister and I are here as a concession to the Webbs' dear friends – my grandparents – whose daughter is delivering her son for slaughter. Our presence in the house is a diversion from what's about to happen to me the moment my family leaves. I will quickly learn that jackaroos do not belong in the house proper.

The meal goes smoothly enough, although I think Mum is expecting me to burst into tears at any moment. I can sense she and I are sharing one thought, and one thought only: Mrs Baillieu's dire prediction. As I sip the lemon cordial I assume Mum, like me, is pondering the mechanics of my death.

'Michael is so looking forward to being here,' she says between mouthfuls, trying without success to bolster my spirits. But all she gets from Mrs Webb is a steely glare after Penny whispers 'Liar' far too loudly. Mum hears it too, and she shrugs her shoulders at Mrs Webb as if to say, *Can't help kids*.

As soon as good manners permit, Mum bundles Penny into the Holden and they're out the gate with hardly a kiss goodbye. At least I don't look like a sissy. As they drive away, I gather my gear and Mr Webb walks me a few paces to what appear to be servants' quarters, located between the house proper and the garage. Yep, I'm right, they're the jackaroos' quarters, and I promptly learn my second lesson about life at Habbies Howe: the words 'jackaroo' and 'servant' are interchangeable.

As we approach, Mr Webb stutters, loudly, 'D-D-Dougie, a-a-are y-y-you th-th-there?'

'Yes, Mr Webb,' comes a compliant, gravelly teenage voice from inside the room. Dougie Summers was lying on his bed reading a book when the boss called his name. In a split second he's on his feet, standing at the door, pretty much at attention like a cadet would back at school.

After introducing us, Mr Webb promptly retreats to the house.

Dougie holds the door open. 'You'd better come in, I guess,' he says with a concluding laugh. I can tell without looking he's sizing me up, which is a worry. His laugh doesn't go unnoticed – I find he finishes every sentence with the same involuntary utterance. It must be a nervous thing, and straight away it endears him to me. That laugh will brighten many a sombre moment at Habbies Howe.

Stocky and much shorter than me, with a round face and light brown, wavy hair that on sunny days will have a red tinge about it, Dougie looks the complete Farmer Joe in his checked shirt, with its several shades of red and blue, and baggy green work pants. Later, when the cold weather sets in, he'll add an equally daggy brown jumper, which makes him look even more of a dork. Dougie enjoys telling the world he doesn't give a stuff what it thinks of him; he'll do his own thing, regardless.

Dougie is nineteen, almost two years older than me. He's a farmer's son from over near the Victorian–South Australian border. I will soon discover he knows everything there is to know about farming, or at least he thinks he does.

Compared to where I just had lunch, everything about the

quarters is tiny: doorway, room size, windows. If I stand up straight I'll bang my head on the ceiling. A small window above the middle of Dougie's bed and another between the two beds at the end are so low, all I can see while standing is the gravel outside. At least in our dormitory at school I could stand upright. And I got a view.

'That must be your bed over there,' Dougie says, pointing to the freshly made one against the inside wall, before adding, 'seeing this one's mine', again with that laugh. He waves a hand past the unkempt bed under the side window. Between the beds, beneath the end window, is a small bedside table and, in the far corner, at the foot of my bed, a chest of drawers. I guess they're for sharing.

'I'll show you the rest of the set-up,' he says, pulling on his riding boots and turning to lead me back out of the room, before I even get to try out my new bed. I follow him back out through the wrought-iron gate. But we turn sharp left and walk just three paces on the cobblestones to another small door on our left. It leads to a separate section of the servant-jackaroo quarters.

These rooms have the same miniature features. Again, I'm being shown nothing more than cramped servants' quarters. The door opens into a dark and dingy sitting room and beyond that a tiny, even darker bathroom without natural light. The sitting room is empty apart from a sagging chair and a lumpy couch, both missing nine-tenths of their fabric. Between them is a small table. A single, uncovered light globe dangles from the ceiling, off-centre.

No TV, virtually no anything, just a dark, uninviting hole of a place.

'That's it,' says Dougie, before he realises he's missed something and points to a closed door on our right. 'Except for Alan's bedroom,' he says, nodding towards it. And then, to pre-empt my question, he adds, 'Annual leave – one week.' Then the laugh again.

Later, Dougie will tell me that Alan Greenwood is twenty-one, but he can't bring himself to say, to actually mouth the words, that

Alan is the senior jackaroo. I sense there may be tension between the two of them.

'One week's leave,' he repeats, more for his benefit than mine, shaking his head almost in disbelief at the miserable entitlement. The idea of holidays hasn't crossed my mind.

The tour of our quarters complete, Dougie takes me back to our room, where he promptly resumes lying on his bed, boots on this time. He picks up the book he's been reading, looks briefly at the page he's on, and lets it rest on his chest, open at the page. He folds his hands behind his head on the pillow and stares at the ceiling. Not knowing what else to do, I push my suitcase against the wall at the foot of my bed next to the chest of drawers. I place the oilskin jacket and stockwhip on top again, and take up a similar position to Dougie on my bed.

And for a fleeting second I remind myself how this will be my eighth year – almost half my life – living away from home. Eight years sharing a bedroom, my suitcase above a cupboard.

With nowhere else to look, I copy Dougie and stare at the ceiling. I notice how cool the room is. Despite the confined space and the fact there are now two bodies breathing in here, it is still noticeably milder inside than out. Obviously, the smaller bluestone bricks, rejected for building the homestead, work well enough to keep the jackaroos' rooms cool.

'So,' says Dougie, his eyes still aimed at the ceiling, 'what crime did you commit to get yourself sent here?' He lets out another of his chuckles at his own words. I want to laugh out loud at him, but I stop myself.

Not wanting to brag about family connections, yet knowing it's the truth, I reply, 'My grandfather's a wool buyer. I'm here to learn about wool. You know, where it all starts.' Dougie makes no comment. He must be processing it, so I continue. 'My grandparents have known Mr Webb forever. They were their first house guests here after Mr and Mrs Webb got married.' Enough already, I tell myself.

Still, Dougie doesn't comment. He stares at the ceiling. I know I've said enough.

'And you?' I ask, keen to get the attention off me.

'It was either here or jail,' he replies, with another full-on chuckle. 'Just kidding,' he quickly adds. This time he glances across at me, I guess to make sure I take it the right way.

In time I will come to realise that Dougie never does tell me how he came to be a jackaroo at Habbies Howe, whether his parents are pals with the Webbs or whether it was arranged by a stock and station agent, or some other third party.

It's a while before either of us speaks. Then Dougie says, 'I guess you know about no car, no smokes and no booze?' He puts emphasis on each item of contraband.

I don't know. Not once have I contemplated such things. Being nine months short of my eighteenth birthday and still unable and ineligible to drive, I've not thought about having a car. Nor am I a smoker, apart from at our school's country property, where we puffed away on tea leaves rolled up in toilet paper – painful as all hell if you got burning tea leaves on you.

The issue of booze is different. My mind jumps to this morning (was it just this morning?) and Mum's plea to me not to drink – how she really does worry about me going the same way as my father.

'No,' I say. For me, right now, cars, smokes and booze come a long way behind a far greater priority – survival. Not that I'm about to tell Dougie what Mrs Baillieu said. No way.

More silence and I ponder Dougie's line of questioning. Have I just exposed myself as a total sook, shown him how much of a loser I am? Should I not have asked him, the moment we shook hands, about cars, smokes and booze? I may as well have thrown in raunchy women as well. Have I so quickly shown my total lack of maleness? Should not my first words to him just minutes ago – as we stood at the door after the boss left us – have been, 'So, mate, what truck are you driving these days?' Or, 'Got a smoke on you? Or, 'So where do we store the cans?'

But I didn't say any of these things. Even now, as Dougie announces the first of the rules, should I be jumping to my feet and declaring, boldly, 'Well, if that's the way things are done, then stuff 'em. I'm outta here'?

No, I lie on my bed and I say nothing. I know to try and be tough in front of my first-ever work colleague won't work. He's probably seen through me already. Even now, if I try to say something daring, my voice will probably crack and I'll give myself away. Where will I be out of here to, anyway? Judging by today's drive, it's a long, hot walk back to the railway station in Seymour.

What choice do I have? I guess there's no opening around these parts for a choirboy.

'Come on,' Dougie says, getting to his feet again. 'I'll show you round.' He must have already made up his mind I'm not worth persisting with, and he's looking for a way to dump me.

Again I follow him out the door in silence, leaving behind whatever self-esteem I might have brought here with me.

Outside, it's hot. Stinking hot – over a hundred degrees (we all still talk in Fahrenheit, though metric was introduced last year). I try to ignore the heat. Instead, I focus on what Dougie is showing me. I like him and I want so much for him to like me. As for Alan, I'm yet to find out. Maybe he's the bully of the pair. And while men don't discuss such things, I'm already hoping Dougie will look after me at Habbies Howe, protect me from whatever harm is being planned. I like the way he speaks, even though he uses words sparingly. I've not met anyone like him.

As we walk past the front of the homestead – which I will discover is in fact the back – he asks, 'So, how was lunch?' Maybe he does still want to talk to me, even if I don't make wild, blokey conversation about fast cars, smokes and booze, and raunchy women.

'It was okay, I guess.' I don't know how else to describe a glass of lemon cordial and two sandwiches, swallowed nervously. 'Mum couldn't wait to escape,' I add.

'You'll be lucky if you ever see the dining room again,' he says, after a pause. I don't understand what he means so I let the comment pass as we walk on.

At the far end of the homestead, the roof again drops low, signalling more small rooms, possibly more servants' quarters.

Dougie opens the small, corner door and I follow him inside. It's a dining room, but with a higher ceiling than the one in our quarters. It looks like it's been recently renovated – and the priority registers in my brain. A laminated table takes up most of the room, with green, vinyl-covered metal chairs tucked in on the sides and ends, leaving just enough room for folk to get past. I count eight places.

'This is where *we* eat,' says Dougie. His comment about not eating again in the homestead now makes sense.

What strikes me most about the room, and totally dwarfs everything in it, is a blackboard fixed to the wall above the mantelpiece at the far end. I can't help but stare at it. It extends from the mantelpiece above the blocked-off fireplace to the ceiling, its surface divided into equal left and right halves. In the far left column of each half are painted in white what I guess must be the names of Habbies Howe's paddocks – I quickly count thirty-two in each half . . . times two . . . sixty-four paddocks – in alphabetical order. Beside each name are two narrower columns where chalk is used, one headed 'Cattle', the other 'Sheep'. The whole thing is so in-your-face in the small room, it's difficult to look anywhere else.

I notice, for instance, the first paddock, Arthurs, has '60 cows' scrawled in chalk in the cattle column, while the paddock at the top of the second column, No. 6, has '400 weaners' written in the sheep column – whatever weaners are. The blackboard looks well used, but it's filthy, with chalk dust and poorly executed rub-outs all over the place, as if the writing is done in haste. An equally filthy-looking duster sits on the mantelpiece. It too is caked with chalk dust, which as any schoolboy knows, renders a duster useless. I make a mental note to come back later and tidy up the mess. What this place needs, I decide already, is some half-decent administration – just the job for me.

What Dougie says next scares the living daylights out of me. Looking at the board, he says, 'The boss will give you two weeks to learn all the names.'

I freeze. The idea of having to memorise anything is a worry, let alone sixty-four paddocks.

'Really?' is all I can think to say, like I'm already grizzling. I should have said *So?* and taken his statement in my stride. Or at least pretended to.

Two weeks? Again, I stare at the sixty-four names. It will be like trying to learn the chemistry table of the elements at school, or worse, Latin verbs. It's one thing to memorise each of the names, but to associate the names with actual paddocks will be something else, at least until I've been in each paddock and have found something physical with which to associate the name, to give me a reason to remember it.

'Yeah,' continues Dougie, with another of his involuntary laughs, 'and he'll expect you to know what's in each one of them by then as well.'

Struth! How am I going to remember all of this? Hang on – will it be death by exam?

Later, I will discover how the boss administers the paddock name test. It will happen during what we jackaroos call 'the Royal Tour'. You get to do it if you're not quick enough to hide on a Sunday morning – or to have considered church. The boss will ma're one of us drive him around a fair chunk of the 10 500-acre property, a journey that can take all morning. It truly will become one of life's more painful experiences, the jackaroo driving the ute or Land Rover with Mr Webb sitting beside him, prescribing with his finger exactly where he wants you to steer, metre by metre, centimetre after centimetre. An entire trip is directed with his index finger, not just across thousands of hectares of pasture – he points exactly where he wants us to drive as we follow well-defined internal tracks, even on a strip of bitumen that bisects Habbies Howe.

Ruling out church, due to not having a car to get me there, will make finding a place to hide a major priority on Sunday mornings.

I stare at the blackboard. It tells a person just about everything he needs to know about Habbies Howe. Apart from nine paddocks simply called No. 1 through to No. 9, and predictable ones like Home and Horse, there is every conceivable name. In time I will learn the relevance of each one. The type and number of stock also tell the observer a story, like how big each paddock is. Daskeins, for example, has 1200 ewes, which makes it one of Habbies Howe's biggest paddocks. Nolans, temporarily at least, is home to eighty heifers. Whatever heifers might be.

Dougie takes me through to the kitchen, where I'm struck by the presence of a machine so big it looks like it should be powering the train to Sydney. I've never before seen a famous yellowy-cream AGA oven and hotplates, a contraption that takes up the entire western wall of the huge kitchen. It runs on oil, although Dougie says it used to run on wood and they still do it that way in poor farmers' homes. The machine has no less than eight hotplates, each with a hinged metal lid, two of which are up to make way for shiny steel kettles. As well, there are four separate ovens: two either side of the central workings, one above the other. Dougie tells me the grand device is never turned off. I notice one kettle is steaming – the Webbs must have made more tea after Mum and my sister left.

'Yeah,' Dougie says, patting the old girl, 'it sure cooks a mean roast. Plus, it stops you from freezing your balls off in winter while you're cooking breakfast.'

He then takes me through the pantry and into a tiny room that houses the boiler, which sends hot water throughout the homestead, the kitchen and our quarters. Two days from now, the device will cause me to have my first panic attack at Habbies Howe. Dougie tells me it will be my job, during my first week at any rate, to keep the thing running – twenty-four hours a day.

It's all beginning to feel like déjà vu, because three years ago at our school camp the units in which we lived each had a similar boiler, albeit they ran on wood, which we cut with axes. And there, if as boiler-boy for the week you let the fire go out, causing the showers to go cold, the mandatory punishment would be meted out by the other boys in your unit. You'd be hunted down wherever you tried to hide and dragged kicking to a cold shower, clothes on and all. Indeed, the only punishment at the camp which was worse was when the student mafia decided it was your turn to be nuggeted, with the entire student population crammed into the dormitory looking on. With four strong boys each stretching an arm or leg, your stripping naked would be done ceremoniously, as would the smearing of shoe polish over your dick and balls. Apart from the sheer humiliation, the worst part was getting the rotten stuff off afterwards.

We leave the boiler room, but not before Dougie checks that the fire is burning well. Coal, he tells me, is better than wood because it burns more slowly and evenly and thus requires less attention. 'Oh, good,' I say, thanking God for His smallest of mercies.

For a second, I wonder if the punishment for letting the fire die will be death by nuggeting.

Outdoors again in what quickly has become suffocating afternoon heat, Dougie leads me across the homestead area to the row of cypress trees on the southern side.

'Horse paddock,' he says, resting his arms on the gate, for which the overhanging trees provide a fraction of merciful shade.

Only sixty-three paddock names to go, I think to myself, also leaning on the gate.

Peering into the paddock, I need to squint to see anything against the glare. My eyes quickly adjust, however, to let me count nine horses. A couple are eating grass in semi-shade, while two idiot horses stand in full sun. The other five stand against the fence under the shade of the trees with their heads drooped low, their tales swishing back and forth like the pendulum on our grand-father clock at home, although here the pendulum swishes at flies.

'Three of them are yours,' says Dougie, without identifying which ones.

Three horses each. Wow. Wait 'til I tell Mum about this. He points to a big red horse, one of the two standing in the hot sun off to the right. 'The red one's mine,' he says. 'I use him first.' Then he points to a grey horse. 'That's Alan's, a real mongrel of a horse. But Alan likes him.'

Dougie sees me looking at a brown horse with a shiny coat standing in the shade on our left. This one isn't as tall as Dougie's chestnut, but the same height as Alan's grey. 'Charlie,' says Dougie. 'He'll be yours. Graeme rode him.' Then, as if it's an afterthought, he gives me half a glance and adds, 'Can you ride?' Again, the characteristic laugh.

'My sister and I had ponies when we were young,' I answer.

'Huh,' says Dougie. I don't think what I just said impresses him, or properly answers his question. The guy surely is the epitome of frugality when it comes to the use of words. Why use four when three will do? Even so, I will soon discover that compared to the eight station hands, Dougie suffers from veritable verbal diarrhoea. No one here turns out to be much of a conversationalist.

He then points to a black horse in the shade. 'If I were you, I'd use that black one when we need to change at lunchtime.'

Suddenly it's all too much information. I choose momentarily to skip his last point.

'Tell me about Graeme,' I say. 'Am I replacing him?'

'Yeah, the poor bastard.'

Next lesson: everyone on the land, and I mean everyone – other than the bosses, of course – is a 'poor bastard'. It's not that they are necessarily financially bereft, or sick or even anaemic, or that they come from unmarried parents. But everyone who makes his living off the land suffers great disadvantage, which makes him a poor bastard.

Dougie looks at me. 'I would have been here, let's see . . .' he says, scratching his head with his right hand, 'about three months when Graeme arrived. In a VW.' He lets out another of his now mandatory chuckles. 'The boss told him to take it home. Immediately. He came back on the train the next day, the poor bastard.' Another laugh.

'Really,' I reply, thinking I mustn't mistake Mr Webb for my easy-natured grandfather.

'Yep,' says Dougie. 'No cars.' I'm starting to think the guy is paranoid about the rules.

My mind turns to what else Dougie just said. I'm learning something new by the second. We'll work our horses hard enough to need a fresh one after lunch. Wow – three horses each. This makes playing pony club dress-ups at Mt Eliza gymkhanas real kids' stuff.

As for Graeme, his name will not be spoken again. Clearly, jackaroos come, jackaroos go.

At dinner, nothing exceptional happens, other than that I learn to keep my mouth shut. It turns out Mr and Mrs Webb eat with us in the jackaroos' dining room, which I find strange given they have a much more posh room in the house proper. Maybe they want to check on our table manners and make sure we don't throw food at each other. Mrs Webb sits on her husband's left and seldom speaks. From the outset there is something about the woman that worries me, and I quickly work out what it is: she absolutely, unequivocally loathes us jackaroos. Then I realise something else. I've never met a female adult who doesn't relate to young people, because in my sheltered life I've never met one who isn't a mother, teacher or boarding school matron, all of whom understand, work with and tolerate, if not love, kids. Mrs Webb has not had children of her own – or been close to any, it seems. Every conversation I have with her will be strained, like it's her versus me – not a skerrick of warmth. I will have more friendly talks with tiger snakes, before I thrust the sharp end of a shovel through their neck.

The place on Mr Webb's right normally is Alan's, but because he's on annual leave, Dougie moves up one. I sit on his right, furthest away from everyone yet closest to the dreaded blackboard.

Susie, the cook, and her station-hand husband, Cliff, will join us for lunch each day, and Cliff again for breakfast – breakfast we jackaroos have to cook – but they take their evening meal in their cottage, tucked away on the southern and least public side of the homestead. I've not yet seen any sign of the couple, but it is, after all, New Year's Day, Sunday, and a public holiday.

And it's over dinner that I learn why the blackboard is where it is. It's so the boss, who sits at the end of the table furthest from it, can look up and see what is happening anywhere on the property. Accordingly, he spends most of my first meal – and every one thereafter – staring at the entries on the blackboard, while he chews. Given he spends many days at farm industry meetings in Melbourne or interstate, the blackboard enables him to catch up on the state of Habbies Howe the moment he gets home. I will quickly discover Mr Webb has an amazing memory and seems able, by looking at the blackboard, to track a flock of sheep or mob of cattle through several paddocks over several months, needing only to read the type and number of animals to remember their movement over time. It also helps to have his jackaroos drive him around the property on Sundays on the Royal Tour to keep him up to speed with which sheep or cattle need shifting to fresh pasture.

'Th-th-those s-steers i-i-in S-Stewarts,' Mr Webb declares to everyone present at my first meal, 'th-th-they've been there l-l-long enough. I'd b-b-better get onto B-B-Bill about m-m-moving them.' It's a reference to Bill Webb – no relation to the boss – the manager of Habbies Howe, whom I am yet to meet. Word has it that Bill Webb was one of three jackaroos at Habbies Howe before the war, and Mr Webb was so impressed with them, he promised to take back as a junior partner whoever among them returned from the war. Bill Webb was the only one who came back.

Already, I'm starting to learn the culture of the bush, of which Mr Webb's remark at the dinner table is typical. He's not asking us jackaroos – who see the manager every day – to tell him the boss wants the steers in Stewarts shifted. That's not our place. He's telling himself out loud what he needs to do, how he needs to pass on the message to the Other Mr Webb. Consequently, there is much that is said at the meal table that doesn't expect or warrant a reply. Mostly at meals the boss will prattle away to himself, or he'll muse out loud about his day or week in Melbourne or elsewhere, giving us a running monologue whether we want it or not. And because no reply is expected, we jackaroos can easily drift off to sleep with our knife and fork in hand, shovelling food into our mouth without it ever being noticed we're actually asleep, totally wiped out after another day's punishment.

I will often find myself puzzling over Mr Webb's monologues. One night he announces to anyone not asleep, 'Had d-d-dinner w-w-with Bill G-G-Gunn last night.' The name means nothing to me. I look at Dougie, who purses his lips and nods his head, as if to say, *That's downright amazing, boss.* When we're safely back in our room, Dougie mimics a drawl very close to the boss's, repeating, 'H-h-had d-d-dinner with B-B-Bill G-G-Gunn last n-n-night.'

'Who's B-B-Bill G-G-Gunn?' I ask, showing my gross ignorance.

'The chairman of the Australian Wool Board, that's who. The biggest of the bigwigs.'

It means nothing to me. But I'm amazed that a man can own most of the state of Victoria, yet find the need to name-drop in front of his lowly servant-jackaroos.

After dinner, I help Dougie to wash up – something we'll do after every meal. He then takes me across the cobblestone courtyard to the door to the house proper, the one through which my family and I entered for lunch. But this time we don't go far into the hallowed inner turf. Just inside the door Dougie turns sharp right into the office, a small, dark room I glanced into at lunchtime.

Against the wall to the right is the messiest desk I've ever seen. It's a disgrace, with paperwork strewn everywhere. The boss needs a good nuggeting for the state it's in. Straight ahead against another wall is a second small yet tidy desk, on which sits a thick, brown book next to an ancient Olivetti typewriter. Dougie plonks himself down in the chair at the small desk, considerately shifting the chair to the right so I can look over his left shoulder.

'Normally, while two of us wash up . . .' begins Dougie, pausing to open the large ring binder at a busy page he happens to find, 'the third guy comes over here and does this.' With his right hand he opens and reaches into the drawer beneath the table top and pulls out a fresh piece of quarto-size paper.

'It goes like this,' he says, as he begins to feed the paper into the typewriter's roller.

While Dougie sets up, I look at the sample page he's opened as another million thoughts race through my mind. As with the blackboard in the meal room, the single diary page tells many stories – yet it begs just as many questions. The entry begins with the date, using the black ribbon centred at the top. Underneath, also in black, is the word 'Weather' followed by a less than sophisticated description of the day's meteorological conditions: such as 'Rained', but not how much rain, and 'Hot', but not how hot. Below, using the red ribbon, are two subheadings, one headed 'Cattle', the other 'Sheep', with phrases like '50 cows from One Tree to Millers' and '400 weaners from Hume to Jeffries'.

What is more intriguing, though, is what appears below. Down the lower left half of the page are listed the names of the ten men and three jackaroos who work on Habbies Howe. Beside the names is the task each person performed during the day. The entries begin . . .

R. Webb	In Melbourne
W. Webb	Above stock moves
A. Greenwood	Above stock moves
D. Summers	Above stock moves
G. Thomson	Above stock moves
G. Bain	Repairs to woolshed catching pens

. . . and so on, continuing down the page.

The detail is so brief the whole thing seems pointless. I'll embellish it, I tell myself, but I decide now is not the moment to disclose my management plan to Dougie.

Once again, Dougie tells me no more than I need to know at this very moment. Yet I want so much for him to tell me about each of the ten men listed: what each man is like, how long he's been at Habbies Howe, what family he has, where he lives (it's obviously not next to the homestead, other than for Cliff, the cook's husband). Will they be friendly? Dougie has no idea how much these things matter to me, how much I yearn to be accepted. How much I yearn to be a man.

Then again, I don't know what Dougie's private needs are. Deep and long and meaningful conversations don't seem to be the way things happen here. Not yet anyway. He tells me what he decides I need to know; nothing more, nothing less. I guess he figures I'll learn the rest soon enough.

I watch as he types: 'Sunday, 1 January. Weather: Hot.' Then, suddenly, without warning, he rips the sheet out of the typewriter, makes two holes in the left side with the punch, and puts the page in the ring binder. The Diary is done for New Year's Day, 1967.

'What about the rest?' I ask in amazement, again showing my gross naivety.

'Nothing happened,' he replies. He stands up and closes the Diary for another day.

You know, I would have thought, as a gesture, he might have typed, 'M Thornton: arrived.'

I guess my name will appear for the first time tomorrow night, Monday, after my first day of work.

If I survive it.

Safe in the knowledge that to get through my days at Habbies Howe I will have Dougie, three horses and eleven fellow workers – ten of whom I am yet to meet – plus, of course, the names and contents of sixty-four paddocks to learn in two weeks, by ten past eight I'm dead to the world.

4

Resignation

In 1841, pastoralist George Taylor took up a selection known as Kobyboyn in hill country twenty-five kilometres east of Seymour, near the hamlet of Dropmore, in northern Victoria. Two years later, Gideon Stewart, a Scotsman who'd not long since arrived in Port Phillip with five hundred sheep and £500, bought it from Taylor. Stewart's wife called the selection Habbies Howe, after a pub twenty-four kilometres from Musselburgh, near Edinburgh. Habbies Howe is Gaelic for Herbert's Hollow.

Gideon Stewart built the homestead in the mid-1840s. It was one of the earliest homes in the district to be made out of handmade bricks (including some tiny ones left over for the servant-jackaroos' quarters). Little wonder the National Trust of Australia awarded the homestead and surrounding farm buildings its premier classification.

In 1973, *The Pastoral Review* described the homestead as being 'based on an Indian bungalow design. The main, central room has a large archway of windows which opens onto a veranda, with smaller archways to the sitting room, bedroom, and two passage ways.' Archways to bedrooms would be news to the jackaroos – we certainly weren't privy to the elegant features of the house.

'Gideon Stewart must have been extremely energetic and hard working,' it continues. 'By the 1860s Habbies Howe comprised nearly 60 000 acres, extending from Avenel Estate (further up the Hume Highway towards Euroa) to within five miles of Seymour. Stewart died in 1863, aged forty-two [little wonder, given the huge acreage he took on] and the property was carried on by his talented wife Georgina who, when she first came to Australia, worked as a governess.'

From 1920 to 1923, Messrs Barrett and Wiseman owned the property, and in 1923, Mr TM Daskein bought it. Daskein's ownership is significant because he employed my boss as his manager. And, in 1937, when Daskein died, Mr Webb and his brother, who runs a property close to Seymour, took out a lease on the property, before buying it outright in 1946.

Richard Cappur Webb took possession thirty years before my time. *The Pastoral Review* noted: 'Under the terms of Mr Daskein's will the Webbs had to buy the stock and plant. They had very little money but were helped in great measure financially by the AML & F Co Ltd [stock and station agency], to which they have remained loyal [clients].'

According to records, 1951 was the best year, as it was for Australia's graziers generally, when wool prices peaked at what's often referred to as 'a pound a pound' (the contemporary equivalent of thirty-seven dollars per kilogram – well above today's price of around $4.45 per kilogram). With wool prices eight times today's, Mercedes-Benz must have shaken hands with a lot of rural Australians back then.

The Pastoral Review reported on the two factors which set Habbies Howe apart: its 31-inch average annual rainfall and its close proximity to Melbourne's Newmarket saleyards, 'making the property's situation ideal'. By the time Habbies reached its peak production in the mid-1970s – eight years after my stint – it carried 15 000 grown sheep, 5000 lambs and almost a thousand breeding cows on its 10 500 acres.

At precisely four-thirty on my first morning – everything at Habbies Howe is done precisely – the wrought-iron gate beside our bedroom door clangs and the boss calls out, 'Are you b-b-boys r-r-ready?' Mr Webb stumbles on past our bedroom towards the garage.

'Come on,' calls Dougie, with unusual urgency in his voice as he leaps out of bed. That Dougie seems to be in a panic shows a whole new side to him, which I'm observing less than arm's length away as, in unison, we throw on our shirts and pants, drag on our riding boots (in my case, embarrassingly big, shiny and dorky) and hurl ourselves at the door, doing up our flies as we exit our room.

Meanwhile, the boss has started the Holden ute and is backing it out of the garage.

After reversing some thirty feet, he puts the vehicle into first gear and swings past our door, just missing us as we dive from our room. We fling ourselves into the tub as he comes by in almost pitch-darkness. Mr Webb crunches the vehicle into second gear. Suddenly, I find myself lying on the floor, my nose just centimetres from the grinning face of the cutest border collie sheepdog.

'What just happened then?' I ask, as the ute's momentum pushes me sideways.

Even though it's dark, there's enough moonlight to tell the dog is drop-dead gorgeous, with beautiful black and white markings. On the ridge of her brilliant white muzzle, small black dots start and extend all the way up to her eyes. She smiles at me with both her ears back – and instantly I have a new best friend.

'That was close,' says Dougie, also catching his breath and steadying himself against the side of the tub. I'm sure Dougie noticed the look of bewilderment followed by terror on my face just moments ago. But he doesn't laugh at me.

'Welcome to Habbies Howe,' he says, with that same laugh. He sees me admiring the dog. 'Name's Skye. Boss's dog. Village whore. She'll let anything root her.'

You don't look like a whore to me, you sweet thing, I want to tell the puppy, but I don't in case Dougie thinks I'm a poofter.

I'm not, but I haven't yet figured out how to be myself in front of him. Although I am a 'sensitive boy', I decide my policy at Habbies Howe thus far is to feign toughness. For as long as I'm able, at any rate.

At the top of the driveway, Mr Webb swings right onto the gravel road and accelerates. Despite the early morning dew, dust rises and flies past us beside the ute. And as hot as the day will become, I freeze in my short-sleeved school shirt. The cold wind stirred up by the vehicle's movement swirls in and around the tub. My arms are quickly a mass of goosebumps, which I hope Dougie hasn't noticed. Goosebumps are for weaklings.

The boss pulls up at the gate into a paddock on our left, which Dougie takes as his cue to jump out and open it. I can't help but notice how he runs to the fence. Running the few metres to open a gate does seem a bit excessive.

'Y-you c-c-can leave th-th-that one o-o-open,' the boss calls out, as he drives through. He then almost stops the ute – but not quite – to let Dougie back in. I will soon find that small courtesies, like actually stopping a vehicle to let someone back in, aren't observed at Habbies Howe. Treat them mean and keep them keen – isn't that the saying? I would have stopped for Dougie and I promise myself I will if the chance ever comes my way. Once I learn to drive, that is. I hope he'll do the same for me.

At this stage I'm far too raw to understand that he leaves the gate swinging outwards so we can bring sheep out through it later.

Gates. To the great amusement of local graziers and just about everyone else in the district, I will discover, it's widely known that Habbies Howe jackaroos always run to and from gates – whenever the boss is around. Later, I ask Dougie about it. He shrugs his shoulders, as if embarrassed, and says only that it's a tradition Alan and he inherited when they arrived. 'That's all there is to it,' he says, before looking away. I can tell Dougie doesn't like the line of conversation, so I drop it. Running to gates is a rule here, and you just do it. A little bit like 'no car, no smokes and no booze'. And no raunchy women.

No questions, no explanations. Just compliance.

'There are bigger issues,' Dougie eventually adds, looking past me out across the paddock.

A few months later, Mrs Webb's teenage nephew Stuart will come from Melbourne to visit, and the boss will bring him out in the ute with us. When it comes to Stuart's turn to do a gate, he must assume the running rule doesn't apply to him and he walks up to open it.

Big mistake.

Alan is driving, the boss in the passenger seat. Dougie and I are riding in the tub.

'D-d-drive o-on,' Mr Webb tells Alan, as Stuart holds the gate open for us.

Dougie and I give Stuart a mocking wave from the tub as we leave him with a seven-kilometre walk back to the homestead.

No one challenges Richard Cappur Webb. Not even a relative.

Daylight is just beginning to dawn as the boss drives along what I notice is a well-worn vehicle track. We continue around the side of a hill towards another distant fence line. It's the first real farm paddock I've ever been in, discounting Horse, next to the homestead, where we only leaned on the gate yesterday.

I breathe in the moment. It's the first day of my working life, and up at four-thirty. Wow.

We come to another gate. Much to my surprise, sitting at it, waiting for us, is a grey Land Rover just like the one we left behind in the garage. It can't possibly be the same vehicle. How did it get here before us?

The Other Mr Webb, the manager, is standing beside his vehicle. I copy Dougie and jump out of the ute, and we approach him.

'This is M-Michael Th-Th-Thornton,' says the boss, also getting out of the ute.

I'm staring at a short, stocky and powerfully muscled, wiry man whom I take to be in his mid-forties. His build reminds me of Ikey, the dreaded PE teacher at school. This Mr Webb has black, wavy hair and thick, dark, bushy eyebrows. He's dressed all in khaki: sleeveless shirt with pockets either side, and long trousers. He looks gaunt, which I put down to hard work, wrestling wayward cattle and disciplining recalcitrant jackaroos. His thin face and trim body – and especially his sleeveless shirt which exposes massive biceps – accentuate his rugged appearance and give the man an unchallengeable air of authority.

I start to move forward to shake his hand, but promptly stop when – and I can only put it down to shyness – he ignores me completely, turns to the boss and says, 'They're all over the shop. I reckon if the boys start round the back and come up over the top, I'll cover the far side.'

I notice he makes no reference to what the boss will do. This is how things are. The manager will never tell the boss what to do. It isn't his place, just like it isn't our place to pass on to him messages that might imply any form of instruction. Indeed, the boss's contribution, while everyone else is working, is to drive down to the creek or to a water trough, and tell Skye to 'Bogey, g-g-girl, b-bogey', which means, jump in the creek or trough and take a bath. Whereupon Skye will dive into the nearest water point.

Meanwhile, the Other Mr Webb and we jackaroos get on with the work.

'R-r-right-o,' replies the boss, excitedly, like he's a little boy who's just been told he can go and play with his toys. I'm amazed that the wealthy owner of such a huge spread should seek permission from anyone to take time off. But Mr Webb must feel he needs it. He gets back in the ute's driver's seat, and with Skye still running around in the back, he drives through the gate and heads towards the creek. Surely, it's too early and cold for Skye to bogey, but the boss takes her down along the creek bank anyway.

I follow Dougie's lead and climb into the back of the manager's Land Rover, still wondering why the man didn't shake my hand. Was it me? Has he so quickly sized me up and dismissed me as not worth the bother? Or is he like this with every new jackaroo? And what's with this four-thirty start caper? My mind races. I notice how sitting in the front of any vehicle at Habbies Howe seems to be by invitation only – for us jackaroos, at any rate.

Just as we're about to drive into the new paddock to do whatever it is we're about to do – given I've not been told what 'They're all over the shop' means – another Land Rover pulls up behind us. That's three, I note, counting the one back in the homestead garage.

'Who's that?' I ask Dougie, as we wait to move off. He turns to glance behind us.

Turning forward, still gripping the truck's metal handrail, he says, 'That . . . is Old Harold, the stockman. Or so the old goat calls himself.'

Knowing it's rude to stare, I glance back again, but only briefly. A small, very old man sits crouched behind the big steering wheel. You'd expect him to wave or at least make some eye contact, given we're right in front of his face, but he stares straight through me, as if Dougie and I and the truck we're in don't exist. I'm struck also by the black smoke billowing from his vehicle's rear end, and the dreadful, howling noise coming from the engine.

Dougie's seen and heard them too, and again predicts my question. 'The old fart doesn't know what a choke is,' he says. This time he doesn't look back.

Old Harold must be in his seventies. He quickly becomes one of the characters in my new life. Slimly built, like Ikey he has bones in his face that stick out further than God meant them to. He also has far more than his share of a nose. As for his clothes, they make him look, well, homeless. Even in summer he wears a blue, moth-eaten jumper tucked into a pair of daggy green strides, the latter held up with old bale twine. His truck is for his exclusive use, so Dougie will tell me later. Of the three Land Rovers, Old Harold's is a short wheelbase, while the other two are 'longs'. His has wooden back-and-side panels which can be let down if ever he feels inclined, which isn't often, to rescue a sick or injured sheep. He lives in a room tacked onto the maintenance shed. Not only is he a poor bastard, he's a mean, poor bastard. He wears stubble on his face that is always, and I mean always, five millimetres long. I will forever marvel at how he manages to keep it that length. Maybe he's invented a razor that cuts whiskers exactly five milli-metres out from the face. If so, he should be making a fortune.

Dougie tells me later how he thinks Old Harold has a million dollars hidden under his bed.

Before our vehicle moves off, I sneak a look into the back of Old Harold's truck, thinking I might see a stricken sheep, or some-thing more interesting, but it's squeaky clean, empty except for an ugly mongrel of a grey, spotted dog that sits in the corner busily licking his privates. I guess neither Old Harold nor his truck – nor the dog for that matter – ever get put under much pressure, unless you count the pressure of the vehicle's engine, which screams all day long because the old geezer doesn't know how to work the choke. And either no one has ever bothered to show him, or he refuses to learn how to use it. How quaint.

For the next however long, under constant and tedious direction from the Other Mr Webb, whose hand I am yet to shake and who barks orders at me endlessly, I chase small groups of fearfully dumb Merino sheep all over the top of the hill. Dougie has to do it too, but either he is far fitter than me, or he knows better how to predict sheep's behaviour. After twenty minutes of running – it's still only something past five o'clock – I'm exhausted. I've tripped over fifty granite rocks, all of which have been positioned deliberately to get me. I'm being used like a sheepdog, and it takes me just seconds to realise it. So this is how it ends, I tell myself.

At one point, when I'm out of sight of the others and game enough to stop and take my first piss for the day, one of the manager's two sheepdogs runs past me, and in less than two seconds he heads a group of sheep that I've tried but failed to turn in the right direction. I can never do on two puny boy-legs what the stupid dog just did on his four.

Having done his job, the dog runs back past me with his nose in the air, as if to say, *Well, aren't you a waste of space.* The mongrel is dead right – and the smart-arse animal would be dead if I had my hands on a gun. And if I knew how to use one.

Eventually, all eight of us – including the dogs but not Old Harold's, which never leaves the truck – finish mustering the sheep. There must be over a thousand of the stupid, grey blobs in front of me, not one of them higher than my kneecaps.

My first observation about Merino sheep – any sheep – apart from the fact their brains are for us to eat and not for them to ponder with, is that the fools progress in a forward direction by running around in circles. It's true, and the secret for man – or rather, dog – is to confront that circle at just the right instant and turn the flock in the opposite direction. It causes the sheep, momentarily at least, to go forward before reverting to circling in the opposite direction. And if you do all of this long enough, eventually the flock will reach its destination. It makes for one hell of a long journey, but I quickly learn that is what this farming caper is all about. It's one hell of a long, painfully slow journey, mostly going round in circles.

Of course, a sheepdog makes it look so easy. He understands the quite simple concept that says that for something to go forward, it needs to move in that direction. So, one dog working on the left of the flock will turn the sheep to the right, and another on the right will turn them left. Result: the group goes forward. Eventually. Amazing, when you think about it.

Incidentally, the fact that two jackaroos are employed to run around on foot behind the dogs dawns on me fairly rapidly as being totally superfluous, a complete waste of human resources. But then, I'm also coming to realise that it's a fool of a jackaroo who tries to reason anything.

I wonder if Dougie has a sheepdog, and later I ask him. 'Yeah,' he replies, 'I've got a poor bastard of a thing. Useless. Never use him. He runs right through a mob and splits them up.' It's an idiosyncrasy about Dougie that I will never fathom. Here is one of the smartest young guys going around, one of the cleverest I've met anyway, who knows everything there is to know about just everything – particularly farming – yet he keeps and feeds at great expense a useless poor bastard of a sheepdog. It's Dougie's soft side, and I've found it already.

We get the sheep out onto the road and for a while I'm able to stop running. It's not yet six-thirty and I've never worked a harder day in my life. Plus, I'm as dry as Dougie's sense of humour. My lips already are beginning to crack, and being the fool I am, I lick them, don't I? Of course, that only serves to make them a whole lot worse.

Then it occurs to me how, at this very moment, if I was back at school, I'd still be asleep.

Yet there is something about all of this that is special. The smell of the dew on the grass and that of the gum trees beside us here on the road are things truly to behold, absorb and remember. Then there's the smell and sound of the thousand bleating sheep we're pushing along the road. If only I could muster the energy to appreciate it all. I really do want to love my new life, even though I'm already wrecked and terrified as to what will happen to me next. I'm a bundle of paradoxes: happy, yet terrified; excited, but exhausted.

The Other Mr Webb has gone ahead and is blocking the way further up the road, beyond the gate into the sheep yards. The boss, having returned from the creek, Dougie and I – and I guess as a courtesy I should include Old Harold – bring up the rear. Meanwhile, Skye continues to run furiously from side to side in the back of the boss's ute, barking madly, thinking she's being half useful.

Dougie and I each walk a fence line, pushing along slow, injured and anaemic sheep, which are called the 'runts'. I can certainly identify with them. I've taken to copying Dougie's every move, to win his and the others' approval. Like him, I wave my arms about madly, calling out 'Ho-ho-ho' as if we're a pair of Santa Clauses, just like yesterday when Mr Webb waved his arms about like a mad person to greet Mum, Penny and me. Was it really only yesterday?

Old Harold meanwhile sits in his idling Land Rover some fifty metres back, resting, as does his slack-arse dog, still licking his privates. A stranger would be forgiven for thinking the old codger is dead at the wheel. He continues to stare straight ahead, as if to say, *Don't bother me, I'm concentrating*. With the manual choke still full-on, his vehicle sounds revolting and a continuous plume of black smoke billows from the exhaust pipe. To which the old fool must be oblivious. Or is he? I wonder. Maybe the old goat has everyone fooled.

Old Harold is a legend. Dougie says the boss employs him for his museum value. 'Why else would he keep the old fart on?' He's my first experience of what is known as a 'faithful retainer', yet I can't think of anything about Old Harold that's faithful. It's the boss who's faithful – to him.

Despite my state of exhaustion, I stare in awe at the sight before me. Here, for several hundred metres ahead of me along the gravel road lies this enormous grey, floating woollen blanket, made up of a thousand sheep. Each animal is interconnected, jammed together as if one, with the fence on either side framing this unique work of art. Being the dreamer I am, I tell myself it's a massive genie's rug suspended in mid-air, with a million goblins underneath busily going about their daily business, bobbing up and down, causing lumps and bumps and waves in the magic blanket as it floats along the road. I almost convince myself I can hop on the rug and ride far away from this place, even back to school – and bed.

If only my friends there could see me now. But then, I remind myself, what friends?

The sun bursts through and lights up the rug in different places, except where trees on our left don't let it happen. Dust floats up from my blanket, as if some invisible giant is whacking it with a gigantic, invisible broom. I could dream away like this for hours, except the dust is gnawing at my lungs and settling on my now stinging, cracked lips. Stupidly, I lick them again.

And however bad all of the running around in the paddock is, what happens all day – and the next day, and the next – in the sheep yards gets much, much worse.

After the Other Mr Webb closes the gate into the yards behind the last of the sheep, we leave them in the holding pens and stop for breakfast. Sure, I'm hungry, but there's no way I can front up to the thought of fried eggs and the energy required to ingest them. Just sitting is nourishment enough. I force down a slice of toast and two big glasses of milk. No one offers me cream for my stinging lips – blokes being blokes, they probably haven't even noticed how red and sore they are. Matron at school would have seen and rushed off to get something to put on them. Here, I'm too scared to ask.

Before returning to the yards at seven-thirty a.m. to begin the day's work proper – as if we haven't done a full day of labouring already – Dougie takes me to the dairy to do the milking. And what a ritual milking turns out to be. We jackaroos normally 'milk' at five-thirty, except on Sundays when we're allowed to sleep in until seven.

Dougie explains that the two tall black and white cows are Friesians, while the fawn one is a Jersey. Together, they provide enough milk each day for seven people at the homestead, the manager's family of five, and the station hands and their families: twenty-eight mouths in all. The dairy cows live in their designated paddock across a bridge on the other side of the creek.

Milking involves locking up the cows' calves in a pen next to the milking shed after work each night, so that by morning each mother will have stored around nine litres of milk – one stainless steel bucketful – for the twenty-eight humans to share. After we finish milking, we let the calves back onto their mothers so they can have whatever milk the mothers produce during daylight hours. Come night, we lock up the calves again.

My first attempt at milking, which I decide is tantamount to masturbation, is a disaster. I can't produce a drop of fluid. Even touching the teats seems pornographic, let alone tugging on two of them at once. However which way I slide my fingers up and down the slippery organs, nothing comes out. Dougie is sitting hard up against his cow with his head buried in her flank, out of sight but within earshot of what I'm trying to achieve on my side. I can hear the rhythmic, dual spurts Dougie is making as milk hits the bottom of his stainless steel bucket. Then, when he fills the bottom of his bucket, which he does quickly, I hear a different, softer sound as milk hits milk. No sounds come from my bucket. I feel even more useless. So far, my contribution to the effective running of Habbies Howe is zero.

'How's it going?' Dougie calls out from his side. He knows I'm a loser and that he'll have to come and rescue my situation after he finishes masturbating his cow.

'I'll get there,' I call back, lying my arse off, but not knowing what else to say. It just isn't working for me.

'Make sure you keep the vaseline up to the teats,' Dougie calls out. 'And roll your fingers down them, like I showed you.'

Yeah, right. Is this *legal*?

Eventually, I manage to extract a few pathetic dribbles of white fluid, which nearly bring tears to my eyes. It's enough to write home about. I'm so useless compared to Dougie.

'Here, let me finish her off,' he says, after finishing his cow, and the third. He places his two full buckets of milk well out of the way, to prevent a wayward dairy cow kicking either one over as she leaves her stall. Losing nine litres of fresh, foaming milk wouldn't be a good look; families would miss out on their daily quota.

Finish her off? Dougie certainly is tactful and generous with his few words. After thirty minutes I've hardly got my cow started, let alone to the point where she needs to be finished off.

Normally, while two of us milk each morning, the jackaroo who draws the short straw cooks breakfast under the constant scrutiny of the boss, if he's not in Melbourne. Mr Webb insists on every egg being placed in the frypan exactly as he instructs. This pedantic approach to the simplest of things drives us jackaroos crazy, especially at six o'clock in the morning. The days the boss is in Melbourne are a merciful relief; the atmosphere in the kitchen becomes jubilant, almost euphoric. Things sometimes even get thrown, just because we can.

Finally, with milking over, we reunite the calves with their mothers and send the lot of them packing back to their paddock. Dougie then pours the milk from two of the buckets into six billies of various sizes, some made of enamel, others cheap tin. The entire

big, third bucket we take to the homestead, where we leave it on
a kitchen bench to cool. Later, Susie will put it in one of the two
big fridges. I soon learn how much milk I can guzzle straight from
the huge bucket without her wising up to me. This, of course, is
long before homogenisation and pasteurisation, and the seven
centimetres of disgustingly thick, gooey, yummy cream that settles
at the top of the nine-litre bucket goes deliciously with the odd
Weet-Bix in a brimming bowl. Little wonder many years later I will
have a quadruple heart bypass. Serves me right. Amazing, isn't it,
how so much in life comes back to bite you on the bum?

The long and hot day working in the sheep yards is excru-
ciating. By eight o'clock my mouth is so dry from the dust and
heat I can hardly swallow. By nine o'clock the sun is melting my
face. By ten o'clock my throat feels like I'm being force-fed razor-
blades. By eleven o'clock flies are working their way into my mouth,
down my throat, up my nostrils – buzzing crazily inside each orifice
as they decide whether to go further. I hardly care any more.

After lunch it's more of the same. I want so much to stop, hide,
cry. Yet I don't have the energy or guts to do any of these things.
Trying to be one of the blokes is fast killing me.

At day's end, totally wrecked, somehow I manage to crawl to
dinner. And while the boss prattles away to himself at the far end
of the table, my mind is a mess. Not only am I wiped out physically,
but I can't see any happy way forward; I feel completely hemmed
in. There seems no way my life here can possibly improve.

Looking at the faces around me – faces that never look at
mine – I feel more alone, more isolated than I ever felt at boarding
school. And at school I *did* live a life of total isolation.

Habbies Howe is far, far worse than anything I ever imagined
it would be.

Dougie and I wash up, after which we make our way to the
office, where Dougie types up the Diary. And, yes, he types:

'M. Thornton: started.' Oh, how I wish, how I ache that he'd add: 'and stopped'.

Within seconds of closing the book, I'm in bed and dead to the world, still with my red-raw, cracked lips, which of course Mrs Webb didn't notice over dinner. Typical.

Tuesday offers more of the same, and by nine a.m. three things consume my mind. The first is why no one tells me what we're doing with the sheep. All they do is tell me to run. 'Run, boy, run. Run, boy, run. Run, boy run.'

Second, there's a dripping tap just two pens away from where I'm being made to run nonstop. Drip-drip-drip. Drip-drip-drip. But I'm too scared, too hopeless, too much of a wimp to stop what I'm being forced to do and to go and put my mouth under it. Even for a second.

'Run, boy, run. Run, boy, run. Run, boy, run.'

I become increasingly agitated, increasingly desperate for a cool drink, any kind of drink. The heat is unbearable. And the tap is just over there, dripping clear water which falls onto ungrateful dirt. It wouldn't cost them anything to let me go to it and put my mouth under it for ten seconds. But I can't, I just can't. I'm too scared of the way they yell at me. Nonstop.

Third – and this is the only comforting, positive thought that pounds away in my brain – I begin to devise a plan to escape this godforsaken, hellhole of a place. But I can't just climb over the rail and start walking to the railway station at Seymour – however tempting a thought that might be – because four men and a jackaroo are watching my every move.

'Run, boy, run. Run, boy, run. Run, boy, run.'

I'm exhausted; dehydrated. I have a thumping headache. I keep telling myself I've got to get out of this place. I just have to find a way to escape. Whatever I've done wrong, please God forgive me.

'Run, boy, run. Run, boy, run. Run, boy, run.'

The words ring in my ears. The bosses never let up. I am so exhausted, so sunstruck, I hardly notice any more who is yelling at me. Anyway, I don't care. I'm out of here as soon as I can work out how to escape. Maybe if I do just drop dead, I'll be saved from all this torture. When it was this hot at school, we jumped in the pool. Oh, school . . . What a wonderful thought that is. Anything, even Ikey's dreaded PE classes, even his stinking rotten wooden horse – lengthways – would be better than this.

'Run, boy, run. Run, boy, run. Run, boy, run.'

I begin to hallucinate. Not about sheep. A skinny, naked teenage girl runs past me, then another, beckoning me to follow them to the cool, dripping tap. It's no longer kelpies running over sheep's backs – it's naked, skinny pubescent teenage girls with tight pointy breasts, urging me to go with them. One of them stands by the dripping tap calling me with her hands and breasts to come and drink with her. My stinging lips and wrecked body want so much to wrap themselves around the tap, her breasts, her . . . But I don't dare stop running.

'Run, boy, run. Run, boy, run. Run, boy, run.'

Suddenly, in the loudest voice, I call out towards the tap: 'I can't come, they won't let me!'

Everyone stops what they're doing. They turn and stare at me. It lasts forever. I look away and stand dead still, as if stuck in time, like I'm feigning death on two legs. When they resume their work, with no one looking, I turn and sink my riding boot into the nearest sheep.

It's Wednesday, and the panic attack happens after breakfast.

For the second day in a row we've been allowed to get up at the normal time of five-thirty. I begin to get the knack of masturbating my Jersey cow – which I secretly call Belinda. Belinda seems happy enough to let me fondle her rubbery, dangly bits. With my forehead resting against her flank while I work, Belinda starts to have an improper effect on me. I turn my face to the side and rub my cheek gently across her furry hide. And for just a moment I forget that I'm milking a cow – three days of scorching heat and lack of water have turned me full-on weird.

I finish milking Belinda by the time Dougie completes the other two cows, although what hand muscles I have are numb from working my sweetheart's parts. The numbness in my fingers and wrists makes lifting my bucket out of the way nigh on impossible.

With breakfast over, I attend to the boiler, only to discover the fire has gone out. I hear Dougie calling to me that the boss is waiting for us. The ute is revving out the front. I have to be out there immediately, but I can't leave the boiler without restarting it. Dougie has already made it clear we jackaroos never leave Mr Webb waiting for anything.

Panic sets in. Hopelessly agitated, I begin to hop from foot to foot. I need to have a piss, but there's no time. Boy, do I need to take a leak. Dougie calls out again. But I need more time to restart the fire. Everything is going wrong. I hate this place, I really hate it. No one will tell me what we're doing with the sheep; I almost fainted a dozen times yesterday; I'm being treated no better than a dog. In fact, I'm being treated worse than the dogs. And now the boiler has gone out. What am I doing here? No one likes me. I'm not a rural. I'm late. I've let the fire go out. I shouldn't be here. I'm not cut out for this farming bullshit. I should be getting ready to go back to school where I belong. I hate being on this stupid farm . . . Tears build, and soon I'm crying, hopping uncontrollably from foot to foot. I really need a piss. I don't know what to do.

Something tells me I should go. I slam the metal door shut and run through the kitchen. The ute is moving, albeit slowly, up the driveway. I chase it halfway up the hill and fling myself over the tail-gate. Dougie watches the whole thing. I look the other way in case he sees I've been crying, but I know he can tell. I'm under no illusion that I'm fooling him or anyone else at this hellhole of a place.

Mrs Baillieu can be right for all I care. Habbies Howe is going to kill me.

Half lying in the ute's tub, I take a deep breath and try to set-tle. Another deep breath and I turn my head to the wind, hoping it will dry my eyes. Part of me doesn't care if Dougie does see I've been crying. I've stopped caring, especially about things manly. I probably look like Clifford back at school before he made his one, last dramatic charge at the wooden horse. The sheep yards are my wooden horse. I need to make a really good run-up like Jonathon did, and fly over them, then keep on sailing into oblivion.

And never ever come back to these lousy bloody sheep yards ever again.

After lunch, I see Mr Webb go to the office. Once Dougie is safely out of sight, I follow him. For over an hour I've been building the courage to do this, to face up to Mr Webb and tell him I'm leaving. If necessary, if he doesn't like what I tell him, I will walk all the way to Seymour. Gone are any feelings that I should just hang in here and hope things will get better. I'm so agitated, so stuffed, so confused. All I can think of is to get away from this awful place, to get away from this bunch of mad, crazy people. He's already sitting at his stupid, messy desk when I knock on the door.

'Mr Webb,' I blurt out, revealing instantly how agitated I am. He turns and looks up at me, no doubt amazed to see me in the house at this time of day.

'Y-y-yes, M-M-Michael?' he says, clearly surprised, but giving me his attention.

'Mr Webb,' I repeat, trying to force a strong voice, 'this just isn't me. I have to leave.' There, I've said it. I know that what I'm doing is pathetic, wimpy, confirming me as a weakling, a total loser. I know I'm proving Mrs Baillieu right. But I don't care – I'm completely and utterly stuffed. All I want to do is to get the hell away from this hole. And I'll do anything in the whole world to achieve it. I don't care what the rurals at school think. I've convinced myself that nothing the boss can say will make me change my mind. I'm telling him out of courtesy more than anything. I'm leaving. That's all there is to it.

Mr Webb stands up. He looks hard at me and says, 'B-b-boy, if you ch-ch-chuck th-this in, y-y-you'll never s-s-stick at anything. N-n-now g-g-go back out there, and c-come back and s-s-see me t-tonight.'

He turns, sits down, and begins to fiddle with his paperwork.

I desperately want to say, *But* . . . But I don't. Something inside stops me. I can't get any words out. I can't even begin to reply because it's not in my nature to argue, not in my nature to be anything but subservient. It just shows how pathetic – how much of a loser – I am. I can't even resign like a man. I leave the office and mope my way back to the sheep yards.

The boss must later say something to the Other Mr Webb – that they've won – because the afternoon in the sheep yards pans out vastly different to the previous two-and-a-half days. First, they stop yelling at me to 'Run, boy, run'. Dougie even whispers encouraging words, coming back through the sheep more than once to explain not only that we're sexing (splitting) the wethers and ewes, as well as classing (ranking) them, but also why we're doing it. At one point the boss even takes me with him on a brisk walk down to the workshop to get an adjustable spanner – he doesn't need to take me, but he says it's so I'll know where to find the wrench next time one is needed to fix the drafting gate. The brief time out of the dreaded yards gives me welcome respite. While we walk, he doesn't mention our lunchtime conversation. And I certainly don't.

It's as if the initiation is suddenly over. As if I've been broken in – or just broken – and now they're starting to put me back together, the way they want me.

As for the follow-up talk with the boss after dinner, it doesn't happen. It's not needed. They've made sure during the afternoon that I'm on the way back.

It's said new school teachers are taught not to smile before Easter. At Habbies Howe, they don't bother to wait until Easter; they break in their jackaroos in seventy-two hours.

5

Charlie

Thursday is a whole heap better. Dougie and I milk at five-thirty; we eat breakfast with the boss along with the ABC news at seven. At seven-thirty, we're waiting under the cypress tree for the Other Mr Webb to arrive, to give us our morning orders. Moments later he pulls up in his Land Rover, winds down the window, and says coldly, 'You boys can get your horses.'

Get our horses. Yippee! Relief at last. It's the best thing to have come out of the man's mouth all week; indeed, it's the only good thing. Yet I don't trust him one bit. I remember what that innocent-enough ride in the boss's ute three days ago resulted in.

I'm amazed how easy it is to get the horses out of their paddock, past the homestead and down to their corral – at a gallop. Simply opening their gate is enough because they know that their feed boxes, which hang off the corral railings at intervals, will be full of yummy chaff.

The change in my mental state is extraordinary. Just looking at the horses as they gallop to the yards raises my spirits and renews my strength. The nine animals are a breath of fresh air.

Dougie shows me which gear belongs to Charlie, and saddling my horse becomes the first task all week for which I don't need Dougie's help. The simple act of doing something for myself, even a small thing, gives my self-esteem a huge boost. Charlie wants to play with his bridle as I place it over his head, but I tell him not to be a prick and to keep his head still.

The heat is so much easier to bear on horseback. Just our movement makes enough breeze to keep the flies at bay and soothe my
still aching, red-raw lips.

We spend the morning in paddocks doing what I quickly decide
almost makes everything else about Habbies Howe bearable. Mustering and moving cows and calves is exhilarating, even though
later I will realise that what we're doing on my first day in the
saddle is pretty elementary stuff. But I don't care; I'm out of those
damn awful sheep yards, and Dougie and I are away from the two
dreadful bosses. What relief.

I trust Dougie, but I don't trust anyone else here.

Sometimes with the manager along for the ride, we jackaroos undertake all of the cattle work on horseback, while it's
Old Harold's job to shift sheep regularly from paddock to paddock using his truck. The boss's rationale for having us rotate
the cattle around Habbies Howe's sixty-four paddocks with
monotonous regularity – which I soon discover is what we'll be
doing – is to keep fresh pasture up to them. This, in turn, allows
mothering cows to produce the optimum quantity of milk and
their calves to put on greater weight, ideally one kilogram of live
weight per day.

The other reason the boss and the manager make us jackaroos
move the cattle around the property with monotonous regularity is
to ensure we never, ever get a moment's rest.

Charlie is great to ride; he has a smooth and even gait, and
I quickly learn just how deft he is at cattle work, at times making
me feel totally superfluous on his back. Even Dougie acknowl-
edges how agile Charlie is on his feet. He's also intelligent, which
is helpful.

I soon understand how vastly different doing stock work is
compared to pony club dress-ups as a small boy – that pathetic,
childish stuff we did at gymkhanas, thinking we were brave.

Mustering cattle on horseback is real man's work. It requires constant concentration and forethought, because, when things go awry, they do so quickly and in a big way.

Mustering our first mob is easy; the paddock is small. We can see all of the cattle in it from the one high point. Even though we know straight away that we have all thirty cows and their calves, as soon as we get them together Dougie stands tall in his stirrups and counts and re-counts them – telling me to do the same, 'Because maths isn't my strong point,' he calls out, with that laugh again. Either we're both dummies at arithmetic or we've got them all, because we both count sixty heads. So does Charlie, by the way.

The hard bit is what I thought would be the easiest: putting the mob through the gate into their new paddock. All I expected to do was to just open the gate and watch them trot through. Not so. I'm in the country now, where if something can go wrong, it will.

A calf, whose mother has already made it through the gate, baulks at the opening and takes off at pace along our side of the fence – on Dougie's side of the mob we're flanking. I watch as, in an instant, Dougie spins round and accelerates at a gallop after the wayward calf, his horse unashamedly farting at us as it takes off. Charlie wants to go after them, and he pulls on his bit to tell me so, but I rein him in. I figure we need to wait in case another calf does the same thing on our side.

Confirming my instinct, Dougie turns in his saddle and yells, 'YOU STAY THERE!'

In seconds, Dougie and his galloping horse gain on the recalcitrant calf, which has its head down as if trying to get extra speed. What a sight. Go Dougie. I keep one eye on the remaining cows and calves, which seem uninterested in the chase; they continue to make their way through the gateway without any sign of belligerence. Meanwhile, the escaping calf, believing this is what it's been put on earth to do, runs faster. This must be the Webbs' way of providing physical distraction for hormonal boy jackaroos, I think, as I watch Dougie gain on his quarry.

It takes him maybe a hundred metres to get in front of the bolting calf. The moment his horse gets its nose in front, the calf skids to a halt, in what must be less than three metres. This is the part that requires the greatest skill from the rider – to stay on board his horse while it stops in its own length. Otherwise, the rider does a Jonathon Clifford and floats through the air like a capeless Superman.

Clearly, Dougie has done this many times before. He not only stays in his saddle, but within seconds he has the calf trotting back along the fence compliantly towards the still-open gate. But it doesn't end as smoothly as all would hope. The calf baulks at the gateway a second time, jumps high in the air and to its left, and hurtles along *my* side of the gateway. A cow, already through the gate, comes running up on the other side of the fence alongside her 'baby', as if to control its wayward behaviour. The cow's presence does exactly the opposite; it serves only to make the calf bolt faster.

'YOUR TURN!' yells Dougie, who stays well back.

'Our turn,' I tell Charlie, kicking him gently in the flanks and pulling his reins to the left. I needn't have bothered. Charlie has already worked things out for himself and I find myself hanging on to the pommel with all my might as he swivels and accelerates in pursuit.

Charlie is brilliant, and the experience for this novice stock-horse horse rider sitting on top at no charge is nothing short of sensational. He's obviously been waiting for his chance to strut his stuff – to show me what he can do – and he sure is in his element as he gallops as fast as Dougie's horse did across the open grassland moments earlier.

Charlie is giving me a lesson, and my role is nothing more than to hang on – and learn.

He copies the wide arc Dougie's horse made. Catching up with the calf is the easy part, although I've never ridden a horse so fast. Again, it's that split second when Charlie gets his nose in front of the calf that counts. The beast stops suddenly; we stop in our own length. Plus, I stay on. If we'd not stopped with the calf, as I will experience on a later occasion, the calf would have waited for us to sail past and then it would have run around and past us – and kept on going. You always need to stop with the beast, and stay with it.

Having done what we needed to do, the rotten calf stands staring at us, heaving huge breaths and expelling a bucket-load of snot in our direction It stares at us for what seems to last for minutes. Then, sensing it can't get away with any more of its stupid antics, the calf turns and begins to trot back.

I think I just learnt why footballers snarl at each other.

This time Dougie is ready. He and his horse are standing at a sharp angle at just the right distance from the gateway. At the precise the moment the calf gets to the opening, Dougie shouts a loud 'HEY!' The calf, given the fright of its life, jumps sideways and literally falls through the open gateway.

Mission accomplished.

'Well done,' Dougie calls out to me – and I sit fifty metres tall in my saddle. His compliment brings me alive; it gives me a feeling I haven't had all week. Indeed, it's a feeling I've not had since . . . I don't know when. Probably being awarded Half Colours for swimming.

While Charlie and I stand back and watch, Dougie walks his horse to the open gate, bends down and swings it closed. His horse follows the gate's arc, without coaxing, and Dougie leans over and puts the chain on.

I pat my horse's neck. 'Good boy, good boy,' I whisper to my newest best friend. (Sorry, Skye. Beautiful dog.)

Right at this moment I resolve to put behind me what

happened over the past three days. Stuff them all, I think to myself. I will stay at Habbies Howe come hell or high water, regardless of what punishment they dish up next, regardless of how hard they try to kill me. Pack of mongrel bastards. (I learnt the expression from Dougie on Monday, in reference to the sheep.)

On our ride back to the homestead, walking our horses side by side – even though we have to rein them in because they know we're heading home to their feed boxes – Dougie pulls out his tobacco pouch and papers and rolls himself a cigarette, like he's done each night in the dairy after locking up the calves. The dairy is the one place where Dougie can confidently have a smoke without being sprung. It's also the only safe place where we can share a quiet beer. So much for the no smokes and no booze edict.

He holds out his tobacco pouch. 'Want one?'

'Yeah, why not. Thanks,' I reply. I've earned myself a smoke, even if Dougie does double up laughing at my pathetic first attempt at rolling a fag.

We both laugh. 'It's not easy rolling the bloody thing while I try to stop Charlie from bolting home,' I say, despite Dougie having just done so on his mount. And so I become a smoker. Peer pressure.

We spend the afternoon doing chores around the sheds, which again gives me breathing space, time to reflect. How unnecessary was that stupid four-thirty start on Monday? And all the shit they hung on me in my first three days here; the way management breaks in a new jackaroo in such a ridiculous, heavy-handed manner. Boys' games, I tell myself. Stupid, childish, bloody boys' games.

During my year at Habbies, I will see two more jackaroos broken in on their first few days. Both boys will get similar treatment to that meted out to me: up at four-thirty a.m. to do some dubious task that doesn't need doing at such a ridiculous hour, pushed to the limit throughout their first three days. Both new boys treated like shit in the same way I was in my first seventy-two hours.

Friday is different again. My harsh new world has only just begun.

At morning orders, Dougie and I are again told by the manager: 'Get your horses.' I wonder if the man says please when he wants the salt passed to him at the dinner table.

What pisses me off most, though, is how we're never told what we'll be doing. Not immediately. It means we can't plan in our heads how we might approach the task we're about to be given. What management doesn't realise – and this despite Habbies Howe's impressive reputation for training jackaroos – is that we aren't learning how to think, just to do. Which is ridiculous given that the whole point of being a jackaroo is to learn to think – on our feet, on the job – and to apply that thinking later to successful farm management practices ourselves, if farming is to be our career.

Dougie and I trudge off to bring in the horses. The bottom line is I don't care what we'll be doing with them, so long as I'm never made to put another foot inside those damn awful sheep yards. Indeed, from this moment on, every time the Other Mr Webb says 'Get your horses', my heart leaps with joy and I give quiet thanks to God for His unbridled mercy.

We saddle up and suddenly the manager reappears and tells us to meet him at The Landing, a small paddock less than a ten-minute ride south of the homestead, so named because it contains a loading dock for heavy machinery, as well as a raised platform for the old Bedford truck's stock crate to sit on when it isn't needed for transporting animals.

When we arrive at The Landing, the Other Mr Webb is already there. He and another man are cruising around the paddock in a white Holden station wagon. Goodness knows where the vehicle came from. We amble over to the car, which is slowly circling two quiet Hereford cows, the only animals in the paddock. Dougie and I bring our horses to a standstill, let loose our reins and watch. And I have to tell you that sitting still on a stockhorse, with loose reins, at eight o'clock on a summer's morning, is about as therapeutic as life can get. I could sit here forever and a day, nestled cosily in my comfy leather saddle, Charlie chomping on fresh pasture while he has the chance.

'Government vet,' declares Dougie, eyeing the red number-plates on the vehicle.

So what? I think. The two cows are 'dry', Dougie says; that is, neither has a calf at foot. But what each cow does have, I notice immediately, is a huge, disgusting-looking growth bulging from one eye.

'Cancer eye,' Dougie says, again reading my mind. 'Common in Herefords.'

I figure Dougie knows exactly what will happen next, but, as usual, he will tell me things on a need-to-know basis. For instance, he obviously doesn't see the need to tell me now that cancer eye is caused by a lack of pigment around the eyes, and when sunlight and dust get in the affected eye, it promotes cancer. And how, while the disease is common in white-faced Herefords, the same thing doesn't occur in black cattle, a truism with which Angus breeders cajole Hereford men mercilessly. I will learn all of this later. For now, ignorance makes life less complicated, even if enormously frustrating for an inquiring mind.

After what appears to be considerable discussion between the men in the circling vehicle, the Other Mr Webb leans out of the window in our direction, and he calls out, 'You boys can bring these cows down to the yards.' He winds up his window and the pair drive off.

I think sometimes Dougie chooses not to tell me stuff because he thinks I won't be able to handle it. Given what happens next, it probably isn't a bad strategy.

We herd the two cows out onto the road and walk them quietly towards the cattle yards, down past the homestead. The cows definitely can see out of one eye only; both keep turning their head further than normal to see where we are, and then back to where they're walking. It's really sad. Neither old girl gives us any grief – not like yesterday with the recalcitrant calf – but then today we aren't dealing with a nursery.

The cattle yards are next to the dreaded, shadeless sheep yards, although the section set aside for cattle is mercifully in shade courtesy of a huge pine tree next to the loading ramp.

No sooner do we put the cows in the first yard, climb off our horses and walk into the yards, than from nowhere the vet produces a rifle and shoots both cows between the eyes.

Fair dinkum, it happens as quickly as that. Excuse me – what just happened then?

The noise from his rifle is incredible and because I'm only centimetres from the vet when he shoots, my ears ring and my heart pounds fiercely. It's my first-ever experience of death, or murder – of either – and immediately I go into minor shock. I stare at the two motionless bodies, blood oozing from a tiny hole neatly placed directly between each one's eyes, in the curly white hair in the middle of each lady's forehead. Both cows collapsed on the ground right in front of me, like sacks of potatoes falling off a truck, their eyes now blaming me, telling me it's my fault, that I murdered them. I shudder involuntarily, then move back two paces in case I shudder again and someone notices. Toughness is the order of the day here.

Still, both sets of eyes follow me. Suddenly, I feel breakfast coming up, but somehow I swallow just in time. Spewing right now wouldn't be a good look.

I'm stunned, speechless. My guts are wrenched tightly. Yet again, my shock and fright are due as much to not having been fore-warned as to the killing itself. No one here gives two shits about me. Why don't these pricks ever tell me what's about to happen? Yet maybe it is better that I wasn't warned. I probably would have run for the train in Seymour – and collected a shelling on the way for deserting the good ship Habbies Howe.

I look across at the vet and his smoking gun and shake my head sideways in disbelief. It's so cruel. Another story to tell Mum in my first letter home if I ever have the energy to write one.

The two men finalise their discussion, which Dougie later tells me has to do with how much compensation the government will give the boss for each beast.

Agriculture, as an industry, I learn to my amazement, has con-siderable clout; huge government subsidies get handed out left, right and centre. The government even pays for your damaged stock. It's why the boss – being the industry leader he is – keeps going to those meetings in Melbourne, and elsewhere: to keep the subsidies rolling in. Does the government reimburse the corner milk-bar owner when a block of Cadbury's goes off in the summer heat? I think not. It's a pity the boss doesn't represent immigrant milk-bar owners, and get compensation for them for their damaged goods. And while the rest of us pay the doctor, farmers get paid even for the doctor's house calls.

'Dougie,' says the Other Mr Webb in his usual gruff way, his voice bringing me back with a thud to the present. 'You can get the knives.'

What did he just say? The knives? Where's my mother when I need her? Someone help.

I turn my attention momentarily from the two dead cows lying directly in front of me to the vet. Casually, he bends over and picks up the forensic evidence of his murderous deed – the two empty rifle shells. The two men then calmly walk through the gate, get into the station wagon and drive off.

With Dougie gone too, I'm left alone with the beasts, steam rising off them, both still staring at me. I move behind them. What is this thing about knives? Is it what I'm thinking? Surely, we're not about to attack the poor things with knives. Where is Bill Peach and the *This Day Tonight* TV cameras when a story so blatantly inhumane presents itself? I know that cattle need to be killed, but can't it be done . . . nicely?

I dry retch – I can't help myself. Fortunately nothing comes up, and no one sees or hears me. Moments later, Dougie reappears with two knives and says, 'We'd better get into it.'

There's no point asking him *Into what?* because he probably won't give me an answer. So I don't ask. We just do.

We spend the rest of the day skinning, gutting and cutting up the two carcasses. I shan't go into the whole gruesome process, save to report that the work sees us peeling or hacking the hide away from bone, fat and meat. The 'contaminated' meat is destined for the kennels and the station's pack of rabbit dogs, of which there are more than twenty. Dougie makes the point that here we're just 'hacking' steaming, flopping sections of meat, which the rabbit dogs will tear apart further when they get their teeth into it.

Of the thirteen men and boys who work on Habbies Howe, two catch rabbits for a living. Between them, Jonesy and Tuff keep the dogs, which represent every breed imaginable, from Dobermans to greyhounds – some that I'm sure were never meant to be bred for any purpose, let alone rabbiting – each dog deft at chasing, catching and garrotting rabbits. Jonesy and Tuff also have a collection of savvy ferrets, which they send hurtling down rabbit holes to chase out the bunnies, whereupon the dogs pounce, lock their mouth around the rabbit's neck and go chomp.

This is how it works in theory. In practice, the two men spend most of their day sitting under a gum tree, reading yesterday's *Sun* newspaper, drinking billy tea and smoking. Occasionally, they will get off their arses long enough to make the dogs catch an odd rabbit.

And to think all of this happens – Australia's horrific rabbit problem, I mean – because in 1859 some gormless grazier in Victoria's Western District imported twelve rabbits from England so he could hunt them. He ought to have been nuggeted, if not shot in the curly white hair between his eyes, and had his farm confiscated.

Each evening at five-thirty, Jonesy and Tuff return to the shed area to feed and lock up the dogs. Our job – that is, whichever jackaroo is about at the time – is to locate each station hand as he packs up for the night and ask him what he did for the day, for the Diary. The rabbiters know this is why we need to ask them how many rabbits they bagged, and this part they never challenge. Their dishonesty comes in their answer; they lie their proverbial heads off. It's my first experience of an adult other than my mother lying directly to my face (that I know of).

'Thirty,' Tuff will say to me, without a single blood vessel in his face giving him away. I'll look down at the hessian bag he's carrying to his car to take home for his and Marg's dinner, and there'll be a tiny lump at the bottom. Maybe two, possibly three rabbits. Tops. Apart from the shock of it, I have to stop myself from laughing straight in his face.

'Yeah, right,' Dougie will say, whenever Tuff announces how many rabbits the two men caught. Yet I notice that Dougie never says 'Yeah, right' to Jonesy, when the older rabbiter tells the same fib. I can tell Dougie isn't the least bit scared of Tuff, but with Jonesy, who mostly wears a scowl on his face, Dougie watches his p's and q's. Another useful lesson for me.

It's also another paradox concerning life at Habbies Howe. We jackaroos can't get away with anything – well, not much – and yet Jonesy and Tuff spend every day sitting under the shade of a tree, drinking tea. And they get away with it. We'll be riding our horses way out in a far paddock – many kilometres from the homestead – and we'll come across the pair sitting around, smoking.

'Morning,' we'll call out.

'Mornin',' will come the reply from Tuff, neither man showing an ounce of embarrassment.

It teaches me another of life's lessons, about how some people put in and some don't.

After Dougie and I hang the meat from the two cows in an old meat shed near the woolshed (not the shed near the yards set aside for killing sheep for the homestead), we take wheelbarrow-loads of still-warm offal to the dog compound and heave it into two big wood-fired open boilers. Dougie shows me how to cook a casserole using meat-meal powder, water and two sets of cows' guts – guts which, just hours earlier, were propelling their owners around a paddock. The meat-meal thickens up the glug, like flour does in cooking. It reminds me of porridge they dished up at boarding school. But Dougie cooks it without the glug island. Still, it's revolting.

Dougie tells me we're making enough gruel to feed the rabbit pack for a month. Of course, knowing all of this will help me enormously in my career as a wool buyer.

My claim to fame on this, my fifth day at Habbies Howe – and this is something I will hold dear to me until I go to my grave – is that I do not chunder during the entire killing. Oh yes, I do dry retch – no one sees me, thank God – and I do want to vomit from the sight and smell of steaming guts as they spill onto the dirt. But I don't chunder. Wrenching a stomach out of a carcass using both hands, watching mounds of partially digested lime-green grass cascade over my arms and hands, is bad enough. And hacking off the beasts' heads with bits of sinew dangling, and extracting the still warm kidneys and the incredibly slippery liver from hard up against the beast's backbone using my fingertips, isn't much fun. And placing all of those flopping bits and pieces in the wheelbarrow certainly makes it a day to remember – but not once do I chunder.

And here's another thing I quickly discover about life as a jackaroo, which leaves me totally perplexed: we never, ever get a *thank you* from management. Over dinner I fully expect the boss to say something along the lines of, *Michael, I guess it was pretty hard for you out there today and I really am proud of the way you coped. In fact, I plan to give both Dougie and you a well-deserved pay rise for how you performed your duties today.*

Yeah, right. Get real. It's all part of being a Habbies Howe jackaroo.

And yet – and I don't know how to justify it – this whole shitty mess in which I find myself embroiled, literally up to my armpits, is starting to grow on me; it's starting to have a positive, exhilarating effect. Despite having spent the day doing one of the worst farm jobs imaginable, during a quiet moment I thank God that I didn't follow through with my resignation just two days ago.

Many years later, my 'resignation' will become a standing joke among the folk at Habbies Howe. Of course, the story will be 'adjusted' – as country folk are wont to do. They will laughingly say the reason I didn't follow through with it was that no one would drive me to the railway station in Seymour. Ha ha. God in heaven knows the treatment here is tantamount to child, or at least teenager, abuse.

During dinner, I decide to hang in at Habbies Howe, at any cost. The place now owes me big time – there must be benefit in staying and seeing it all through – and I'm not about to let management off the hook. I've even learnt to conquer the flies. And I've seen death close-up – and it wasn't my own.

What more could they possibly dish up that could kill me?

I'm about to find out. My first week at Habbies Howe is far from over.

Over dinner – and without any mention by the boss of our pending pay rise for the fantastic day's work we did with the knives – Mr Webb declares to anyone still awake at the table, 'Th-th-the s-super will be here t-t-tomorrow.'

So what? I think to myself. Why do I need to know about a truck bringing petrol? As usual, Dougie wises me up to nothing.

Saturday. Dougie and I get up as usual at five-thirty, we masturbate the dairy cows and cook breakfast under the pedantic eye of the boss. 'Not th-th-there w-with th-the egg, boy!' he screams at me. He makes me move the egg all of one centimetre across the frypan. The old man is full-on weird.

We eat, wash up, check all vehicles for oil and water and fill them with juice, and we're back in our quarters having a ten-second lie on our beds after cleaning our teeth – me still not having a clue what I'll be doing on a *Saturday* – when I hear the sound of loud, huffing air brakes descending from the top of the rise into the valley which is Habbies Howe. It's the same hill that Mum drove me down less than a week ago – the same hill over which in my dreams I've escaped a zillion times since.

Dougie doesn't move and I dismiss the truck as being the one the boss mentioned over dinner, the one bringing petrol. As usual, Dougie keeps me in the dark. Yet, my brain slowly begins to ask: if this is the truck bringing petrol, why are its brakes so loud? Why is it such a *big* truck? Why is it huffing so? Why am I becoming ever so agitated?

The huffing air brakes grow louder and louder as the truck gets closer to the front gate, the noise accentuated by the echoes coming off the surrounding hills.

'Here it comes,' says Dougie, finally swinging his legs off his bed and getting to his feet. As usual, I copy his every move, as if we're twins joined at the hips.

We're almost down at the sheds when the truck lurches its way through the front gate and heads left across dry grass towards the sheds, towards us.

It turns out it's a full-blown semitrailer. I notice it has an exceptionally long, flat tray, on which sit tightly stacked yet quite small, white plastic bags. The bags look harmless enough, although at only one layer high, I should be twigging straight away that something fishy is going on.

I've completely misunderstood the word 'super'. It's not petrol, it's fertiliser – *superphosphate*, the white powdery shit that comes straight off a ship from the tiny island of Nauru. It's an additive famous for making grass grow in much of south-east Australia.

The catch – everything we do at Habbies Howe I now realise has a catch – is that each innocent-enough-looking small plastic bag of 'super', as it is far too affectionately known, is deceivingly heavy. Deceivingly so, that is, until I try to put the first bag on my back. The truck is carrying a hundred and forty-four bags of the stuff – twelve tons (super's still supplied in the imperial measure) – which at twelve bags to the ton means each bag weighs 83.3 kilograms. I weigh seventy-five.

It works like this: the driver trolleys each bag to the back of his truck, whereupon Dougie and I take it in turns to put one on our back, with our hands up over our shoulders. As we do, the driver grins at us, as if to say, *Why the hell are you two dickheads working here? You look far too bright to put up with this shit.* Well, I hope he's thinking the second part.

And here's where the fun begins: we're required to carry our bag into the shed and place it precisely where Mr Webb wants it put, to where he's pointing. My problem – Dougie is much stronger than me and it isn't as big a deal for him – is that once my bag of rock-solid fertiliser begins to slide sideways off my soon red-raw back, there isn't a single thing in the whole wide world I can do to prevent it crashing to the ground exactly where it wants to go; never, of course, where Mr Webb wants me to put it, finger-pointing or no finger-pointing.

'Ch-christ, b-b-boy. N-not there,' he yells at me. My bag has fallen three millimetres from where he wants it, but still it's not good enough for his ultra-pedantic nature. He makes me move every bag I deliver to him the three millimetres, not caring one iota about the lifetime of chiropractic care I will require.

After ten bags, my back is a blister. After the seventy-two, I'm like a convict oarsman who's been lashed mercilessly the entire journey from England to Botany Bay.

But, hang on, there's something else that's fishy about all of this. This widespread pile we've been making is covering far too big an area for just one truck-load. What gives?

Derr! Hello! Snap! Idiot, Thornton! *This isn't the only truck-load.*

When the truck is bare and the driver climbs back in the cab with his mocking grin intact and drives off, I stagger to our servants' quarters and collapse face down on my bed. In unbearable agony, I figure the five-metre-square pile we've made – of which we've barely begun the second layer – must mean there are more truck-loads, many more truck-loads, to come. My back makes me pray I am horribly, horribly wrong. Each time I backed up to a bag, put my hands behind my shoulders, grasped the bag's top corners and pulled it forward onto my back, it was like someone was twisting the corner of a house brick into my shoulder blade. It stayed that way, the pain of the brick grinding its way into bone, until I again heard, 'Christ, b-b-boy. Not th-there', as the bag I was lugging cascaded off my back onto the pile, always in the wrong place.

Before I can count to fifty, I awake to the sound of more air brakes huffing their way into the valley. Again, I pray for forgiveness for whatever I've done in life to deserve this punishment.

In all, *six* trucks arrive; seventy-two tons of the rotten shit. Four hundred and thirty-two bags on each of Dougie's and my backs. At the end of the day I am totally and completely stuffed. I lie on my bed, unable to move – again with not a single word of praise from the proprietor – and I ponder how, somewhere, in some developed country, to which I promise myself I will emigrate the moment my aching back heals, there must be laws to prevent employers doing things like this to good young boys; to this good young boy, at any rate.

Hey, did this Alan guy choose a good week in which to take his annual leave? Or is every week at Habbies Howe like this? I would have had to lug one hundred and forty-four fewer bags if he was here, I worked out in my head while shepherding yet another bag in dread to Mr Webb.

Oh. And what, you may ask, is the remuneration for a first-year jackaroo at Habbies Howe? Nine dollars a week.

Nine dollars a week.

Plus all I can eat, if I have strength to eat, which I don't. That saves the Webbs more of their precious dollars. I've hardly eaten anything all week. Little wonder I'm half anaemic.

Yet, despite my physical and mental pain, I'm still alive, and I'm still a jackaroo at Habbies Howe. I had my chance to leave – kind of – but I didn't go. No one could have stopped me, or so I convince myself. Yet nothing, nothing will make me leave now. I'm owed, big time.

Something else is happening to me. Despite the brutal nature of the work, I'm beginning to gather the father-figures that have eluded me all my life. Even though we don't get praise for what we do, somehow I know our work is appreciated. And as my year at Habbies Howe progresses, I will come to learn how high the community's regard is for Habbies Howe's jackaroos. Every grazier and farmer in the district – and far beyond, it seems – knows that being a jackaroo for Richard Cappur Webb is tough. People respect us; they tell us so to our faces. Me, tough? This, to a fatherless city choirboy who all his life has been put down by adults and boys – and his mother – alike, becomes the turning point for me. It gives me confidence, self-esteem, courage; things I've only ever read about. Blow the rurals at school – I'm a Habbies Howe jackaroo, to whom important people show respect.

It's odd how we are respected off the property but not on it. Other graziers and their wives and sons look up to us as Dick Webb's boys, yet on Habbies we're treated like shit. But still, I don't care. I'm learning to hold my head up high. It isn't about bragging, it's about having a quiet, inner self-confidence. It's also about ridding myself of lifelong feelings of inadequacy and aloneness. At last.

One Sunday, the chairman of the board of what later becomes part of Westpac, a man who owns an adjoining property, will invite us to lunch. For such outings the boss lets us take his ute. We dress up in our white moleskins, put on our 'going out' shirts and polish our riding boots.

While we aren't allowed to have grog at Habbies, as soon as we arrive at Bungle Bori, Mr Kimpton thrusts one of those big, bottle-size cans of Foster's into each of our hands. It's heavy, it's heaven, it's . . . better than sex (not that I know what that's like). Mum's plea with me not to drink at Habbies Howe isn't applicable, I decide, because we're not on Habbies Howe – we're next door.

Being forward, I say to Mr Kimpton, 'It's really kind of you to invite us.' (*Especially given you've got three drop-dead gorgeous daughters wandering around the house*, I think to myself.) 'But you don't know us. How come you've invited us to your home, if it's okay to ask?'

We're standing on the deck of his house, which has views of a fence on a faraway hill. It's the boundary fence that Bungle Bori shares with Habbies. Yet, like all of Habbies Howe's boundary fences, it's on this side of the hill – no one gets to look into Habbies Howe.

'I don't know you personally,' Mr Kimpton replies, with a smile, 'but Habbies Howe jackaroos are always welcome here.'

So there you go. I look across at Dougie – and he smiles at me. And I know that he knows.

Nothing more needs to be said.

Habbies Howe's reputation extends far beyond the Highlands district of north-east Victoria. The property and its reputation for training jackaroos is legendary throughout Australia, even beyond – among people in primary industry who count – as I will discover later.

We're invited to twenty-first birthday parties by people who don't know us. Young guys our age will come up to us and shake our hand. We get treated as special wherever we go, almost like royalty. It's so different to how I've spent the rest of my life – so wonderfully, heavenly different. It even makes cutting up murdered cows and lugging unbearably heavy bags of super worth it – and possibly even working in the sheep yards.

No longer am I the school weakling, the loser in a group of boys and men. I'm a respected Habbies Howe jackaroo. Here, I'm not carrying any school-related baggage; I'm a new person. I'm even starting to look less dorky in my moleskins and my size thirteen riding boots.

If only my father were alive – and sober – to see it.

6

Alan

It's Sunday, the day after the 'super' punishment, and exactly one week since I arrived at Habbies Howe. Mid-afternoon, Alan Greenwood, the senior jackaroo, returns from his week's annual leave, and immediately the dynamics among us jackaroos change. It's my first experience of a workplace pecking order, and the comfortable, close-knit, almost brotherly relationship I've built with Dougie over the past week suddenly is turned on its head. Dougie becomes sullen, withdrawn – even the laugh vanishes. A definite coolness comes over the jackaroos' quarters.

For me, Alan's return is no big deal. I'm still at the tail end of the pecking order. Yet Dougie becomes quiet. He loses his full-on confidence the moment Alan enters the room, silencing himself halfway through a sentence – something he never did before. Then, he had no reason to hesitate: he was in charge.

During my first, painful week, Dougie was my rock. More than that, he and I became close. Now, that closeness seems suddenly to have disappeared. He becomes remote, distant.

At twenty-one years of age, Alan is clearly in charge. Like Dougie, he's also from the Western District, but the more posh part near Glenthompson. Also, he was a jackaroo elsewhere before coming to Habbies, the added experience earning him even greater authority. Who are we to argue when Alan has done it all before on another property?

You only have to look at the three of us to see who comes last in the line-up. It isn't just the four years in age that Alan has on me, and the two he has on Dougie, that sets him apart. Alan has a presence about him; he looks and speaks well beyond his years. He could tell people he's thirty and they'd believe him. And while his complexion is dark like mine, that's where any similarity between us ends. Alan has physical strength, which he finds the need to demonstrate more often than I think necessary. I'm the puny one among the Habbies Howe's jackaroos – clearly the one who gets told to clean up.

It's as if the jackaroos' quarters are the bull paddock, where males are required to kick up dust to prove which of them has the biggest balls. Big balls seem to be important here.

Pleasingly though, Alan, like Dougie, has an outrageous sense of humour. Late one afternoon the three of us are returning in the boss's Land Rover after completing a job out in a paddock. Alan is driving, with me in the middle and Dougie on the passenger side. Alan is teaching me – totally irresponsibly, of course – how it's possible to change gears without using the clutch (although Land Rover surely included a clutch for a reason they thought important). Trouble is, the gears don't change quite as smoothly as Alan would want them to, and he snaps off the forty-centimetre-long, floor-mounted gearstick at its base. And what does he do with it? He takes it into diner and he puts it on the table at the boss's place.

'Who p-p-put th-th-this here?' shrieks Mr Webb, as we go to sit down.

'I did, boss,' says Alan, defiantly, impertinently – outrageously defiantly and impertinently.

I expect Mr Webb to explode, but instead he stares at the gearstick, and says, 'I d-d-don't w-want it, Alan. P-p-put it b-back where you f-f-found it.'

I'm sure all hell would break lose if I tried such a prank,

starting with the small matter of how Alan addressed Mr Webb and not forgetting the sheer act of vandalism. Yet nothing happens; there seems nothing with which Alan can't get away. I can see him as the playground prankster at primary school: not a bully, but the prankster. He'd be the one leading the riot, yet somehow slipping away before the authorities arrive. You know the type.

After dinner, Alan makes an announcement. He tells the boss separately, and then Dougie and me, that he'll be finishing up at Habbies Howe in April. So here I am, within moments of meeting the senior jackaroo, coming to terms with the fact that I'm soon to become jackaroo number two. Yes!

Plus – and here's the good bit – there'll be a new number three *under me*.

I go to bed, just eight days into my new world, and in the still moment before the angels take me away I revisit all that has happened. My back still feels like it's broken from yesterday's unloading of the super. My lips are ever so slowly beginning to heal. I've no idea what's to come. One day at a time, as they say. Yet, despite all that has happened, I decide it will be fun working with these two guys, at least until April with Alan. Neither of them seems to be a bully, which is a blessing. And both seem to know heaps of stuff, which, hopefully, they will pass on to me.

Certainly, Alan doesn't need to know about my attempted resignation on Wednesday.

On Monday, we begin making chaff – supplementary feed for the cattle, horses and sheep. It's an annual ritual that starts in autumn with the growing of oat crops, then in December the crops are cut and the stalks bound by a machine that the station hands use to make old-fashioned, tenth-century sheaves. In late December, the sheaves are stood upright in bundles to form stooks, making them look like miniature tepees, to dry them out in readiness for the next stage. Enter the jackaroos.

Dougie's and my task is to throw the sheaves onto the truck and trailer for threshing back at the chaff shed, one of the buildings at the homestead. And if all this sounds like an antiquated and costly way to feed livestock, you're dead right. But then, that's why places like Habbies Howe have jackaroos: for good, old-fashioned hard labour. Wrap up the whole shebang as 'Appropriate Training for (dopey) Graziers' Sons' and you have a regular supply of dumb-arse boys from totally bluffed families that never twig to the outrageous scam going on. The unwritten rule of employing a jackaroo, I learn quickly, is to find the most mundane farm task possible and then make the boy do it for as long as you can get away with it. If there are no mundane tasks for him to do, then you invent one.

So Dougie and I are dispatched to the paddock with the sheaves, to heave them up to one of the station hands, who stacks them on the tray of the old Bedford truck. And when the truck is chockers, it's promptly replaced by a tractor and trailer driving along behind – the timing of the departing vehicle and the arrival of the other one perfectly scheduled to ensure neither Dougie nor I get a moment's let-up. But I don't care because I'm overjoyed that, away from Alan, Dougie becomes his old self. He talks again. Even the laugh reappears.

Heaving the heavy sheaves of oaten hay onto the truck and trailer using long-handled pitchforks makes even my swimmer's muscles ache after four straight hours on the job. Meanwhile, Alan, who is back at the shed, lets it be known later in the day that he has the easier job. Well, of course he does.

At the shed, the sheaves are fed into the front of the thresher, a stationary machine that cuts up everything – including thistle heads, other weeds and fingers – into tiny pieces. It gets its power via a thick, black rubber belt that runs from a rotating dooverlackie on a tractor parked in front. The piece of continuous black rubber spins furiously and noisily and has a will of its own – it can fly off either piece of apparatus as and when it wills, killing anyone in its path. I'm very happy, thank you very much, to be working in the paddock with Dougie, away from the lethal belt. This time it's the station hands whose lives are at risk.

The resulting chaff is dispatched up an augur – a metal cylinder with a giant corkscrew inside – which rises on a seventy-degree angle up some thirty feet to a hole in the centre of the chaff shed roof, where the chaff falls down into the middle of the floor into a cone-shaped pile. It's Alan's job to spread it evenly across the floor of the shed before the cone builds up, which would eventually see it block the hole in the roof and cause the chaff to spill out onto the ground.

For this, the first day of chaff-making, Alan mostly just lets the cone grow, to give him something to shovel tomorrow.

After our day of heaving, Dougie and I have just enough energy to lock up the dairy calves. Alan then arrives at the dairy with three cans of beer from Old Harold's fridge. To store our beer there, the old fart demands one can in return for our three. I'm getting to know Alan, and I find it intriguing that he deems it necessary to gloat about having had an easier day than us. Dougie and I are stuffed, having had no down time all day, while Alan has spent the day napping. The door into the chaff shed is positioned on the far side from where the threshing takes place – where four station hands busily work the lethal machine. Consequently, no one notices, or has time to check on Alan. The bugger even rolls and smokes without getting sprung.

On Thursday, our fourth consecutive day tossing sheaves, Mr Webb turns up with a car-load of Japanese visitors to see chaff-making in action. The boss always has important visitors at Habbies – mostly dark-suited businessmen from the wool industry – whom he loves to show his jackaroo-slaves hard at work. Who wouldn't brag about running such a rort of an employment scheme?

First, he brings the rubbernecks out to the paddock to show them what Dougie and I are doing with our pitchforks. The visitors stand around pointing and giggling. At us. The only thing missing is the Other Mr Webb standing over Dougie and me with a whip. One of the Japanese says something in his native tongue and the rest of the group turn hysterical.

Have you ever seen the sharp end of a pitchfork fair through a giggling Japanese cranium?

Mr Webb drives them away, just as Dougie says something he shouldn't have about the war.

The boss then decides to show off the end product. After watching the station hands work the threshing machine – fortunately the rubber belt doesn't fly off and kill one of the visitors – the boss directs the official party to the action at the rear of the shed. And there is Alan, sprawled across half-filled bags of chaff for his comfort, dressed only in his undies but with his privates dangling out one side for all to see. He's sound asleep, complete with rake resting upright in his left hand, like Friar Tuck minus the frock.

'The boss could have bloody well warned me,' Alan later complains. This time he does get a lecture from Mr Webb.

No sooner do we finish making chaff than it's decided the Other Webbs will have a new house. In truth, it probably was decided months ago, but because we jackaroos are employed on a need-to-know basis, we're informed about the enterprise the day we begin work on this seriously inappropriate project for jackaroo labour.

A new house. So what, you ask? Ah, but you fail to understand the role of a jackaroo. The Macquarie Dictionary defines a jackaroo as 'an apprentice station hand on a sheep or cattle station'. The Australian National University's Dictionary Centre goes further, describing 'a person working on a station with a view to acquiring the practical experience and management skills desirable in a station owner or manager'. Now, am I missing something here, or can being put to work as brickies' labourers for the better part of three months be described as approximating the work of an apprentice station owner or manager?

It's important to know that we jackaroos have no recourse. Only in Queensland are jackaroos covered by any industrial award, courtesy of the Australian Workers' Union, under whose bailiwick station hands and indeed all pastoral workers are covered. The bottom line is that if you don't like being a jackaroo, it's hoo-roo.

Also, we know that Mr Webb can replace any of us within hours. We're reminded constantly, in not too subtle ways, that Habbies Howe has a five-year waiting list for jackaroos. I know. My name was put on it when I was twelve. The boss milks the existence and implication of the list for all its worth, saying he can replace any one of us in a blink. He hangs it over our heads like a partially suspended death sentence. I'm quickly discovering why Habbies Howe is so famous.

The first decision regarding the Other Webbs' new house is that it will be built on exactly the same spot as the old one, in which the family will continue to live while their new home is built. What I find amazing – and this is a great learning curve for me – is that this small point of detail (moving the old house sixty metres so the new one can be built in its place) fazes absolutely no one other than me. And even I quickly fall into line – and become an expert house mover-builder, or builder-mover, or builder's labourer, as it turns out.

We simply jack up the old weatherboard house – virtually with the Other Mrs Webb still inside it – and place three telephone poles underneath it. After lowering the dwelling onto the poles,

we use Habbies' impressive Caterpillar D8 bulldozer as the lead
vehicle – along with the two big Massey Ferguson tractors three
metres either side to help – to drag the old house forward some
sixty metres. Piece of cake.

'STOP!' someone cries, just as the house starts to creep forward. No one has thought to disconnect the telephone line.

That no task is too difficult is a wonderful lesson for later life.
Instead of looking at life negatively, we focus always on what can
be achieved. It is far superior to whinging about what can't be
done. A can-do mentality pervades the place and dominates our
lives. All part of learning the work ethic, I guess.

Towing away the old home is the easy part. We then set about
digging the foundation trenches for the new house, and after that
we distribute by wheelbarrow fifteen million bricks to various
points along the trenches. The truck delivering the bricks can't get
all the way down the Other Webbs' driveway. Of course it can't!
Never mind, says management to the builder; we have numbskull
jackaroos who can cart the bricks anywhere you want them taken.
I can just see the Other Mr Webb bragging to the builder: *Would
you like a few barrow-loads wheeled into Seymour? My boys
would love to do that for you . . .*

Summer turns into autumn and still we're digging trenches,
as well as carting hundreds of wheelbarrow-loads of bloody house
bricks.

The builder must think we jackaroos are a dozen bricks short
of a load. Here are three extra pairs of hands to help, at no charge.
Yet we're sure the boss must be getting a massive discount on
labour costs for prostituting his jackaroos so blatantly. And if he
isn't getting the massive discount for it, then more fool him.

Doesn't the builder have an apprentice, you ask? Yes, but the
poor lad really is a few bricks short. He spends most of each day
brewing tea for his boss, or staring into space.

Occasionally, the boss's conscience will get the better of him (after all, our families back home think we're learning to be farm managers), and he'll drag us off the building site and send us out on our horses to do cattle work. And every time he does that – and usually less than an hour after we saddle up – the Other Mr Webb will find us and send us back to work on his new house.

Thus, many an afternoon is spent carrying bags of cement or wheeling bricks for the builder, our horses saddled and tethered to the nearby fence, laughing at us. Charlie must think I'm a real lackey.

We build the house to lock-up stage, then finally I'm allowed back on Charlie.

One Sunday morning, I'm far too slow in hiding from the boss. In fact, I forget completely about the need to do so. I'm lying on my bed, reading. Alan and Dougie are far quicker than me; they've both disappeared in different directions. Without warning, as usual, the gate next to our bedroom clangs.

'Are y-you b-boys th-th-there?'

Shit. 'Yes, Mr Webb,' I reply, jumping to my feet like the simple servant I am. I have my riding boots on before he stutters 'th-th-there'.

As he passes our door, he sees me about to come flying out. 'Oh, come on th-then, M-M-Michael. W-w-we'll go and l-look at some p-p-paddocks.'

Oh, no. My mind races back to the comment Dougie made on my first day, about how Mr Webb will give me a fortnight to learn the names of each of the sixty-four paddocks, and what stock is in each one. The fortnight is well and truly up, and suddenly I wonder if it was arranged for Alan and Dougie to absent themselves this morning.

The boss continues to walk to the garage, but stops next to one of the sliding doors, turns back to face me, and asks, 'C-c-can you d-drive the u-ute, M-Michael?'

In total unmitigated, stupid, youthful, unforgivable foolish naivety, as I catch up to him I answer, 'I can't drive the ute, Mr Webb, but I can drive the Land Rover because it's got the gears marked on the gearstick.'

How stupid, how dumb, can a boy be? I must be certifiable to have said it. And to think I once thought I had the brains to be a doctor. I haven't learnt the first golden rule of life on the land, which is to say absolutely nothing unless it is absolutely essential.

'CH-CHRIST, B-B-BOY!' the boss explodes. 'N-N-NEVER TRY TO D-D-DRIVE TH-THE T-T-TRUCK BEFORE YOU C-CAN D-DRIVE THE U-UTE!'

He turns and stumbles on towards the Holden, no doubt wondering why he ever agreed to have his dear old friend's dopey halfwit of a grandson as a jackaroo.

Keep your shirt on, you silly old fart. What's the big deal? Gearsticks are all the same, aren't they?

I presume he's angry with me because it must be cheaper to replace the gearbox in the ute, compared to the one on the four-wheel drive Land Rover. Nonetheless, it becomes my first full-on reprimand. So what if I bugger up the gears on the Land Rover? The old goat has four of them: Land Rovers, that is. Well, that's how many I've counted – the boss's, the manager's, Old Harold's and the rabbiters'. (I will later discover a fifth – the dozer driver's.)

Mr Webb opens the passenger door of the ute and climbs in. As he does, he motions to me to take the driver's seat.

'Oh, shit,' I whisper, but do as instructed.

As it happens, he turns out to be an excellent driving instructor. What makes him so is his patience, once he becomes focused on teaching me and not beating me up. Having settled from the blasting he just gave me, slowly and without further hysterics he ensures I have my left foot pressed firmly on the clutch and then explains how to put the column gearshift lever into reverse. Then, before he lets me reverse out of the garage, he makes me put the gear lever in and out of reverse several times. It's a good thing he teaches me to start by going backwards, because if we go forward we'll crash through the garage wall, fly down the hill and drive straight into Stewart's Creek.

The boss's driving instruction style is unique. He points constantly with his right index finger where he wants me to drive. Along the short strip of bitumen road that bisects Habbies, I do think it's a touch excessive, but even then he points with his finger where I'm to steer. Once we're in a paddock, the pointing becomes truly animated. Every inch of our journey is prescribed not by some yet-to-be-invented GPS system, but by the boss's right index finger.

Then comes the moment of truth. Oh no, I think – someone save me. Stopping at a gate several kilometres from the homestead, as he climbs out of the car to open it, Mr Webb asks, 'What's th-th-this n-next paddock called, M-M-Michael?' He stumbles on to open the gate, leaving me to sweat it out in the ute.

I haven't a clue. I've not yet ridden my horse anywhere near this part of the property.

As I drive on through the gate and wait for the boss to get back in, I consider my options: I can say the name of another paddock and pretend I've made a genuine mistake – thus at least appearing to be half intelligent and possibly get three out of ten – or I can tell the truth and say I've no idea. And get whipped.

'I don't know, Mr Webb,' I reply, as he gets back in.

'Th-th-that's n-n-not g-g-good enough!' He yells at me. 'Y-you sh-sh-should have learnt all th-th-the p-paddock n-n-names by now!'

'Yes, Mr Webb,' I say. If nothing else I know how to come

across suitably admonished and contrite. After all, I've had lots of practice at it all my life.

The boss doesn't ask any more paddock names on this Tour, and by the time he next drags me out on one, I will have learnt all sixty-four names – and what type of stock and how many head are in each paddock. Yet, the incident causes me to ponder why things are done the way they are at Habbies Howe. I wonder if Mr Webb really did expect me to know the name of this far-flung paddock, which has had no stock in it since I've been here. It's full of tall, untouched grass.

As soon as we get back to the homestead, I go to the meal room and check the name of the paddock on the blackboard. There's no record of stock having been in it for months and no sign of recent rub-outs on the blackboard. Mr Webb deliberately asked me the name of a paddock whose name he knew I wouldn't know. Why did he do that to me? Again, I find it strange how a man with so much finds it necessary to belittle and trick an inexperienced boy.

The old codger certainly is building up a well-deserved quota of nuggetings.

He's an enigma. He was so patient teaching me how to use the stupid column gearshift on the ute. Yet he goes and bullies me over the name of a paddock he knows is a mystery to me. The boss will remain a paradox and the strategies he uses to ridicule a raw jacka-roo will remain a puzzle.

But then, I remind myself that this is Habbies Howe, where some jackaroos don't last long.

7

Bad Day

It began yesterday afternoon. We loaded a bunch of portable steel-mesh panels onto the old Bedford truck and took them to Near Hill, a paddock so named because it's located five kilometres from the Habbies Howe homestead. At least it has a hill. Farmers have quaint ways of naming things.

First, we made a holding yard, about the size of half a tennis court, then a narrow race with a swinging gate at one end to separate the lambs from their mothers. We then built a smaller holding pen and after that an even smaller one, about the size of a small car, for us jackaroos to catch the lambs for 'marking', whatever that means.

Our final task yesterday was to roll out a length of wire netting to make a funnel along the fence line that leads into the temporary yards. You and I would twig that the funnel represents a trap, but not so fearfully dumb Merinos, which are slow to cotton on, even to death.

It's another four-thirty a.m. start, and yet when we get to Near Hill the Other Mr Webb and Old Harold are already here, the headlights of their Land Rovers providing just enough light for the manager to push the sheep he's mustered down the funnel-trap into the holding pen. Old Harold, for his part, sits in his truck, concentrating, the choke full on, black smoke billowing. His assistant, the slack-arse kelpie, as usual sits in the back licking his privates.

'Decided to show up, eh?' Old Harold calls out as we run past his truck to help the Other Mr Webb with the sheep. Truly, if we weren't typing the old goat's name in the Diary each night after dinner, there'd be no reason to believe the old fart exists.

As the last ewe enters the yards, the Other Mr Webb shuts the gate behind her. We draft the lambs from the ewes, then let the hysterical, fretting mothers back into the paddock, although most choose to stay close-by, bleating madly for their offspring. We're left with some five hundred lambs, those born early in the season now big and chunky, the younger ones nothing more than anaemic bags of skin, bone and yellow, runny poo, and all of them – along with me – plainly wondering what will happen next.

I help Alan and Dougie to push some fifty lambs into the car-sized catching pen. I then watch as they each catch one and sit it on the outer rail of the pen facing away from him, the lamb's two left legs gripped tightly in the jackaroo's left hand, its right two firmly in his right. As usual, I copy them and catch myself a mid-size lamb, its woolly legs amazingly soft and cuddly in my fingers; cuddly, that is, until the little bugger begins to kick like all get-up.

The collective bleating of the lambs under our feet and their fretting mothers just outside is enough to make the noise of a city jackhammer sound like a whimper. It stifles conversation, not that anything is ever said when either Mr Webb is around, anyway; everyone stays deadly quiet and serious.

Three men work outside the pen: the Other Mr Webb and two station hands. This year it's Warwick and Chas's turn to be involved in lamb marking. Warwick is the first to come by – a tall and imposing man in his early forties who lives with his wife, Joy, and their four kids in a cottage way up a track at the northern end of the property. He inoculates each lamb in the loose skin just under where the front leg joins the body, with an injection called 'Five-in-One'. It's a vaccine, I learn, to prevent the most common diseases in sheep in southern Australia, and from which Merinos can drop dead in an instant: blackleg (destroys muscle action), pulpy kidney (causes death from restricted gut activity), black disease (infected liver), tetanus (death from infected wounds usually incurred during crutching and shearing), and malignant oedema (a general infection common in Merino sheep). And you thought your woollen suit just happened.

Next along is Chas, who uses a pair of metal ear piercers to cut a V in the lamb's ear – left ear for girls, right for boys. I watch oozing blood flow from each lamb's ear down onto Alan's arm, but that's nothing compared to what I'm about to witness.

The shape of the notch represents the year of birth. It enables the sheep classer to later look at a sheep as it runs through a drafting race and confirm its sex without having to check under the animal, and determine its age without looking in its mouth at its teeth.

I've already described how farm tasks require considerable practice – this is no exception. Inserting the notch requires the operator to slice off just enough ear: too small a notch and it makes it difficult for the classer to decipher; too deep a cut and he might slice through a vital blood vessel. The work suits Chas, a quiet and squat, blond-haired, oval-faced Polish 'New Australian' who performs his duties methodically, without uttering a single word all week.

Third along is the Other Mr Webb with his innocent-looking, yet, as I'm about to find out, lethal pocket-knife. Girls get off lightly; they lose only their tail. He performs the manoeuvre by grabbing the top half of the fluffy tail in his left hand. I then watch in horror as he runs his thumb down through the yellow pooh until he finds the gap between the first and second knuckle. He then places the blade of the pocket-knife in front of his thumb. Slice! Depending on the angle at which we jackaroos sit our lamb on the rail, blood either spurts from the place where the tail hitherto was attached – straight onto the faces and clothes of anyone outside the pen in the line of fire – or, if the lamb is slouched back, the cavity quickly fills with blood and promptly congeals. Spurting blood is by far the most fun, because then folk have to duck. The secret is to pretend you got someone by mistake. Shit just happens.

For a boy lamb, it's a whole other story. The poor guys loses his exceptionally brief yet precious manhood in the eight seconds it takes the Other Mr Webb to slice open the lamb's scrotum, squeeze his two little testes into open air using his thumbs and forefingers, bend down and draw the balls out with his teeth, sinews and all. He spits them out and the waiting sheepdogs pounce on the delicacies.

How utterly, horrifyingly gross. Surely, there's another way to do this. (There is. Most farmers use rubber rings which are stretched over the scrotum using a set of reverse pliers, eventually causing it to fall off. But why waste money on rubber rings when you've got perfectly good teeth that can do the job?) Are things getting weirder around here, or what?

After one lamb, the colour of the manager's mouth resembles a Pro Hart effort with a can of crimson paint. My mind, however, is with the poor, unfortunate lamb. Feeling for him as well as for my own burgeoning manhood, I squeeze my knees together and make one of my involuntary shivers.

I can't believe what I've just seen, and I promptly resolve to improve my standing with the manager forthwith. The thought of that pocket-knife . . . and his teeth!

On the third morning of this bizarre if not warped enterprise, it happens. Alan and Dougie have been given a turn with the pocket-knife, as I have with the inoculating gun and ear piercers.

Without warning, the Other Mr Webb, in his usual bland drawl, says, 'Michael, you can hop over and have a shot with the knife.'

Me? Have a shot with the knife? No thanks. But what do I do? I consider my options: faint, vomit, feign a heart attack, climb the nearest gum tree, stage some kind of foaming at the mouth, cry, quit.

Momentarily, all of my new-found confidence, my self-esteem, even my . . . *maleness*, goes flying out of the pen. Again, I'm left cursing my deranged grandfather for having dreamt up this stupid idea of sending me to be a jackaroo for this bunch of warped crazies. I think of saying: *Mr Webb, sir, nice sir, really nice sir, I really am very happy working on this side of the rail. Thank you anyway for the kind offer. And by the way, I do like that crimson motif on your face. Indeed, I've been admiring it all week. It kind of goes with your bloodied khaki outfit. Don't all of you other guys agree?*

But of course I don't say anything of the kind. I drop the lamb I've just picked up and ever so slowly I 'hop' over to the rail. Damn it, I'm fine earning my nine dollars a week catching and holding fluffy lambs for other macho heroes to get their rocks off. Why make me bite out lambs' balls? I neither need nor want a testicular morning tea. Basically – and I have no qualms admitting to this minor point – I'm actually not into sucking on testicles.

The Other Mr Webb hands me the dreaded knife. Everyone is waiting for me to catch up.

I can't tell you how relieved I am when my first client is a girl. I grab her tail with my left hand. Starting at her anus, I run my thumb down through the sickening yellow faeces, along her bony tail to just past the first knuckle, with everyone watching, as if they all are medical students and I'm Dr Christiaan Barnard about to perform a heart transplant. I begin to hack at the dip between the two knuckles, my poor little patient fairly screaming her precious head off.

'Not like *that*,' calls the Other Mr Webb, curtly. 'Here, give me the knife. You have to do it in one firm action. Look, like this.'

Having snatched the knife from my hand, he slices off the partly hacked tail with a quick, downward thrust.

What I haven't realised is the brute force with which he's been administering his knife, even though I've watched him perform the procedure a thousand times from the other side of the rail.

My second attempt mercifully is also with a girl, and I give the knife such a strong downwards thrust, I almost yank the poor lamb out of Alan's hands. The tail quivers in my fingers, and the shock of feeling life still in it causes me to let go and throw my hand in the air, as if I've been clutching a redback spider and I've only just realised it.

I quickly duck to avoid Alan's miserable effort to spray me with spurting blood.

I mouth a genuine sorry to the lamb, which Alan lets drop to the ground without pity. It staggers away to find its mother – tailless, blood dripping off its hind legs onto the ground.

Why is everyone here such a mean, heartless bastard?

My third victim – and this is because charming Dougie deliberately hunts him out for me – is a *boy*. This time, the manager stands right next to me. And before I can begin to foul up, he puts his right hand over mine. With the knife in my grasp, he guides my hand as I slice open the scrotum with one continuous thrust of the blade. It's only the second scrotum I've ever fondled.

I actually do a fair job of slicing it open. The manager then lets go of my hand and I turn the still-open blade inwards under my right wrist, something I've seen him do hundreds of times.

For a moment I stare at the insides of brazen maleness: the open cavity. It all looks exceptionally gooey in there. I stare at the two little lumps I'm about to wrap my teeth past. With my two thumbs and forefingers I take hold of the base of the fluffy purse and squeeze. The little fellow lets out a huge bleat as his two little grey, oblong testes see daylight. Each capsule has tiny blood vessels running along its length just under the skin. I can't look. I close my eyes as, in fear and trembling, I bend forward, not wanting to watch or feel that which I'm being made to do. Still squeezing, I pass my teeth over the two small protruding lumps and close my jaw behind them. Then with my jaw clamped I stand up straight, like I've seen the Other Mr Webb do so often. The noise emanating from the poor little lamb's lungs goes from a shrill bleat to a dull groan, as if the poor little blighter has expelled his all – which he just has. I feel the warm testicles slide around inside my mouth, while outside slimy, slippery, gooey sinews dangle from my chin.

'Quickly. Now the tail,' barks the Other Mr Webb.

Everyone is waiting. I spit the balls onto the ground, and a kelpie, patiently waiting nearby, rushes in and makes off with them. I feel blood congealing on my chin.

I grab hold of the tail and, because it's my third try, I find just the right spot with my left thumb. I slice off the woolly thing with a hard downward thrust of the knife. Blood spurts high in the air, which I manage to duck even though Dougie tries hard to squirt me.

And I think about the nuggeting ritual that gangs of boys performed on innocents at our school's country camp, and how much more fun it would have been if – after stripping the poor kid naked, with the entire year group watching on – the leader had sliced open the boy's scrotum using a sharp pocket-knife and bitten out his balls. They could have charged folding money for that.

For all seven years at boarding school I wrote to Mum weekly, yet at Habbies Howe I haven't had the strength at night even to lift a pen. Cruelly, I want so much to tell her about lamb marking.

Oh and by the way, Mum, you know those lovely school shirts of which I'm so fond? Well, they now have a crimson look and they've been dispatched to the incinerator.

8

Simon

It's late April, lamb marking is over, and Alan leaves as he promised he would.

Simon McDonald arrives and straight away we have a big problem. Sneaking a look out our bedroom window, I see what the problem is with Simon the moment he climbs out of his brother's car. Well, I do once I work out which of the pair is Simon.

Like Alan and Dougie, Simon is from Victoria's Western District, and for a moment I wonder if they purposefully breed boys there to fill Habbies Howe's jackaroo quota. It sure is some system the boss has going here, this never-ending supply of cheap boy labour.

Simon is tall and lean, but not as tall and lean as me. He has light brown, wavy hair and thin features. And, like Alan, Simon has worked on another property between school and coming to Habbies, which I feel he is somewhat quick to imply, if not say straight out, gives him seniority over me.

Like hell it does.

Simon has also tried agricultural college, but that didn't click for him, he says.

I couldn't care less that Simon has been around a bit, or that he started agricultural college, or that he's nineteen and I'm still seventeen. I'm now Number Two, I've put in, and no new chum is about to steal my status. If I was still at school, I'd probably let him trample all over me. Not any more.

Things begin for him the same as they did for me the day I arrived, in January. The brothers are ushered into the homestead dining room for the mandatory sandwiches and lemon cordial. Then, as soon as good manners allow, the brother escapes, just like Mum and my sister did. Mr Webb then brings Simon to our quarters and introduces him to Dougie and me, before quickly retreating to the house proper.

Dougie, of course, has already moved into Alan's single room, which means I now have a new room-mate. I've not had a bedroom to myself since I was nine.

No sooner has the boss gone back inside the house, than he reappears, calling out, 'Hey, M-M-Mike, are y-you th-th-there?'

The boss often calls me Mike to try to be friends, but I don't get sucked in by that crap. As long as the old man never tries 'Mick'.

'Yes, Mr Webb,' I reply, compliantly, leaping at our door as we always do. I haven't even had time to tell Simon about the 'no car, no smokes, no booze' rule, or to ask him how he came to be at Habbies. Or to tell him how, for me, it was either here or jail.

Moments later, the boss is standing by our door.

'Th-th-the Webbs need some f-firewood. T-take S-S-Simon w-w-with you.' With that, he turns and stumbles his way back across the courtyard to the house.

I know what this is about, and it has nothing to do with firewood. Things are about to turn nasty. For Simon.

'The manager doesn't need any firewood,' I tell him as we walk the ten paces to the garage next to our quarters. We climb into the Land Rover. I drive, to make the point that I'm in charge, even though I'm yet to get a driver's licence. 'We took a load of wood down to the Other Webbs last week.'

'So why are we doing it again?' Simon asks.

Even though it's a fair question, I don't reply. How dare this new boy ask me something. A new jackaroo is on a need-to-know basis only. Isn't that right?

We arrive at the house with our load. The Other Mr Webb is outside waiting for us. He beckons Simon aside. This time I do see a handshake. I begin to unload the firewood, alone, all the time keeping one eye on the pair deep in conversation several metres away. Like I say, our trip has nothing to do with firewood.

Moments later, Simon returns to the truck. He says nothing for several minutes. He stands next to the vehicle, staring at the wood in the back. I can tell he's deep in thought and that he's getting angrier by the minute. His face now flush, slowly he picks out a piece of wood with his left hand. He throws it behind him without looking where it lands. It continues like this, Simon working at a fraction of my pace, not looking where he's throwing his wood. Blood vessels in his neck begin to take the strain.

'Fuck him,' Simon suddenly blurts out, his face now ashen. 'Fuck him. Fuck him.'

Yeah, I think to myself. Been there, done that, a million times. I wait a few moments, so as not to appear as if I need him to tell me what I already know, because that would give him an advantage over me, and I'm sure as hell not about to give him that. I continue to do most of the unloading.

Finally, Simon tells me what I already knew.

'The prick said if I don't shave my beard off by tomorrow morning, I won't be here to meet the men.' As he speaks, he drops a piece of firewood back on the tray and he begins to stroke his precious beard with his left hand, as if to calm the thing from the stress it's going through.

'Hmm,' is all I can think to say. Well, what else am I supposed to say to the poor bastard?

No car, no smokes, no booze, no raunchy women. And now, no beard as well.

'Fuck him,' repeats Simon. 'Fuck him.'

We unload the remaining firewood without conversation, just

Simon's constant expletives. As we finish, I can tell Simon's emotions have moved from grief to anger, and are rapidly approaching blame. As we climb back into the Land Rover to head home, I figure he's about to ask why we don't stand up to the pricks. How he's worked in Western Australia, and how he was allowed to have a beard there.

Moments later, he blurts out, 'Why don't any of you stand up to the pricks? I've worked in Western Australia and I was allowed to have a beard there.'

Simon, being Number Three jackaroo – and me being Number Two – should know better. I'm under no obligation to answer such a question, to entertain such insolence.

He looks across at me and again asks, 'Why don't you stand up to the pricks?'

Again, I don't answer. Not straight away.

'If you hang around long enough,' I eventually reply, my eyes firmly on the road ahead, both hands gripping the big black steering wheel, 'you'll begin to understand why.' I'm referring in my mind to the parties to which we get invited, and how every man, woman and son in the district looks up to us; how they regard us as special, verging on royalty. Because we're survivors, because we're tough, because we're Habbies Howe jackaroos.

I'm still working on earning the same adulation from the daughters.

I don't say anything more to Simon. It's up to him if he decides to snatch it on his first day. Dougie secretly showed me in a back copy of the Diary where one jackaroo's name appears for just one day. What a wimp. Simon can do as he damn well pleases. We all know the boss has a five-year waiting list and can replace any of us within minutes. It's certainly not a pleasure I'm about to give the old fart, that's for sure.

And yet, being the softie I am, I relent in my thinking, and

I recall how on my third day, after I told Mr Webb I wasn't cut out to be a jackaroo, during the afternoon Dougie told me to hang in, that things would improve. And I remember how puzzled I was that Dougie, who seems so worldly, so experienced, so manly, put up with all the shit management hangs on us. Four months on, I now know why we put up with all the shit: it's because we're Habbies Howe jackaroos, that's why.

'I know it's hard to believe,' I eventually say to Simon as we lie in bed, before I turn out our light, 'but believe me, it's worth it in the end.'

It seems, however, that my counselling skills aren't much chop. In fact, they're useless.

'Fuck him,' says Simon, for the umpteenth time. And, with that, I lean over and turn out the light.

Nothing more is said.

Simon's behaviour has worn thin. I start to wonder how much of it is sheer pride. He and his stupid beard are beginning to piss me right off. In the moment before sleep, I ponder what will happen if Simon does decide to bugger off. He seems a nice enough guy, and I'll be sorry if he goes, but there is nothing more I can do or say. If he does go, he'll be replaced in a flash. For me, I've been through the shit stage – and I'm hanging in here for the long haul. I'm now second in seniority, after all. I'm also toughening up. Even the hair on my angelic face has gone from fluff to bristles.

Plus, I still have scores to settle with certain people connected with last year's football tour.

Simon can do whatever he bloody well likes. It makes no difference to me.

In the morning, once we finish milking – a new experience for Simon as it was for me four months ago – and after we eat the breakfast Dougie has made, Simon emerges from the bathroom. Minus his beard.

Nothing more is said.

As I lie on my bed prior to going down to the tree for morning orders, I ponder the bosses' reason for outlawing Simon's beard. It can't possibly be because it was dangerous, or unhealthy. What harm could a bit of extra hair cause? Why make such an issue of it? We know jackaroos on other properties are allowed them; a jackaroo at the Seymour pub one night looked like he'd gone missing for ten years in high country. Yet here both Mr Webbs obviously have a thing about facial hair. It must be a discipline thing – all about conformity and image. Come to think of it, I'm surprised Dougie, being the radical, hasn't tried one on. Maybe he has.

It makes me wonder more generally about the way things are done here. Why does life have to be so regimented, so militaristic? Is it because there are three of us, and three boys have the capacity to become unmanageable? Maybe if I was a sole jackaroo I'd be living with the Webbs and I'd be treated more like a son than a servant. After all, Damian, the jackaroo on the boss's brother's place, close to Seymour, says he eats in the homestead dining room with his Mr and Mrs Webb. Glendoxey is a smaller spread, with few workers, which I guess makes Damian's experience there more intimate than ours here. Thems are the breaks when you're a Habbies Howe jackaroo, I guess.

Going to the movies in Seymour of a Saturday night is our chief form of entertainment. (Saying 'of a Saturday night' instead of 'on' is country-speak, and the art of using appropriate language in the bush needs to be worked at. In the company of bosses we jackaroos will say 'on', whereas when we're with the station hands we'll use 'of'. We keep our gentrified tongues for the Webb families – and for going out.)

A movie outing involves obtaining the boss's permission to

take his ute into town. Once there, we go first to the theatre to see what movie is showing. One of us writes down its name in case our brains don't work properly the next morning. Then we drive to the pub where we settle in for the night, but not before asking if anyone in the bar knows what the movie is about. We ask this because every Sunday morning over breakfast, without fail, the boss will quiz us on the movie's storyline. I'm totally convinced Mr Webb knows we've spent the night at the pub, that we never once have set foot inside the picture theatre, yet he never accuses us of lying to him.

But we know that he knows.

Life at Habbies Howe is chock-full of surprises – each new assignment a real education. For me, at any rate. One day it's decided that a new bridge is needed across Hughes Creek – to give the boss easier accessible on Royal Tours, I presume. The project is awarded to Gordon, Habbies Howe's resident engineer. He isn't a qualified engineer, of course, but every station worth its reputation has to have one, and Gordon's the next best thing because he once worked as a labourer on the roads. And because no one here knows enough about things like building bridges to argue with him, that seals the deal and puts Gordon in charge.

First, Wes, the dozer driver, deepens the creek in the place designated for the bridge. It takes him just thirty minutes to dig out a furrow in the middle of the watercourse with the big Caterpillar D8, making a channel deep and wide to fit, and then roll into place two big concrete pipes, positioning them in line with the flow of the water.

Gordon, meanwhile, teaches us jackaroos how to make two, ten-metre-long form boxes, complete with reinforced steel mesh, which, when filled with concrete and allowed to set, will become the main load bearers for the new bridge. The bearers need to be strong enough to take the weight of any of the property's vehicles, except of course the bulldozer, which doesn't need a bridge. Wes, the overgrown kid that he is, drives the big D8 through Habbies Howe's creeks just for fun. Only Wes is allowed on the dozer, worst luck.

With the bridge built, we move on to other adventures. I'm convinced the boss chooses jobs just to be mean, like on the night of the first autumn rains when he waits until midnight before calling us out of bed to clear leaves from the gutters, rain bucketing down.

I guess he believes no one under twenty-five ever gets pneumonia.

By far the happiest time for me is mustering and droving cattle. The furthest boundary fence to the north is a two-hour ride, the furthest south only thirty minutes. I much prefer riding north.

Solitude: that's what it is. The only sounds one hears out here are the frequent squeaks of saddle leather, or Charlie bobbing his bit up and down over his teeth with his tongue, or a hoof stepping on an occasional rock. There might also be a snort from up front, or a fat 'plop-plop-plop' from down the back. A half-hearted breeze causes leaves to rustle high up in the gums as we ride underneath; wind will gently waft through grass either side of us. High above, the Melbourne-to-Sydney plane doesn't exactly skywrite but leaves a pencil-thin white signature in its wake for us to follow. There's not a living soul within cooee, just Dougie or Simon and me, daydreaming our way across a wide-open paddock, our horses chauffeuring us to the place of the next confrontation with a mob of cattle. Our horses know by heart where the gates are, even if we sometimes have to detour a few metres off line to avoid a snake warming itself in the afternoon sun. Occasionally, Charlie will shy at something innocuous, like a stump or a bolting rabbit, and he'll ruin my daydream.

Sometimes we'll be told to take a cut lunch with us. At other times we return to the homestead for lunch, then saddle our second horse for the afternoon's work. I'm sure the manager expects us to complete every cattle move in record time and report back to him breathless for the next chore, as soon as we finish the task at hand. But we don't. We take our time, especially on the ride home, often getting off our horses and walking in front of them – if only for a change of pace – each of us with a smoke dangling from our mouth, our horses walking a metre behind us, their reins draped loosely over our shoulder.

Often, we'll let our horses walk most of the way out to the paddock we're to muster, or at least until we have to push a mob of cattle out of the way, like over a hill. Sometimes, when we feel time is against us or the weather looks threatening, we canter part-way out to our destination. Importantly, we need to save our horses for the actual work of mustering, cutting and droving – and retrieving wayward, recalcitrant beasts.

Amazingly, returning home after completing a cattle move requires the most energy. Our horses know which direction is home; they know that chaff is waiting for them in their feed box. Charlie is no exception. As soon as we close the gate behind our mob of cattle, it's as if intuitively he knows it's time to bolt home. He begins to fidget and pull on his bit. Unless, of course, we get off and walk in front of them. Then they act completely the opposite – they mope along behind us, resigned to the fact that galloping home today is not an option.

The boss would be furious if he sees we've raced our horses home. He can tell by the sweat on them. Yet, boys being boys, we often let our horses have their head, at least through a couple of paddocks, although I admit to not ever attempting to jump over a closed gate.

Sometimes I'm sure we're told to shift stock just for the hell of it, or because management can't dream up anything torturous for us to do. More than once, we muster and move the same mob of cattle twice in consecutive days. I even wonder sometimes if the bosses realise.

One winter's morning, the Other Mr Webb gives Simon some erroneous task and tells Dougie and me to get our horses. He says he'll meet us at his house. It's a sunny day and Dougie and I ride out dressed as usual in long pants – Dougie in his green strides and me in my blue jeans – both of us wearing short-sleeved shirts. However, by the time we reach the manager's house, some twenty minutes to the north, huge clouds have developed in the south-west. The potential of the looming storm doesn't bear contemplating.

The Other Mr Webb, having had more time to see the change of weather coming, meets us dressed in full wet-weather gear. The three of us set out, riding north – in silence, as always – through four or five paddocks towards our destination. I keep glancing over my left shoulder at the dark clouds developing behind us. Moments later, it becomes so dark it's like one of those eerie moments when day thinks it's night.

Just before the rain begins to tumble – and with the harsh southerly wind now upon us, sending loose grass and tumbleweeds flying past us on both sides – I notice a dead cow a hundred metres or so to our right, lying up against the fence. Now, if there is one attribute we jackaroos at Habbies Howe must have, and demonstrate, it's *observation* – the hallmark of a good stockman. Yet on this occasion I can tell neither the manager nor Dougie has seen the dead animal. Normally, both of them see a problem long before me. For fun, I wait until we are well past it – so neither can claim to have seen it first – before I say, 'Mr Webb, what do you want to do about the dead cow?'

Well, does the man spin in his saddle. Standing abruptly in his stirrups and twisting his body every which way, he snaps, 'Where? Where?'

I can't help myself from saying, 'Behind us.'

I take the lead and swing Charlie towards the fence, my two riding companions following.

'Grass tetanus,' the manager declares even before he sees the dead animal close-up.

It begins to pour – really pour – and in seconds Dougie and I are soaked to our skin. But we continue on and move two mobs of cattle, the manager as dry as chips under his broad-brimmed hat and Drizabone oilskin jacket, Dougie and me sodden and shivering our butts off in our sodden saddles. Water streams down our faces, and our hair is bedraggled and in our eyes. Our visibility is reduced almost to the point where we're useless participants.

Not a word is spoken until, finally, the Other Mr Webb declares, 'You'd better get on home.' Yeah, right. All I can think is that it must have been a lesson designed to teach us to think ahead and to come to work better prepared. Yet, there was no storm looming when we left the homestead.

In later life, whenever rain begins to tumble, I expect to hear the order come from somewhere behind me: *Get your horse.*

The boss teaches me to crack my stockwhip. At this kind of thing he is superb. Like when he taught me to drive the ute. Basically, teaching is about having patience.

Mr Webb gets me to sit astride the top rail of the horse yards, which puts me more than two metres off the ground. He then climbs up and sits behind me.

Holding my extended right forearm in his hand, he teaches me to lift my arm high above my head with my arm straight, and then to force the whip down, firmly and in one continuous action to effect the cracking noise. He then repeats the action, using his hand on my wrist maybe ten times before finally letting me try it on my own.

Here is a man, to whom so often I've shown less respect than I ought, taking the time one-on-one to teach me something practical.

Yet he remains a mystery. Again I wonder at how we're given fair dinkum shit jobs, about which we whinge and bitch and moan, yet we still do what's required and bounce back for more.

One night when Dougie feels particularly aggrieved over some issue he threatens to quit before his time is up. Mr Webb tells Dougie he couldn't care less if he chooses to leave early – as harsh as that might sound – and again mentions the five-year waiting list. I quickly realise the boss doesn't mean malice; he's just showing Dougie who has the upper hand.

Later, in our quarters, Dougie gives me one of his standard laughs, saying, 'I told the old fart I'd stay, just to piss him off.'

Yeah, right.

As we go to bed, I think again about Mr Webb sitting up on that rail with me, holding my forearm in his right hand, teaching me to crack a stockwhip. And a sense of gratitude overwhelms me. It makes me realise how, because of the many and varied opportunities I'm being given here at Habbies Howe, I'm slowly but surely shaking off my lifelong feelings of inadequacy.

Basically, I'm growing up, I guess.

9

Professional

As an avid reader of the rural press, one section I find most intriguing is the lists of farmers and the prices they receive for their cattle. What interests me especially is how one farmer will get $1000 for a steer, yet another farmer will get just $500 for a beast the same age. Is it breeding, pastures or supplementary feed (hay, silage, grain)? Is it the stocking rate (how many animals run per hectare) or the way farmers look after their animals (husbandry)? Or all of the above? I'm fascinated as to what it is that gives these farmers the edge over others.

The net return for a beef-cattle enterprise – after allowing for costs – is a far better way to determine success, because one grazier might, for example, spend a fortune pumping expensive grain into his or her animals, and naturally they will be heavier. But at what cost? And when you take into account the labour cost involved in feeding out the grain to those cattle, and the capital and interest cost of the mechanical grain feeder and storage facilities, the farmer who receives $1000 for his or her stock might indeed come out behind their neighbour who gets just $500 but doesn't go to the expense of buying in – or growing, storing and feeding out – expensive grain.

Of course, at Habbies Howe, in many ways I already have my answer – and also incidentally the reason Richard (Dick) Cappur Webb has a five-year waiting list for jackaroos. Habbies Howe regularly has its name at the top of the cattle market prices. These top prices are achieved because everything at Habbies Howe is done so well. Both Mr Webbs have a knack of selecting quality livestock (and jackaroos) and managing the land to maximise its capacity for production.

One reason Habbies Howe succeeds is it's use of the best commercial bulls found in Australia. The foundation Herefords at Habbies Howe, all those years ago, were bought from a stud property in central Queensland. The end result is proved in the most important place of all: the livestock marketplace.

The Webbs avoid overstocking their paddocks. As well, we jackaroos rotate the animals around the property with such relentless monotony, continually giving cows and calves – and ewes and lambs, for that matter – fresh grass to eat, which must contribute to their size and condition, and hence the prices achieved.

The aim of beef-cattle farming is to turn the cows' milk and grass into meat on their calves. Farmers receive roughly two dollars per kilo of live weight per calf. The aim is to have calves put on one kilo – two dollars worth of meat – per day. And that, friends, is the simple economics behind raising beef cattle: two bucks a day.

None of this ever is explained to me at Habbies Howe. As good as the training and discipline are here, I will need to wait until much later to learn about the all-important financial side of farm management. What we do learn at Habbies – and we do learn heaps – is the practical side. Plus, we learn it on the run – literally running to open gates.

Some six years after my year at Habbies, I will read about the boss's long-term objective for the property in *The Pastoral Review*. Mr Webb's aim is to build the Habbies Howe herd from nine hundred to 1500 cows. Such growth in production will be achieved through more-intense grazing practices, principally by reducing the size of the paddocks to make grazing them more intense and efficient – in shorter bursts – and by sowing higher-quality grasses and clovers. Also, management will construct more dams to service each of these newly created paddocks. The dams will, of course, be in addition to the no less than seventeen permanent creeks that run through Habbies Howe.

Incidentally, the magazine article doesn't give one ounce of credit to us hard-working, loyal and clear-thinking jackaroos, who have always provided the slave labour for these highly commendable projects.

Improved pasture development is seen as critical to the higher productivity, and more than one-fifth of Habbies Howe will be re-sown with improved grasses and clovers. What I don't know is that the oat crop that we so diligently carted in and cut up for chaff back in January, is in fact the first phase in a three-year, big-picture pasture improvement program. Indeed, after the oats were taken off the paddock in January, the paddocks were lightly ploughed and then sown with phalaris and cocksfoot, two of the most popular pasture grasses sown in Victoria, and Mt Barker clover, a legume. All of this with a hundred kilograms per hectare of superphosphate. I will take the memory of lugging the shit with me – along with boxes full of receipts from my chiropractor – to my grave.

Phalaris, a tall, lanky grass with a long fluffy seed head at the top, like a pipe-cleaner, can often be seen growing beside country roads. It can also be a killer weed, seriously poisonous, especially to cattle if it's allowed to become too rank. But then, that's the same with everything on the land: it's either too much or too little, boom or bust, feast or famine.

I'm not allowed to plough a paddock or sow a crop or new pasture. These are jobs for the station hands. I am, however, dispatched one day to harrow two paddocks – towing behind the station's smallest tractor, the small grey Fergie, a collection maybe three metres square of short metal rods welded together, some with spikes. The purpose of the harrows is to spread out sheep and cattle shit evenly across a paddock – and thus give the entire paddock a good smattering of the nitrogen that is present in the dung. Harrowing is a simple task, ideally suited to a jackaroo, who can thrash the small tractor around a paddock, starting at the outside and working his way towards the middle in ever-decreasing circles. What makes it fun – and this might be the reason we jackaroos are never allowed to use the bigger tractors for the more serious work of ploughing and sowing – is that we can charge around in top gear at breakneck speed, bouncing all over the joint and throwing up sticks, cow shit and even small rocks in our wake, some of it even flying forwards and landing on the driver. It's totally irresponsible behaviour to drive any machine or vehicle like this, but someone has to do it, and, anyway, it's another rite of passage for a jacka-roo and good fun. Except, with all the bouncing, my teenage guts become a twisted mess, and when I climb off the tractor after one particular hairbrained circuit of a paddock, I spew green bile for a good minute.

Another important consideration in this farming caper, I learn, is the need to keep a pocket diary. And what a good lesson that will turn out to be for later life. Take calving and lambing. Bulls need to be put out with the cows and heifers in the first week in June – cattle having a nine-month gestation period. For sheep, it's five months. The timing is organised so cows and ewes will drop their calf and lamb in early autumn, which means you check for problem births in both species simultaneously. It also enables calves and lambs to be old and strong enough to cope with the onset of the cold winter. Then in spring, the young ones will put on lots of weight.

The need for a diary is driven home to me one Sunday during another Royal Tour, with the boss this time making me drive him around the southern end of Habbies Howe.

Peering over the boundary fence at a small soldier-settlement block, Mr Webb says, 'The silly c-cove f-f-forgot to p-put his rams out one y-y-year.'

What an idiot, I think. 'Really? I guess that's why it's important to keep a diary, Mr Webb.'

What a greaser I am.

Much as these times spent with the boss can be painful, with his pedantic pointing and surprise tests, we can learn a bit if we keep our ears open. On another Royal Tour Mr Webb explains to me the skills required in handling men. He tells me how a friend, back when both men were in their early twenties, was overseer on Brunette Downs in the Northern Territory, at one time Australia's biggest cattle station. The property is 13 000 square kilometres (bigger than Vanuatu) and runs 65 000 cattle. Mr Webb's friend was told to take the stockmen to shift a mob of cattle from a paddock roughly the size of Sydney. In those days there were no helicopters or motorbikes to assist with the mustering; everything was done on horseback. The stockmen, so the story goes, were just waiting for the new overseer to make a mistake. His age and position – and his wage packet – caused resentment from the other men, all of whom were older and were used to working things out on the basis of age and experience, not by who took greater responsibility.

'They w-w-were ou-out t-t-to teach my f-f-friend a lesson,' Mr Webb tells me, pausing briefly to get out of the Land Rover and open another gate.

The moment the team entered the paddock, all smirking, the boss continues, his friend said to them, 'I h-haven't g-g-got a c-c-clue where to start. Y-you b-b-blokes teach me.'

It was a w-w-win–win situation. His friend acknowledged the stockmen as having superior knowledge, which increased their self-esteem. And, by deferring to them, the new overseer earned their respect and got them onside. He also got the cattle mustered and learnt on the job how to do the task the next time, without the need to ever ask the men again.

'Never b-b-be t-t-too proud to l-learn from anyone, M-M-Michael,' Mr Webb says to me. 'Y-y-you c-c-can learn s-s-something from anyone, even th-th-the fellow s-s-sweeping th-the streets down in M-M-Melbourne.'

That's how we jackaroos are taught things at Habbies Howe: out in the paddock with the boss, listening to his stories and advice, all with a purposeful, poignant message.

Many years later, I will sit on panels interviewing people for jobs and will wish some of the applicants had Richard Cappur Webb as their mentor. So often, I will want to say to a candidate, 'Just tell the truth and say you haven't any experience in this or that aspect of the job, but that you're willing to learn.' Not many people will do that for fear of showing weakness, and missing out on the appointment.

I learn so much from Dick Webb and I can see why so many people love and respect him (even us jackaroos). Yes, there's still the five-year waiting list, and the threat of it hanging over our heads. Yes, we can walk away from Habbies any time we want. But we don't – we stay for the experiences and the lessons we learn.

If only the old bugger would rid himself of his unfortunate habit of getting us out of bed at midnight to clear the homestead gutters in teeming rain.

One day, Mr Webb thanks us.

It occurs in August, just on winter's end, before Dougie leaves. If I was riding Charlie at the time, I'd have fallen off him. The boss never thanks or congratulates us for anything, ever. He must be seriously ill.

It happens while we're feeding out hay. All through winter

we've been feeding hay to the cattle and sheep – a brain-deadening task – and so far we've fed out 40 000 bales the station hands made the previous summer. The bales are what are known as 'small squares'. It is some years before the big round 'Texas' hay bales will be introduced into Australia.

We've been working hard at emptying two haystacks, in a childlike way having competitions to see how quickly we can load the truck. And, boys being boys, we stack each load onto the old four-ton Bedford truck higher and higher, trying to break the world record for the number of bales we can load onto the old girl without the hay falling off before we reach the destination paddock.

Even more foolishly, we dare one another to ride up on top of the load as we drive. And, of course, the higher we stack the hay, the more precarious the ride is for the jackaroo on top – and the greater the likelihood of him coming crashing to earth along with a hundred bales of hay.

Of course, if we get caught playing the goat, we'll get yelled at. If both things happen simultaneously – getting caught and the load tumbling off the truck – we'll be in even deeper shit. Hay doesn't sit comfortably on a truck, so the odds of a calamity occurring along bumpy tracks are high. But you learn to have a go – to 'takes your chances'.

This day the boss materialises from nowhere while we're in the process of loading the truck (and not sitting down having a smoke, thank the Lord). Each bay of the four-bay haystack holds around 4000 bales, and, being the dopes we are, the three of us have been working faster and faster, having set ourselves the goal of emptying the bay this afternoon. Goodness knows why we set ourselves such goals, all for nine dollars a week (in my case, at least).

The boss forces a cough as he comes around the corner, like he always does when he comes anywhere near our quarters, in case he might catch us doing something we oughtn't to be doing.

Suddenly, as if from nowhere, he's standing beside the Bedford. At this stage we have the load stacked only seven bales high. Kids' stuff.

'W-w-well done, b-b-boys,' he says, looking at the near empty haystack. And with that, he turns, walks back to his ute, climbs in, and drives off.

'Well I'll be . . .' says Simon. 'What the fuck just happened then?'

'It was a mirage,' I reply. Either that or Susie put something in the water this morning.

All three of us are in a state of shock. We look at one another, not knowing what to say, not knowing how to react.

The one thing we've not been taught at Habbies Howe is how to accept praise.

10

Best Day

It's the first week of spring, I've just turned eighteen, and I'm in for the best day of my life.

As usual, the Other Mr Webb parks his Land Rover under the big cypress tree to give us our morning orders. The manager always tells us jackaroos what to do before he goes on down to the sheds to give the station hands their day's instructions. Simon, who's still smarting from having to shave off his beard on his first day back in April, thinks I'm a greaser for putting the manager's milk billy in his truck the moment he arrives each morning. 'Why don't you make the prick get his own friggin' milk?' But I can do whatever I like given Dougie finished up last week.

I'm now the senior jackaroo.

The manager addresses Simon first. 'You can help Gordon with the drains,' he says. Simon isn't happy at the news, and without so much as a nod he turns and sulks his way down to Gordon's shed, head down, kicking a pine cone with his riding boot as he goes.

Simon can't win a trick. Like a few weeks ago, when the big, new, shiny Massey Ferguson tractor arrived. We jackaroos and a bunch of station hands all gathered around the spectacular beast, testosterone frothing everywhere; each man and boy present hoping he'd be given first drive of the flash machine. But what did the manager do? He chose Simon – *Simon* – to put the big red tractor in the homestead garage. What he didn't take into account, and nor did

Simon, was how its exhaust pipe extended a good metre above the garage doorway.

Crunch.

Not long ago, in a fit of rage, the boss told us how each of us jackaroos costs him $5000 a year in breakages. I tried to think of what I'd broken at Habbies Howe and all I came up with was my back.

With Simon slinking off to Gordon's workshop, it leaves just the Other Mr Webb and me standing under the tree. Suddenly, I feel embarrassed. My face turns hot red. It's always been Dougie and me, two if not three of us standing here getting our orders. In the pause my face goes even redder. The man is physical, wiry, strong, while my frame – even though I have begun to bulk up some-what – would still hardly bother a tape measure. It's impossible not to notice the man's emu-egg biceps below his sleeveless khaki shirt. My arms you wouldn't mention in a letter home. His build comes with twenty-something years managing Habbies Howe, its prob-lem men and wayward jackaroos.

'You can get your horse,' he says to me, expressionless as usual.

Get my horse? A million thoughts race through my mind. Will he and I be doing cattle work together, given no one else is left under the big tree?

'You can let the cows out of Glenlyon and put them in One Tree.'

The words run off his tongue with such ease, I hardly take them in. Not immediately.

Hang on – what did he just say? My mind reels. What does he mean by 'you can'? Doesn't he mean 'we will'? Is he telling me what I'm now thinking – that I'm to do the job on my own?

Hundreds of worries swamp my tiny brain, as if suddenly I've been asked to define time.

Glenlyon is the biggest of Habbies Howe's sixty-four paddocks and one of the most difficult to muster. I've only been in it once – the day we all went there to build a new fence. Plus, there are cows and calves in No. 9, which will need shifting first. Ditto Jeffries, which has a bunch of young heifers in it. Third, as if these impediments aren't enough for someone – me – attempting to do all of this on his own, I'll need to bully the cows and calves from Glenlyon across Hughes Creek, hugely swollen from the winter rains. Shit.

Is this a test or what? Of course it is. But still I stand staring at the man, waiting, hoping for him to suddenly burst out laughing and say, *April Fool!* – except it's September, and the man has never told a joke in his life. Is he for real? I've never once been sent out to move a mob of cattle on my own, and this is way too big a task for one person – a boy – me, alone.

Or is it? He could so easily be sending Simon out with me, but he's not.

Again, I fleetingly glance into the man's eyes, half of me desperately hoping to hear *And I'll meet you at . . .*, the other half of me praying he'll add nothing and let me prove myself.

He adds nothing, but what he does do almost makes my knees buckle under me – this hardest of hard men smiles at me. Just like Mr Donnet did when he told me he'd be my swimming coach. For some reason, my mind jumps back further to Ikey West. *Weak knee, eh? Like the rest of you.*

Dopey me suddenly figures it out. The Other Mr Webb is acknowledging my new status as the senior jackaroo. He's giving me a task equal to my new place in the pecking order. It will be up to me to prove I can do the job, and deserve the title of Senior Jackaroo.

I offer him half a red-faced smile in return. My problem is, I don't know how to handle a compliment, because I've never been paid one.

I turn on my heels and begin to stride towards Horse paddock to fetch Charlie, all the while holding my breath, my fists

clenched tightly by my sides, waiting to hear him call out behind
me, *And I'll meet you at* . . . But it doesn't come. I quicken my pace
so I wouldn't hear it even if he does say it.

Then I do hear his voice. 'Don't forget your lunch,' he calls out
from a distance.

I haven't thought about lunch As I stride to Horse paddock
in my rapidly fading blue jeans and my now well-worn-in but still
monstrous riding boots, I find I have a whole new spring in my
step. I might be as scared as all shit at the job I've been given to do,
but boy, is the adrenalin pumping.

I put positive thoughts into my brain. I can do it, I tell myself.
Who needs Dougie, anyway?

I smile at the way the Other Mr Webb said I can 'let' the cows
and calves out of Glenlyon. 'Let' them is farm-speak for force
them. It has nothing to do with letting them, as if all fifty cows and
their calves will be lined up at the gate just waiting for me to open
it and let them through, then on through three more paddocks to
complete their journey. Get real. It will be about finding all one
hundred beasts, bringing them together in one mob, counting them
several times to make absolutely certain I have them all, and then
droving them to and through the gate, then onwards through the
other paddocks to their final destination – One Tree.

Plus, somehow, I will have to cajole my animals across a heavily swollen Hughes Creek. *Let* them, my arse.

Making my way across to Horse paddock, I muse further about
the language of the land. People talk about a two-year-old bull or
ram being 'ready to work', meaning he's old enough to have sex,
to sire offspring. Hey, if having sex qualifies as work, pass me the
sign-up sheet.

As I reach the gate to Horse, I'm deep in thought as to how
to get my mob across Hughes Creek. Cattle don't like to get their
feet wet in winter. In summer, they can stand in water for hours

on end. But try to force them across a high, fast-flowing, swollen creek after a cold and bitter winter, and cows and calves are likely to bolt in every direction rather than cross.

'Get ready for some serious cattle work,' I say to Charlie as he and the other eight stockhorses race past me through their open gate and head at full gallop towards the horse yards. Charlie's reply is to fart fair in my face as he flies by.

As I saddle Charlie, I still can't believe what I've been told to do. I notice the Other Mr Webb deep in conversation with Gordon down at the sheds. He must have finished with me and moved on to the other workers.

I tighten Charlie's girth and whisper to him what our task is, making sure no one sees me. If people saw me speaking to my gorgeous horse, they'd probably have me certified – label me madder than Old Harold. And Old Harold *is* mad.

In response, Charlie, the cheeky prick that he is, puts back his ears, tucks in his head and tries to bite a hole in my left hip, as if to say, *Well, come on then, you useless piece of shit, climb on board and let's get this show on the road.* Charlie is always telling me things like that, and I love him for it. I climb on and give my best friend a big hug, again making sure no one is watching.

We ride up to the homestead, where Susie must have been given prior warning because she has my lunch packed ready for me. Susie's a great cook; she always makes cupcakes or something else special for us late in the afternoons. I thank her verbally – it's long before the days of people hugs.

As I ride past the Other Webbs' home, I hear a Land Rover approach and my heart sinks. Is this where the Other Mr Webb tells me to wait while he gets his horse? He pulls up next to us.

'Don't forget the cows in No. 9,' he says, with another of his new-found smiles, like he's just realised the other cattle will be in our way. Will it make him change his mind and now decide to come with me? No, he doesn't say anything more, just puts his Land Rover back into gear and releases the clutch. Phew, I think as the vehicle begins to slide away. It is just me after all.

'And the heifers in Jeffries,' I call out. He gives an acknowledging wave with his hand as his vehicle accelerates.

There I go. One-upmanship. There always has to be one-upmanship among us jackaroos and between us and management. It seems we always have to prove something, to show management we've been thinking on our feet. I've learnt to play the game beautifully. Indeed, I believe I've mastered the technique. But maybe too well. The manager was genuinely just trying to help, to warn me about a mob of cattle he realised will be in my way. And what did I do? I've gone and gazumped him by telling him about another mob in another paddock he hasn't thought of. Why do we do these things to each other? How much better would life be if we could speak openly and communicate without this game play, or fear of criticism or repercussions if an idea we have is wrong or won't work? Why can't we trust one another to be ourselves and speak our mind without fear of ridicule?

Then I think, Get off the grass, Michael, you loser. I've just done what I'm supposed to do: beaten the man on his own turf. It isn't about sharing knowledge and information, it's about me showing the man that I have balls. That's what a jackaroo's life is all about.

I watch as he drives off. And I smile, because . . . because I'm a Habbies Howe jackaroo.

'You'd better do the job good,' I tell Charlie, in language I know he understands. I can't say he gives me a snort in reply, although I wish I could tell you he does.

Halfway to Glenlyon, we come across Jonesy and Tuff in No. 3, supposedly rabbiting but in truth sitting beside their truck having an early smoko. It isn't yet eight-thirty and the pair have already slacked off, their assortment of mangy rabbit dogs lolling about, some pretending to be asleep, others actually so. Not one of the dogs cares less about chasing rabbits or about Charlie and me as we pass close-by. One sits next to Jonesy, his head to the side, eyes wide open, pleading for a morsel of whatever his master is eating. Another brainless bitch is lying in the back of the truck with her head hanging over the side of the tray.

'Mornin', men,' I call out, as Charlie and I go by just metres away.

Tuff, the half-civil one of the pair, at least raises his mug of tea in acknowledgement. Jonesy is reading yesterday's *Sun* newspaper. He doesn't look up. I'm convinced Jonesy despises us spoilt, silver-spoon jackaroos.

The dog in the truck momentarily raises her head, then quickly lets it flop back down when she sees I'm not bearing any form of compensation. What a life.

With the rabbiters well behind us, Charlie and I are again alone in the awesome, huge valley that is Habbies Howe. And despite feeling anxious about the task ahead of us – actually I'm shitting myself – I can't be happier. It's spring, I've just turned the magic eighteen, and all is wonderful in my narrow-focused, yet gloriously simple and uncomplicated world.

Habbies certainly is an amazing property. Everywhere I look, whether forward to the north or backwards to the south, to the top of the hill on my left or to the one further away in the distance to the east, everything is green, with shiny granite boulders jutting out of the sides of the hills. Even here on the flat country there are permanent springs oozing never-ending, fresh, clear water into Habbies Howe's many dams and creeks. They're the source of the green strips I noticed among the dry grass when I first drove down the winding road with Mum and Penny. The springs provide valuable green pick for livestock during hot and dry summer months. The stunning greenness of the property is also due to the dreaded superphosphate, the memory of which I carry in my permanently wrecked back.

All of this is owned by one man: Richard Cappur Webb. Talk about an empire. It makes me think. I wonder if the boss ever drives alone to the top of one of these hills and sits there and admires it all. And whether, after first looking around him to check no one is watching, he lets out a chuckle, and says, *All this, mine.* Or if he ever contemplates the Bible verse which says everything in fact belongs to God ('For every animal of the forest is mine, and the cattle on a thousand hills', NIV Bible, Psalm 50:10), and considers that he is nothing more than a temporary steward of this amazing patch of God's awesome benevolence. For me – ex-choirboy that I am – having attended up to three Sunday chapel services for eight years, I've no difficulty in believing the truth of God's ownership of all that we have. As for Mr Webb, I think in his own way he knows God is the one true Boss.

The lingering winter chill is fast fading and the warm spring sun brings fresh pastures alive after their long dormancy. As for the cattle, mobs of which we pass on our way to Glenlyon, the cows and calves still wear their dark red, furry winter coats. They busily munch on the early spring growth. On my way back in a few hours' time they'll be lying down, resting and content, their stomachs full. I've learnt that if cattle aren't napping by eleven o'clock, there isn't enough feed in their paddock. At Habbies, cattle are always napping by eleven.

Starting in No. 9, Charlie and I get the cows and calves together with relative ease. We push them in a westerly direction over the hill and way down to the creek. I'm banking on this lot finding enough fresh grass along the creek to keep them occupied for at least two hours. Hopefully, that's where they'll stay, out of sight but not out of mind while we bring the cows and calves from Glenlyon past them on the near side of the hill. Because, if they come back over the hill to see what's going on – and the two mobs get boxed – it'll be the end of the new-found smiles from the Other Mr Webb.

The heifers in Jeffries are more difficult. I'm not sure if some might be last year's daughters of the cows I'll bring past them, and although it's months since they were weaned off those cows, I can't risk a mother being inquisitive about her older daughter, and, again, the two mobs getting boxed.

Jeffries is a big paddock, and Charlie and I aren't about to take chances. After mustering it, we do the mandatory head count – eighty – which Charlie confirms. Farmers, if nothing else, are good counters, and these experiences as a jackaroo will make me a counter for life. I will forever count the number of people in a room, train or bus, or the bricks in a wall. And more: I'll count how many people in the room are rams, how many are ewes, how many men are wearing ties, and so on. It becomes an addiction.

Charlie and I push the heifers much further away than is necessary, almost ridiculously so, and in doing it we create for ourselves a catch-22 situation. The longer we spend pushing the heifers out of the way in Jeffries, the more chance the cows in No. 9 will wander back to where we first found them – directly in the way of where we'll bring the cows from Glenlyon. But, as I say to Charlie, we need to make sure the heifers are well out of the way. Better safe than sorry, Charlie reminds me. What a smart horse.

We take the heifers all the way to the boundary fence; it's two hills further than we need to push them. Yet, it's a gamble in timing that Charlie and I feel we need to make.

Poking along behind a mob of cattle might seem, on a television screen, like a piece of cake. Yet, deceivingly, like anything worth doing well, it requires total concentration. An animal even slightly distracted can take off at a whim, requiring the drover to leave the other cattle to their own devices and chase after it. My adrenalin, let alone Charlie's, is flowing faster than the swollen Hughes Creek we're about to tackle.

Mustering the cows and calves in Glenlyon is far less of a problem than we expect. God has put them all on our side of the paddock to make it easier for us. In less than twenty minutes we have them together and walking towards the gate out. At the gate, I find the highest point closest to the mob and stand in my stirrups to count heads: fifty cows and their calves all present and accounted for, a hundred beasts in all. I count them a second time, then a third to be sure.

'Is that what you make it, old boy?' I ask Charlie, sitting back in the saddle. He puts his ears back to signal I'm spot on. I bend forward and give him a hug in return.

Once through the gate, the challenge is to get the mob down to and across Hughes Creek, which is flowing a lot faster and higher than I expected. On our way out I crossed at an easy place, but one far too narrow to bring the mob through now.

Lesser stockmen might give up at this point, make some excuse, but not this jackaroo; I have far too much to prove. Plus, I like the way the Other Mr Webb has begun to smile at me.

Charlie and I get the mob down to the creek without any fuss, the natural leaders among them quickly working their way to the front. Leaders like to know first what's going on. They have more blind courage, they take more risks. Yet none of them, including the leaders, will have a bar of crossing the creek – the flow is far too furious for even the bravest of them to put a hoof anywhere near water. I can hardly blame them for not wanting to get wet. So, for maybe five minutes, Charlie and I let them stand and settle. The only thing not on hold are Charlie's and my eyes, which dart back and forth, looking for any sign of restlessness, any sign that one or

more of the animals might be about to try to make a break for it
back into the paddock.

I glance again at the furiously raging water, and the words
'Webb' and 'sadist' come to mind.

It's time to make a move, before the mob does. Charlie knows
what to do. With the gentlest of nudges in his flanks with my
boots – the same boots my sister teased me about on New Year's
Day – we charge the mob, me yelling my head off like a full-on
lunatic. The effect, of course, is to frighten the cows nearest to us
so they jump backwards towards the bank. They in turn bump
the animals behind them into the creek. Once these cattle are
in the water, wet and with little other option, they do the right
thing – they get to their feet and struggle to the opposite bank.
Dozens more follow them across.

'Good boy,' I say to Charlie. 'Good boy. We've got them
started.'

The cows and calves still on our side aren't convinced they
should follow the leaders, partly because Charlie and I, having made
our charge, are now positioned between them and the water, blocking their way. We quickly move away from our spot, but not before
a bunch of cows and calves take off back into the paddock – at
speed and in different directions. Some left, some right. The natural
instinct for cattle is to run along the bank to look for another place
to cross, wanting to join their friends on the other side, but only on
the condition there is an easier way to achieve that goal.

I quickly estimate that the cows and calves running in a westerly direction – maybe fifteen in number – need retrieving first.
They have the whole paddock ahead to potentially get lost in.
Charlie and I gallop after them, quickly get to the front of the
group and turn them back towards the crossing. Enough beasts
still are crossing at the spot to act as role models, and the ones we
just hunted back promptly follow them across. Phew.

We then take off at a gallop again, this time in an easterly direction, riding well out from the creek in a wide arc so as not to encourage these tearaways to bolt even faster. Thunderous bellowing is coming from cows and calves now on the other side of the creek, grieving for family and friends still on our side, yet to cross. If we can just get around this lot, turn them back and get them across, we'll have everyone happily reunited. The alternative – failure – doesn't bear contemplating.

The cows and calves we are now chasing, I call the Desperates. Every herd has them. They will fight you to the end. And this lot has a good start on us. We gallop hard and soon catch up to the slowest cow and calf. As always, as soon as they see Charlie's nose in front of theirs, they stop in their tracks. Cattle do seem to have an amazing sense of reality; mostly they know when enough is enough. The first pair, not necessarily mother and child, promptly turn and trot back to the crossing where they can see friends on the far side. The remaining Desperates – possibly three cows and three calves from what I can see – are still well out in front of us. The chase is on in earnest.

We pick off a cow. She slides to a halt as we fly past. She makes huge skid marks in the wet ground with her hoofs as she comes to a halt. Then a calf also stops in its tracks. It's all a numbers game for Charlie and me. I bolster my spirits by imagining that we've got them across Hughes Creek. Once we have them all on the other side, they'll calm down and become compliant. I hope.

Stockhorses are amazing animals and Charlie loves every minute of the chase. Crashing through metre-high bracken – not having a clue what's underneath it – he gallops after our prey, hurdling logs and smashing through smaller blackberry bushes. At times like this you need to put absolute trust in your horse. It's scary stuff, yet the manager expects nothing less of us.

We close in on another calf. My eyes can't watch the ground

and the beast when, galloping at full speed through scrub, my right riding boot now is actually in contact with the red hairs on the Hereford steer's rump. It's Charlie's job to avoid fallen trees and stumps, even the odd granite boulder.

The calf suddenly gives up the fight and stops in its own length. Ditto the next cow. But we can't hang about to argue with the cow, even though I can tell she isn't a happy camper. She snorts snot at us, some of it landing on the leg of my jeans as we fly past.

We race on, and I take a quick glance back; both beasts are trotting back to the crossing.

Charlie and I still have one cow and one calf to go. Both he and I are soaked in sweat. Within seconds we're level with the last cow, which promptly decides enough is enough. She stops, digging her hoofs into the wet ground, before she too turns back.

'Dopey shit of a thing,' I tell Charlie. He snorts in agreement as we race on.

The final calf must think it's really brave – but I have the psychological advantage, knowing that in the not too distant future the lousy animal will adorn a butcher's front window. I can see the slaughterman's knife poised. Another advantage I have is that I know we're getting close to the corner of the paddock and there'll be nowhere for the calf to go. The Glenlyon fence comes down a steep section of the hill to meet Hughes Creek, with a giant, overhanging granite boulder blocking the way for man or beast to navigate. It means a dead end, a natural corral: the boulder, a fence, dense scrub and a heavily overgrown section of creek. End of story.

Still galloping, we draw alongside the mongrel of a calf, its head down as if pretending to ignore us while travelling at full speed. I say a few words – the language isn't the kind you'll hear at my grandparents' dinner table over roast beef and Yorkshire pudding. We're that close, if I want, I can bend down and pull out a clump of the steer's red hide. We gallop on, yet still the calf won't call it quits. It runs like it's possessed We're seconds away from entering the natural corral, not that the gormless calf knows it. We have him cornered; it's just a matter of time. Yet Charlie and I don't want the corral to do the job for us – we want to win the fight on our terms. Isn't that what life is about? Winning at all cost? I wonder if Graeme, whom I replaced at Habbies and who rode Charlie before me, was as courageous on him as I am. Was he tough, like me? Am I as good a rider as him? Surely, as Charlie and I hurdle yet another log while still touching the steer's rump, I'm as good a jackaroo.

All of a sudden, the lousy steer gives up the fight and slides to a standstill – *just* before the impasse. Charlie too stops in his own length, and what's more I stay on board. Yippee. *We've won.*

The steer stares at us, its lungs and guts heaving, steam pouring off all three of us. With a shake of its head, the calf sends a blast of snot at us, another appalling habit it learnt from its mother. I flick the snot off my right leg with my finger, and relax momentarily, to let Charlie stare the calf out while he and I get our breath back.

I can tell Charlie is ready to keep going, so I let him take a step closer to the Hereford. It makes the steer jump backwards, duck and turn. Knowing it's useless to try anything untoward, the mongrel steer begins the long trot back to the crossing, with Charlie and me riding right alongside him, two metres away from his right rump this time – all the way, just in case the prick of a thing tries to pull something stupid. My hands are ready to jerk on the reins if the calf suddenly stops.

Just before we get to the crossing, we fall back and let the calf approach the water alone. Once there, he realises he has no option but to join the other ninety-nine beasts on the other side. They're all milling around, watching intently. I figure our calf won't misbehave; he's way too stuffed to try anything stupid. Plus, his mother is now standing on the other side, calling to him to come across and have a suck on her teats. The steer belly-flops into the water like an obese child collapsing into a suburban swimming pool. He promptly gets swamped by small waves, yet somehow – not without a few gurgling noises – he manages to get back on his feet and he mooches his way over to the other bank.

Then Charlie tries to jump the creek, but it was never going to work. By the time we make it across my riding boots are full of water and my jeans are soaked to my thighs. But who cares? Charlie and I are on a roll. We've shown the world we can do it.

I've shown the world I'm fit to be called senior jackaroo.

Fifty cows and fifty calves. Again, I count them. Nothing right now is sweeter than counting one hundred – exactly. Charlie and I count them a third time. They all stand around obligingly still for us. Not one beast looks like bolting anywhere. Their fun is over.

But we can't linger. We still have work to do, so I let Charlie give the order. With the gentlest of nudges in his flanks, he lets out a regular snort. It has just the right effect: the cattle turn and begin to trot away from us, towards the gate into Jeffries, some five hundred metres to the south. These cows have done it before, but not their calves, which are tired and happy just to follow mum.

Charlie also knows – and this is something I'm convinced about – exactly where we need to take the mob, given the way we pushed the heifers out of the way in Jeffries, and the cows and calves in No. 9 earlier. It's an amazing thing about a good stockhorse: not only does he know our final destination with the mob, but any time Charlie sees a cow begin to wander off the path (the vehicle track we're following) even before I notice, he begins to move to the left or right to shepherd it back into line. At times like this I almost feel redundant in the saddle.

Fortunately, when we get to Jeffries there is no sign of the heifers, or the cows and calves in No. 9. We get our mob through both paddocks in a breeze.

With the job done and the gate into One Tree closed behind our mob, our cows and calves straight away begin to chomp on the fresh, early spring pasture. I climb off Charlie, stretch my leg muscles to get rid of the cramps, then sit down and lean against the gatepost to eat my totally squashed and sodden sandwich. Charlie is happy just to stand in front of me, his head hanging low, his reins drooped across my boots. After the sandwich I roll myself a smoke. I offer Charlie one, but he declines – they aren't his brand.

And I think, for the last time, about the boys in my peer group back at school.

What would they know?

Have they mustered a mob of cattle like this, alone?

Have they galloped at full speed through metre-high bracken?

Have they jumped logs and crashed through stinging black-berries chasing recalcitrant cattle?

Have they forced fifty cows and their calves across a rapidly flowing, swollen creek, alone?

Have they driven cattle through paddocks with cattle already in them, alone?

I bet my balls they haven't.

It's time to move on. And it's also time to move on, literally. Charlie is nudging my leg with his nose. He's busting to get home to his feed box full of yummy chaff, before I send him packing back to his paddock. Get a wriggle on, he tells me, as he gnaws away at my riding boot.

As we ride past the entrance to the Other Webbs' home, as if by coincidence the manager suddenly materialises from nowhere in his Land Rover.

'How did it go?' he asks, looking up at me from the cabin. I'm not the least bit fussed that his eyes go straight to my still-soaked jeans and the sodden riding boot that hangs loosely in the stirrup, just inches from his eyes as he sits in his vehicle. Again, the smile.

'No worries,' I reply. Well, it's half true. By now I'm well into the lingo of the land.

The smile says it all. He knows exactly what I had to do.

He says nothing more, and it's the best day.

11

Shearing

For the month of November, in what must be another gesture to my wool-buyer grandfather, Mr Webb puts me in the woolshed to learn about shearing and wool. It will take a month to shear Habbies Howe's 12 000 Merinos. And not one of the mongrels will do a single thing to assist in the process.

Shearing is an amazing phenomenon, not to be compared with a haircut. Imagine if your friendly barber or hairdresser had to put you in a headlock to cut your hair.

Knowing as he does that I'm to have a career as a wool-buyer, Mr Webb tells me to stand next to the wool classer and learn what I can from him about wool qualities. Unfortunately, it's a stroke of benevolence not shared by the Other Mr Webb, who, whenever the boss's attention is diverted, or when he's in Melbourne at one of his graziers' meetings, drags me out of the woolshed to perform a farm task. Some nights the boss returns from Melbourne in time for dinner and he quizzes me in front of everyone at the table as to how the day's shearing fared. Of course I lie and make up some answer I know will please him, earning glares from everyone at the table, including Mrs Webb, all of whom know I've spent the day clearing drains with Gordon. I'm caught between a rock and a hard place. I can't say the Other Mr Webb pulled me out of the shed. Sometimes, I half expect the boss to look at me across the table and tell me I'm lying, because he's already spoken to the manager, who's confessed to having had me work outside. We jackaroos, being the ages we are, are selfishly preoccupied only with our own self-importance; we never discuss the fact there may be tension, possibly even raging fights, between the two Mr Webbs. My presence in the woolshed, away from doing real and often necessary farm work, probably creates such tension.

Shearing is a contracted job at Habbies Howe, which means the contractor brings his own entire team of workers with him. At Habbies, his line-up comprises eight shearers (two of whom are 'learners'), four rouseabouts, a wool classer, a wool presser, and an old geezer, like Old Harold, whose job it is to pen up the sheep. Plus, there's the cook and his offsider. Seventeen men, plus the contractor himself, whose role consists of hiring and firing, making sure the diesel-driven motor that powers the shearing mechanism doesn't crash – which it has a predilection to do several times each day – as well as paying the wages and stopping brawls.

The cook, who goes by the name of Cookie, is stumpy and has the look of a lean ferret. He's also missing most of his teeth. Plus, he's crazy, telling me how, while on a flight to an interstate shearing gig, he began to chat up a magic chick sitting next to him. The girl foolishly asked him what he did for a living.

'I'm a caterer,' Cookie told her, proudly making his false teeth jiggle before her eyes.

'Really,' replied the girl. 'And what do you cater for?'

'Just about anything you like, baby,' Cookie replied.

The budding relationship, he regretted, ended there.

The Habbies Howe woolshed is located some two hundred metres from the homestead and, like the homestead, is listed on Victoria's historic register as a 'building of significance'. It's significant, all right. It's where we shear the flamin' sheep. A hundred metres to the north of the woolshed are the shearers' quarters and mess.

Unlike some shearing sheds in western New South Wales and Queensland, which have up to thirty or more shearing stations but where only eight or ten have been in use since the 1950s glory days, the Habbies woolshed has eight stands, all of which are used.

The shearers' day begins at seven-thirty a.m. and consists of four 'runs', each lasting exactly two hours, a half-hour break for morning and afternoon smokos, and an hour for lunch. The working day ends smack on five-thirty. Faster shearers will shear up to a hundred and twenty Merinos in a day. Learner shearers – the name given to apprentices – will shear between eighty and ninety. This means, for the Habbies Howe shed, more than nine hundred sheep are shorn daily.

Some New Zealand shearers, working on lambs and using much wider combs on their handpieces, enabling them to take off more of the fleece with each stroke – which they are allowed to do in that country because they have different union rules – can shear as many as two hundred sheep in a day. (The current Australian record for an individual shearing Merino lambs in an eight-hour day, set in Western Australia in 2002, is five hundred and seventy. That's a lamb every fifty seconds, which sure is pumping.)

It's not uncommon to see a shearer up and out of bed at five-thirty each weekday. I see a number of them moving around in the distance when I head on down to do the milking. At six-thirty, the team presents itself in the dining room for breakfast. Cookie and his offsider will have been up since four o'clock. I see at least three shearers take a large bottle of beer with them to their breakfast table.

Like all meals put in front of shearing teams, breakfast needs to be seen to be believed. The quantum of food is extraordinary: four hundred rashers of bacon and one hundred greasy fried eggs for a team of eighteen men and boys. I'm not exaggerating. Plus there's enough cereal, porridge, toast, coffee and tea to feed a battalion.

Prior to the first shearing run, the shearers clean and oil their handpieces, and change and sharpen their combs and cutters. Like the old thresher used for making chaff, the shearing apparatus runs via a series of belts which feeds back to a diesel motor that powers the whole shebang. A shearer's handpiece is attached to the overhead mechanism by a section of metal tubes with joints, which enables a 180-degree manipulation of the whirling mechanism that rotates inside, to make shearing possible. And like the electric razor a barber uses, above the stationary comb sits a small cutter with thirteen teeth that agitate back and forth above the comb. Combs need sharpening after twenty sheep are shorn, and replacing after a thousand sheep are done. Cutters need sharpening after ten sheep and replacing after five hundred. That's one heck of a lot of combs and cutters for Australia's 140 million sheep industry.

It's worth adding that with all moving and rubbing metal parts, including the overhead drive shaft and the spinning belts that lead back to the diesel engine, as well as eight handpieces all powering along at once, the noise level in the woolshed is fearful.

Shearers work precisely to time and union rules; they begin their working day not one second before, and never one second later than seven-thirty. Upon the sound of the bell, they dive into their individual pen via a two-way swinging half-door, and they grab the easiest-looking-to-shear sheep (i.e. with the fewest wrinkles in the skin), or the closest. Shearing continues nonstop until the bell rings again, precisely at nine-thirty a.m. A competitive shearer will keep one eye on the second hand of the big clock on the near wall and will time himself to finish his second-to-last sheep for the run twenty seconds before the nine-thirty bell. This allows him to dive in and grab and shear one more sheep to maximise his tally for the run.

There's a reason for this competitiveness. The shearer who shears the most sheep in a day is called the 'gun', and the gun has ultimate say as to what happens in the shed. He also earns the most money. Learner shearers in particular look up to him. The rouse-abouts will sweep the gun shearer's workplace first before clearing another shearer's area if push comes to shove.

Older shearers aren't too fussed about the pecking order. Like old rams, they're happy just to knock out their quota each day; in their case, maybe twenty or so sheep per run. For the young shearer, it's a different story. Every second of every run is precious, and for this year's shed three shearers compete for the honour of being the gun.

Working in the shed for four weeks, I get to know a bunch of men I'd not normally be drawn to. At night, after dinner, they invite me into their dining room to talk, drink their beer and play the most popular card game played in the bush – 500. I deem it an honour to be allowed into the shearers' world, and I have no hesi-tation in telling them so. Small courtesies like this are important in the bush. The men tell stories about who the gun was at Habbies Howe in the '50s, stories that some nights continue well into the wee hours, and which are told with great animation, considerable embellishment and much lubrication. Gun shearers' names are men-tioned with the same reverence afforded to top VFL footballers.

After sufficient Bundy and Coke, tales take on greatly exagger-ated dimensions.

'Shut the fuck up, Gibson,' a senior shearer lets out one night. 'You told the same fucking bullshit yarn last night.'

Gibson must be in his mid-sixties, and that's being generous. He's almost ready to hang up his handpiece and sit on his veranda with his missus at Shepparton, but not quite.

One way a shearer gets a head start over his peers is to allow a young rouseabout, who dreams of one day becoming a gun shearer, to start off a sheep for him. Union rules allow for boys to enter a shearer's catching pen two minutes before the bell sounds for a new run and to begin removing wool. By the time the bell sounds, the quicker of the boys might have removed the belly wool and perhaps the neck wool; he might even have begun to work along the sheep's back leg. The practice is called 'barrowing' and this too is competitive. The moment the bell sounds, the barrower quickly hands the handpiece and sheep over to the shearer. Even allowing for the mess the rouseabout might have made, which the shearer will need to clean up before he delves further into the shearing, it still gives him a head start.

The gamesmanship at the end of each run is amazing. The fastest shearers will watch one another out of the corner of their eye as the clock ticks towards the final seconds. Upon finishing their respective sheep, and with the bell still seconds away, each man will literally throw himself into his catching pen to grab anything that stands on four legs, sometimes even leaving his handpiece running, bouncing on the 'board', to save time turning the handpiece back on.

The role of the rouseabouts is to gather up the fleece and to throw it weatherside-up over a large rectangular sorting table, three by two metres, the top of which is made of parallel lengths of dowel separated by gaps as wide as the dowel itself for off-cuts of wool and other crap to fall through onto the floor below. An adult sheep's fleece will easily fill a six-square-metre wool table. Having thrown the fleece, the rousabout then runs back to where he picked it up and sweeps the area clean of odd bits of wool and sheep shit, the latter shorn from the sheep's rear legs and backside before the shearer finishes his task.

At the sorting table, two shedhands remove the rough ends from the fleece, as well as more odd bits of junk and dried shit. One then rolls it up and hands it to the wool classer, who classifies the four-to-five-kilogram bundle of wool being of an appropriate grade. The quality of the wool varies according to the overall parameters of each property's wool clip. Fleece grades are known as 'AAA' for finest, 'AA' for coarser wool, and 'A' for the strongest fibred fleeces. What is AAA for one farmer might be a different quality of wool for another farm, but still his best.

The wool classer's helper – in this case, me – then places the fleece in one of a number of big, walk-in bins, ready for the presser to turn into bales of wool. I can tell that Ivan, the wool presser, has been hand-picked purposefully for the task, straight out of one of those muscle man magazines. In his Jackie Howe, his biceps bulge, the size of footballs. The moment we shake hands I know we'll be best friends for life.

Ivan-the-presser works two large, green wooden boxes made of solid oak and hinged together at the top, each measuring one metre square and one and a half metres deep. Both bins are open at the top. Into each bin Ivan stuffs around twenty-five fleeces, climbing into each box every so often and stomping on the wool to enable him to squeeze in more fleeces. Using a clever rope and pulley system, he swings one box up and flips it over on top of the other box to make one new, tall box. Finally, he uses a massive metal ratchet to screw down the contents of the top box so that all of the wool is now crammed in the lower box, inside a hessian or plastic liner. After fastening the bale, Ivan uses a stencil and black shoe polish (at last, a Habbies Howe nuggeting) to inscribe the property's name on the top and front of each bale. Under the name he stencils the description of the wool inside: AAA, AA or A for fleeces, BLS for bellies, NKS for necks, PCS for odd bits and pieces, or LMS for lambs' wool.

The bales are then ready to be dispatched to the wool sales in Melbourne, where more often than not my grandfather and his team will buy it and ship it to England, to be made into silky-smooth coils of washed, carded and combed wool known as 'tops', prior to being on-sold to a spinner for turning into cloth.

After a century of letting people in other countries (my relatives) make their fortunes at our Australian woolgrowers' expense, you'd expect some bright spark to have found a way to 'add the value' here; by this I mean, undertake the entire manufacturing process here in Australia. Why are we so backward in this country? Consider this: when the Italians finally get their hands on our wool (our relatives in England only go so far as to make tops, and then on-sell them to the Italians who make the suits), the wool will have achieved a *3000 per cent* mark-up in value. Yet ninety-five per cent of the time and labour to get the wool to its end-point will have been expended by the dumb-schmuck Aussie woolgrower and shearing team, who work their butts off. So, who are the mugs, then?

All shearing teams have characters, and Old Frank, the 'penner-upperer', is no exception. Old Frank's job, often with the contractor's help, is to bring sheep into the woolshed from the outside yards, and to keep each shearer's individual caching pen full. He's beyond shearing, and when he isn't penning up, he helps the rouseabouts to keep the board swept clean.

On the third morning, Old Frank is sweeping the board when, suddenly, he throws his broom on the floor, jumps on it, and yells, 'You bastard of a thing! You've been playin' up all week.' Frank has issues. It's a broom, for goodness sake.

The shearers return to their dining room for lunch, yet for morning and afternoon smokos, crazy Cookie and his offsider bring tea and coffee, and tray upon tray of homemade cupcakes, biscuits and scones with oodles of butter and jam – enough to feed Fiji – to the woolshed. And if anyone complains there isn't enough food – which some shearers do just to stir the poor bastard – Cookie sends his offsider back to the kitchen to fetch the extra tray he's held back just in case.

If these feasts aren't enough, wait 'til you see what gets laid on for lunch and dinner: several huge metal baking trays stacked with golden spuds so crunchy they explode the moment you put a fork within poking distance of them – because that's how the shearers demand them. Plus, there will be at least six legs of lamb or mutton – baked or boiled. Then there's the truck-load of greens, for which Cookie raids and clears out the poor greengrocer in Seymour on a daily basis. Main course is followed by tray upon tray of cooked dessert, with enough custard and cream left over to paint the shearers' quarters three times over.

There's a reason for Cookie's productiveness: simply, he wants to keep his job. Shearers are demanding when it comes to their food, and they are able on a whim to vote a cook out, sometimes without reason or warning. Later, I will experience an unpopular cook being replaced without ceremony between breakfast and morning smoko. It happens that quickly. An out-of-work shearers' cook will be waiting in the nearby hamlet ready to get the call.

It isn't uncommon to see a shearer, after work, carrying his towel, razor and a bottle of beer to the shower room. After that, if it's a Thursday, he might be seen washing his car in readiness for a weekend at home, wherever home might be. Or, if he isn't going anywhere for the weekend, he might be sitting on the veranda outside his room reading the previous day's tabloid, with the mandatory bottle of beer beside him for company.

The month I spend with the shearers is a time I will treasure forever. Whether it's alongside the men in the shed during the day or playing 500 with them at night, these men are the real thing. There are no affected English accents here; these are people without pretence, men of substance, down-to-earth guys with good hearts who work damn hard to make a living.

Which is not to say shearers aren't tough. I quickly learn the rules and conventions that separate the shearers from all the others in the team, including the contractor, who, after all, is their employer. Then there are the conventions that separate the entire team, including the contractor, from the grazier.

Disputes between graziers and shearers of course are legendary. (If you haven't already done so, do get the film *Sunday Too Far Away*, starring Jack Thompson – it's a beauty.) Shearers like to stir, to take the mickey out of rouseabouts, especially those still wet behind the ears. Early one morning, the gun shearer calls one of the young rouseabouts over and tells him to fetch a left-handed screwdriver so he can adjust his equipment. The boy runs off to Gordon down at the workshop, who in turn sends him back for more information. Is it a Phillips-head left-handed screwdriver the shearer wants? The poor kid is dumbfounded.

It's a sad day for me when shearing ends at Habbies Howe for another year. The night the team leaves, I return to the shearers' quarters. Cookie's kitchen is pristine yet deadly silent. I think about the meals he dished up, quantities of food I will see only once again in my life.

Now, the shearers' mess is like a ghost town; silent and eerie. Even the AGA ovens (wood-fired), which only exuded warmth for a month, are cold and uninviting. Kettles and saucepans are tucked away in cupboards for another eleven months.

In the dining room, I take a chair from the stack and sit down at the place where, each night for much of the past month, I've been allowed to play 500. It's here that I heard fascinating stories about times of old, yarns about different shearing teams that have come and gone from Habbies Howe over the years, shearing records, good and lousy cooks, and stories about inept and naive rouseabouts.

And for the first time since Dougie left, I feel alone – and miserable. I run my fingers over rude words dug into the table and wish that soon I could wake up from my dream and once again there'd be laughter; once again the room would be abuzz with men.

On the way back to our quarters I have a final walk through the now deserted woolshed. The shearing mechanism is silent, the diesel motor cold. Gone is the thunderous noise which at the start of shearing, for me at least, made it impossible even to think, let alone hear people speak. The sheep pens and wool bins are empty, save for a mouse which gnaws at a piece of fruit left lying on the floor near the wool press. It sees me and scurries away minus the fruit.

Frank's recalcitrant broom is leaning where he left it, by the gun shearer's stand.

If only I'd known how alone I'd now feel, how much I'd miss those men, I would have lingered with them longer into the nights. But then, regrets are pointless, unless you learn from them.

I perch on the wool table. I cast my eyes around, looking at each stand, and envisaging the man who occupied the space. Why can't I go with them to their next shed? The truth is, I don't even know if there is a next shed, where it might be, or if they're still together as a team. Maybe they've gone their separate ways, what with different sheds requiring different-sized teams. There aren't too many sheds around these parts that require as big a shearing team as that needed for Habbies Howe. What I've just experienced over the past month is unique in this part of the world.

And then I wonder if for all the men I'm now missing so badly, one shed is just like all the others: a bastard place where a bastard boss rips off hard-working shearers and dopey rouseabouts. Where a contractor is so tight he'd rob his grandmother while she sleeps. Where a shearer has his old age delivered to him by the time he's forty, his body riddled with rheumatism and back pain even before he memorises his first grandchild's name. Where the owner-grazier would slice your wages if it weren't for the might of the union.

I ponder the cheeky, delinquent boy rouseabouts, who spent the past month giving cheek to the shearers, and generally driving them nuts. I think about the naive red-haired Justin, who was so dumb he couldn't even figure out that being told by a shearer to go fetch him a 'short time' was a joke. And how the guys working the board that morning were one boy short for the entire run because dopey Justin couldn't figure things out. And how the kid got so bamboozled he broke down and cried, and how I didn't do anything to reassure him, which made me equally guilty of the bullying. I shudder – with remorse. I should have defended the poor kid; I should have stood up for the underdog. My lack of action, my lack of fortitude, was shameful, worse than that of the shearer involved.

Sitting on the wool table, I resolve to stand up for underdogs in future. I resolve to stop being so self-possessed and to be more concerned about the needs of others – and never again to be a guilty bystander, regardless of where that places me.

I sit and ask God to help me to be more like that in future.

And I let a single tear scroll down my cheek because these men who I just got to know – and who befriended me unconditionally – I will miss forever.

12

Leaving

Every Tuesday a jackaroo is dispatched to slaughter four 'killer' Merinos to feed the twenty-eight men, women and children who live on Habbies Howe. I notice my turn at killing comes round far too frequently.

Station hands have an amount deducted from their pay for the meat they order each week, so it's vital we jackaroos present the butchered meat to them neatly. Their super-critical wives don't want their lamb chops and Sunday roast hacked about by some upstart of a silver-spoon jackaroo – our perceived privileged backgrounds being the real reason behind any complaints they make about us (and they do complain about us) to management.

Some fifty or so of the property's more scrawny wethers are set aside in Woolshed paddock, located between the woolshed and the shearers' quarters, for this rather unpleasant end at the hands of a mean boy. 'Killers', as they're called, are the runts of the total flock. Praise God I wasn't born a sheep.

I begin by yarding all of the sheep, because like the stock-horses, indeed all farm animals, the best way to get herd animals to do what you want them to do is to get them all to do it.

Once yarded, I choose the chubbiest four wethers, pounce on the fattest one and drag it into a small pen. I repeat the exercise three times before I let the rest back into their paddock. This time 'letting' them means exactly that: the remaining sheep are let off, earning a reprieve until next week's lottery of life. It's murder-by-weight: the leaner you are, the longer you live. (Years later a roadside billboard selling weight loss will read: LOSE WEIGHT – THE ALIENS WILL EAT THE FAT ONES FIRST.)

I drag my first victim into the killing shed, a small, stand-alone wooden building with a concrete floor and flywire windows that run from knee height to the roof. The floor extends up to the flywire, so it can all be hosed down afterwards, to remove all grisly evidence of the killing.

I find slitting the sheep's throat without thinking long about it least painful – for it and me.

The procedure then follows pretty much along the lines of when Dougie and I were made to skin the two Hereford cows, except here, with the meat destined for human consumption, the job needs to be done more carefully, and indoors in clean surroundings. Each sheep, once dead and with its hide punched away from its flesh around the sides and almost to the backbone, is hung upside down from a hook in the centre of the roof. One then pulls the entire hide down and off the sheep with a single firm, downwards tug.

After gutting the sheep, the ritual ends by grabbing a Land Rover to take the four carcasses, now neatly wrapped in white mourning sheets courtesy of Susie, the cook, to another meat shed located just outside the homestead kitchen. This shed, which is better built, with flywire that actually does its job of keeping flies out, is under the shade of a leafy oak tree. Leaving the carcasses hanging in the shed for two days allows the meat to remain cool while it cures.

The jackaroo is also responsible for dressing the carcasses (another weird term, which really means undressing – cutting up), two days later. And, as with all things, there is a right and wrong way to prepare meat for the kitchen. Splinters of bone among loin lamb chops caused by multiple hits with the meat cleaver are unacceptable. Each blow with the weapon needs to be executed with one confident, solid whack. Producing a neat line of chops, each one an even thickness, takes practice, but once perfected it makes for a good feeling when, over lunch, Susie says to as many as seven people, 'I don't know who did the killing this week, but my, it was done well.' Susie knows exactly who did the killing, because she will have handed the mourning sheets to the jackaroo personally. And everyone else at the table will know who did the killing because, after Susie makes her comment, the face of the jackaroo responsible will be flush with embarrassment.

The only parts of the carcass not eaten by humans are the flaps – the thin pieces of meat and fat that cover the stomach – which the boss steals to give to Skye when no one is looking. That is, providing Skye isn't bogeying, or lending herself to a boy dog.

As with everything, killing becomes a competition in perfection between us jackaroos, something which is encouraged if not orchestrated by management. Second best is never good enough; we have to perform, we have to show the authorities we're the best.

And here's a thing. Years later, whenever I peer into a butcher's shop window or I'm in one of those supermarkets where butchers cut up meat in front of your eyes, I can't help but look to see if they're doing a good job. No splinters of bone in my meat, thank you.

With shearing over, December is upon us and my year at Habbies Howe is quickly coming to an end. In a few weeks' time I'll be on my way to Yorkshire to work in my relatives' woollen mills, to learn about wool qualities and the manufacturing processes, before returning to Melbourne to become a junior wool buyer in my grandfather's firm at the end of next year.

It's my final Sunday, and as with most things, Mr Webb has

a plan. As soon as the breakfast dishes are done he commandeers me for a Royal Tour – my last. An hour later, we stop at a gate. Before he gets out of the Land Rover to open it, he looks across at me and asks, 'D-do you r-r-really w-want to be a w-w-wool buyer?'

'No,' I reply without hesitation. 'I want to stay here.' I start to choke up.

The boss looks into my eyes and says, 'Y-y-you'll be f-fine, s-s-son.'

He gets out and I watch as he stumbles up to the gate – more briskly than usual.

On my final evening at Habbies, after locking up the dairy calves for the night, I collect my can of Foster's from Old Harold's fridge – hating the fact I have to give the poor bastard one as commission, especially if Dougie is right and the mean bastard does have a million dollars stashed under his bed. I return to the dairy, sit on the rail and reflect on the year past.

What a whirlwind of experiences it's been for a fatherless, sorrowful, city boy.

A choirboy, now a cowboy.

Never mind how on my first day I was made to chase sheep like a dog, though I was never remotely likely to be anywhere near as proficient as them at heading the fearfully dumb Merinos.

Never mind having to skin, gut and cut up two cancer-eyed cows in my first week.

Never mind the fact I will require a lifetime of chiropractic care after lugging the super, as well as heaps of Chinese medicine, and incurring a million lectures on posture.

Never mind that I've worked six days a week, and on the seventh day, the day God said we're to rest, I've suffered a Royal Tour.

Never mind that I was made to get up at midnight in teeming rain to clear out gutters.

Never mind how I've had only five days off in twelve

months – four of which were on the weekend – and that I needed a reason and permission from both Mr Webbs to take them off. And two of them were to see the Habbies Howe wool sold at auction.

Never mind about the 'no car, no smokes, no booze' (and no raunchy women) rule.

Oh, and no beard.

Never mind not having seen TV for a year except on Monday nights when we trudged two kilometres across snake-infested swamp country to watch *Peyton Place* at Gordon and Beryl's place, carrying one torch between the three of us.

Never mind how one Saturday night as I stood outside the pub in Seymour – on a trip 'to the pictures' – someone I hardly knew asked me to hold his can of beer for a second, and how the police were waiting and watching, and immediately flashed their spotlight in my face, and how they charged me with drinking in a public place. I hadn't even taken a sip from the can. And how at breakfast the next morning I told the boss what had happened, and how the next day he organised for me to go into Seymour to be severely yelled at by the police sergeant. Yet no charges were laid because Dick Webb had made the call.

Never mind any of that.

I've learnt how life on a sheep and cattle station works – on one of the biggest and best sheep and cattle properties in Victoria. I've learnt to take responsibility for tasks I've been given. I've learnt the work ethic, which will stay with me for life – it will include a life-long habit of getting out of bed at five-thirty: I've learnt too well how to be a servant-jackaroo.

Easily my happiest moments here have been riding Charlie. We understand each other, and so we should – we talk to one another every day. Chasing steers on horseback has been nothing short of sensational. What a lucky eighteen-year-old I am to have been getting paid to do it (however paltry a sum). And all those times

I've walked across paddocks with Charlie loping along behind me, his reins flopping loosely over my shoulder and him nudging me in the small of my back, telling me to get a wriggle on. Never once has he run off and left me.

I've learnt to be interested in and to care about the fragility of nature long before it becomes politically correct to do so. I've even learnt, albeit late in my year at Habbies Howe, to stand up for the underdog, something I vow I will always do in future, regardless of personal cost.

I've learnt not to complain – well, not too much – and to accept how fortunate I am in life.

I won't forget the time Damian, the sole jackaroo on Glendoxey, Mr Webb's brother's property just this side of Seymour, came to spend a weekend with us, to see how we do things at Habbies. And how on our way to the dairy in pitch-darkness at five-thirty on the Saturday morning, he'd stopped, turned to me, and asked, 'Is there any particular reason why you milk the cows in the middle of the night?' I just laughed.

I've learnt not to seek compliments, which is a good thing because they don't come that often. And because I don't know how to handle them even if they do come.

Enjoying my can of beer alongside the three penned-up dairy calves, which aren't happy with me for denying them their mothers' milk for the night – they give me the big stare – I think back to my first week, and how I tried in vain to extract milk from their mothers. Now, milking is so natural; I can fill a nine-litre bucket with frothy, foaming fresh milk in minutes.

I've learnt how to move a house, should the need ever present itself.

I've learnt how to build a new fence across a steep gully, using thick-gauge fencing wire which, once strained but before it's pulled down and secured to the massive wooden posts firmly embedded in the ground in the hollows, hangs several metres in the air. And how, once the wires are tied down on the posts you can play a Brandenburg concerto on them, they're so tight. Real men's work, that was.

I've learnt how to castrate a lamb using my teeth – sinews and all – except I can't quite see where or when that will come in handy.

I've learnt how to tie a load firmly onto a ute, truck or trailer using clever half-hitch knots, a skill for which in later life I will earn from impractical, city-bred males a respectful, 'Where did you learn to do that?'

Probably, more than anything, I've learnt to think. It's something you don't necessarily get taught at school, where answers are spoon-fed and you learn processes and systems.

And so, on this, my final night, just as the sun is about to set, I climb down from the dairy rail, dispose of my beer can, and walk to Horse paddock to say goodbye to my best friend.

I hug Charlie and bawl my eyes out at the thought of never seeing him again.

But the tears are also because I've survived my year at Habbies Howe.

So there, Mrs Baillieu!

PART TWO

Next Horizons

13

England

My family's plan is for me to spend twelve months at our English relatives' woollen mills in the Yorkshire city of Bradford – the epicentre of the world's wool industry – where I will learn to recognise different grades of 'greasy' wool, before returning home to become a junior wool buyer. I'm to learn by standing next to the Yorkshire wool sorters as they sort Australian fleeces. I will also observe the manufacturing process wool goes through in the family's three factories.

Again, my year is mapped out for me to the letter, so it seems.

I'm given a room in a two-storey, Tudor-style boarding house along the main drag heading west out of Bradford. It's bigger than all three jackaroos' rooms at Habbies Howe put together – sheer luxury, my own bedroom.

My three fellow lodgers, with whom I eat dinner each night at the one large table, are an eighty-something-year-old Jewish pensioner called Mr Symons, a nineteen-year-old Malaysian engineering student cum ten-pin bowler called Ben, and a chubby man whom Ben and I think looks and speaks in a way that makes him definitely shady, and who is likely at any moment to be carted away by the police.

It's the first week in January and snow is deep on the ground – so vastly different to the dry, summer heat of Victoria I just left behind. Mum and Penny have come to England with me to 'help me settle in', whatever they think that means. I don't need help settling in – I've never had it before, why should I need it now? They move into a budget hotel a good distance down the road, and I see them twice briefly before they head home.

Regardless of my luxurious surroundings, within a few days I'm dreadfully homesick for Habbies Howe. It isn't fair. I got thrown into a totally new world at Habbies, I was broken into tiny pieces and then put back together the way they wanted me. And now, suddenly, my world is again turned upside down, another year living out of a suitcase; half a lifetime away from home in a strange environment.

I also can't get Charlie out of my mind. Not that family members here know or give a rat's arse about that. It's not part of the plan. But how do you just move on and give up your past, especially when it's a past you've loved so much? I just hope the jackaroo who replaced me at Habbies is taking good care of my best friend. He'd better be.

The boarding house is run by strict Methodists, who have a no-grog rule. Not again, I think. But I quickly find a way around it, even though Old Harold isn't here to share his fridge.

Again, I'm told by my mother to be on my best behaviour as my grandfather's reputation hangs on my every move, regardless of which country I'm in, so it seems. 'And stand up straight,' she tells me before finally leaving for home.

At work at the woollen mills, I'm given a white coat and labelled a 'fine' apprentice – meaning I'm not really an apprentice at all, but an upstart of a distant relative from the colonies with a silver spoon in his mouth, who thinks himself superior to the other workers in their dull, dark blue coats. I'm to stand and watch different wool sorters sort their quota of Australian wool, which they do by pulling apart, removing and dividing parts of the fleece according to the thickness of the fibres in any given clump of wool. Each line of even-quality wool is then sent down for washing, carding and combing, processes involving huge pieces of ugly yet intriguing black machinery that I will soon get to see in action. The end result is the coils of silky-smooth tops which are on-sold to spinners, who turn them into cloth.

A bale might have fleeces generally considered to be '64s count', one of fourteen grades used worldwide to classify greasy wool according to the diameter of its fibres. Numbers range from 80s for the finest wool to 36s for crap wool (the kind they turn out in New Zealand). This count or number refers to the hanks of yarn, each five hundred and sixty yards long, that can be spun from one pound of wool top. For example, 64s wool yields 35 840 yards (five hundred and sixty times sixty-four) of yarn from one pound of top.

As if all of this isn't hard enough to try to get one's mind around, almost as I arrive in Bradford the world's wool industry adopts a new way of measuring wool, called the micron system. The system's proponents say it more accurately measures the actual diameter of a fibre of wool. One micron is one-25 400th of an inch, which can't of course be seen by the human eye, but is confirmed in a lab. Fortunately, counts and microns correlate, and 64s wool comes out at 23 microns.

Taking his bale of what the wool classer back in the shearing shed in Australia believed was generally a line of 64s, the wool sorter will remove clumps of finer wool (e.g. 70s or 74s, or 21 or 19 microns) and coarser staples (62s or 60s, or 25 or 27 microns). It's brain-deadening labour at best, and I get more satisfaction from conversations I have with the wool sorters, whose ages range from close to mine – eighteen – to men in their mid-sixties; men who've stood at the same table sorting the same Aussie wool for all of their dull working lives, real poor bastards who've experienced nothing more exciting that life has to offer.

After three weeks of standing next to wool sorters, I can't wait to be given my own table – to be given my own bales – reasoning that if I have to be here, I may as well do it myself.

It doesn't take me long to get a feel for what is 64s quality wool, or to tell a 60s fleece that has been put in a 64s bale by mistake. In the same way, I quickly learn to distinguish between 64s – used for making poor people's suits – and 80s wool, super high-quality stuff which Italian manufacturers use to make filthy-expensive suits for people who live in Toorak or Potts Point. The coarser the wool, the easier it is to determine its quality, because the crimps (or corrugations) along each staple of wool are bigger and wider apart.

Wool-sorting rooms take up the entire top floor of each of the company's three mills, one of which is located in the centre of Bradford, another on the eastern fringe and the third a few kilometres west of the city. (Some seventy sorters in total are employed.) The firm doesn't only manufacture Australian wool, and I quickly learn to identify South American product – it comes in bales taller than me, bound with metal hoops. Their wool isn't a patch on ours. New Zealand bales are dumpier than Australia's. And you never know what you'll find in a bale, anything from heavy, metal bale grabs, to six-month-old copies of *Playboy* or the *Daily Telegraph*. One sorter opened a bale from Cape Town only to find a farm labourer curled up halfway down. 'Was he dead?' some idiot asked. One can only assume the poor bastard was napping in a half-made bale over lunch, and was still asleep when the wool presser resumed work. At least he would have died in relative comfort.

The family must recognise they're short-changing me, because on my third day I get paged and told to meet a middle manager in the head-office car park at eight o'clock the next morning. There, I'll be shown my car for the year.

When I arrive, busting to see which of the Daimlers and Jaguars lined up in Executive Row will be mine, I'm a tad disappointed that the manager points to a small, red Austin 1100 (an up-market version of the Morris 1100 we have in Australia) tucked away in the corner. But it's my first car, and 'Christine' has bucket seats and she hunts along like billyo. I fall in love with her immediately and won't have a bad word spoken about her, even though I feel dreadfully guilty whenever I think of Charlie.

All goes beautifully with Christine until one day I take my eyes off the road and prang her into the rear of a Volvo, whose idiot driver stopped unnecessarily at a children's crossing. (What's the difference between an echidna and a Volvo? The echidna has the pricks on the outside.) Later, the PA system in the factory where I'm sorting wool bursts into life. 'Paging Mr Michael, paging Mr Michael.' (The Poms and their class system really are unbelievable.) I pick up the nearest wall phone. It's Uncle David, the director of the firm, who's been designated as my chaperone for the year. Can you believe it? A chaperone.

'YOUR CAR IS NOT A TOY,' Uncle David roars down the line. Yeah, fair point, except that the stupid Volvo stopped without warning, I tell him. He's not impressed. Christine gets carted off to a repair shop, and I keep my fine-apprentice title – and her.

Given my status, I'm allowed to sort just four bales of wool a day, as opposed to the men, whose quota is eight. I finish by lunchtime, although usually I string it out to the early afternoon. Then I leave the factory. No one ever comments on my leaving early.

One day I decide to go exploring and find myself at the firm's testing laboratory. It has a huge glass front. Inside, I can see a lone girl standing at a bench, cleaning specimen dishes. I reckon she must be no more than seventeen, only a little younger than me. Hmm. I venture inside the lab and introduce myself.

Sharleen's accent is seriously Yorkshire, like everyone else's in this place below director level. (The directors all went to posh private schools and speak the Queen's English.)

'Is Melbourne by the sea?' she asks.

What a dumb question, I think, but at least she isn't given to searching interrogation. I give it some thought. 'Yes,' I reply.

'What colour is it?' she asks next. Is she serious?

'Which do you mean?' I reply. 'Melbourne or the sea?'

'The sea, silly.'

'Oh,' I say, having been put in my place. I need time to consider it. It's not something I've thought a lot about. Anyway, I need to examine her body more closely, especially two small pointy bits half out of her white coat.

'It's blue,' I tell her, finally, my mind certainly not focused on sea. Sensing Sharleen isn't completely satisfied with my answer, I add, 'And when you get into really deep water, it looks kind of green.' I hope I'm not leading the poor girl astray.

'Really?'

'Yes, really. Haven't you ever seen the sea?' I ask.

'No,' she replies without a skerrick of embarrassment, as she wipes clean another specimen dish.

Bradford lies at nearly the narrowest part of England, the sea being just sixty miles to the west and some seventy to the east. I figure the poor girl hasn't had much of a life.

'What's the furthest you've been from Bradford?' I ask.

'Hoodersfield.' Huddersfield is a twenty-minute drive south of Bradford. The poor girl needs to get a life – providing it isn't one with me.

Two days later, out of the blue another white-coated middle manager asks if I'd like to earn a couple of hundred pounds. Sure, I say, typically for a naive, loopy eighteen-year-old. He gets me to meet him in his car outside the east Bradford factory a week later at lunchtime. He has me sign two cheques – one for £10 000, the other for £20 000. And he hands me my two hundred pounds. I have no inkling as to how he or the people with whom he's in cahoots opened a bank account in my name without my knowledge or permission, where the original money came from for the investment, or how I was able to both release the initial funds and the profit to them on the same day. The entire episode will forever remain a mystery. The only part of the scenario that isn't a mystery is the two hundred quid burning a welcome hole in my pocket.

The wool-sorting floors are run by supervisors, who wear white coats like mine. Apart from maintaining discipline on the floor, the supervisors stand next to various trapdoors in the centre of the room, each door measuring about a metre square. He calls out a wool quality, and in turn, wool sorters bring up their big wicker wheelie basket full of that quality. While the wool sorter holds up his basket, the supervisor sends the wool down the chute, checking for off-sorts. Clumps of wool inconsistent with the main sort get handed back to the sorter, who stuffs them between him and the back of his inclined basket, which he balances with his hands. He then takes the rejected wool back to his table. Mostly, very little wool gets rejected. The job itself might be mind-numbing, yet these wool sorters do know their wool qualities.

Another young white-coated, yet far more senior family member did his apprenticeship just prior to me. One day, so I'm told, he took his bin to the supervisor, with wool he believed was 64s quality. The supervisor, because he wanted to have a story to tell his grandchildren, rejected almost all of the young executive's wool. The entire floor fell silent, each sorter pretending to work but in fact watching from the corner of his eye to see what would happen next.

Examining the rejected wool, the young executive separated out a small handful from what he'd been given back, and tipped the rest down the trapdoor, defying the supervisor's ruling in full view of thirty blue-coated subordinates.

The supervisor was left staring down the hole, speechless. No one dared say a word.

I might be wearing a white coat, and I might be a distant relative, but there is no way I'd try such a stunt. I know my place, and I'm way too far down the family's greasy pole to try something like that. Plus, it's just not me – it's never been me – to defy authority like that.

Yet my inner streak of social consciousness is developing, so one day, much to the bewilderment of the Yorkshiremen with whom I work, I venture downstairs from the top (sixth) floor to where another bunch of workers take wool from the big bins below the trapdoors and lug it to yet another trapdoor, to be dropped down to the scouring machines on the fourth floor.

What I hadn't realised is that all of the workers just one floor below us are Pakistani immigrants. Here I am, just one level down, yet it's like suddenly I've been transported to Pakistan. The two races have different rosters – they come and go at different times, and they never mix with, speak to, or even pass one another. The class system might be carefully exploited by the executive class, but so it is here, perhaps even more so, by England's downtrodden working class, men more racist than their bosses.

When I enter their floor in my white coat, the Pakistanis can't work me out; they stand frozen. Am I a boss, as my coat suggests? But surely I'm too young. I walk up to the man closest to me, who stands stiff as a statue, expressionless, worried. I offer him my hand. Nervously, he extends his. We shake hands. I smile at him. His face breaks into a nervous half-grin, then a full smile. He starts to laugh, a laugh that gets louder. Not mockingly, but a relaxed, happy laugh. Other men step forward. We take turns to shake hands and smile at one another, and bow our heads as we go. Smiling is the language we can share.

After the handshakes, again we stand motionless, my brain working overtime to think what to do next. I think of how Mr Webb's friend got the stockmen at Brunette Downs onside and, looking into the bin from which they've been taking wool, I get an idea. I step inside the bin and pick up an armful of wool, and carry it to the hole in the floor and throw it down, as I'd seen them doing. The white-toothed Pakistanis giggle as, one by one, they begin to pick up armfuls. And so it is that I spend my morning working with the Pakistanis. And, despite their lethal garlic breaths, I have a ball.

'What the fook made you go down there and work with them pillocks?' asks a young wool sorter when I eventually return upstairs for lunch.

'You can learn something from everyone,' I tell the young Yorkshireman, who is just two years older than me and already a raving, committed racist.

'Aye, you can,' the wool sorter replies, 'but not from them fooking pillocks you can't.'

One day during my wanderings at the farthest mill in Bradford's west, I chance upon a group of five middle managers I've not met. They're in the dispatch area standing in a circle, trying to fit as many end-product wool tops as they can into a latest-technology vacuum packaging unit. It's an open-topped, aluminium box roughly one by two metres and over a metre deep – about the size of a short yet tall and chubby coffin. A thick plastic bag lines the insides of the box, with extra plastic spilling out over the top on all four sides. With the box full of wool tops, the plan is to wrap the ends of the plastic bag around a hose that leads to a powerful vacuum device which sucks out all of the air, shrinking the package to two-thirds its original size for more economical shipping.

For maybe fifteen minutes I watch as the managers try different configurations, each in turn trying to get as many tops as possible in the container. The best they manage is twenty-two big coils of wool.

'May I have a shot?' I ask, eventually. Puzzles always fascinate me.

'You certainly can,' says their leader, who has absolutely no idea who I am, but deferring, I guess, to my white coat, my handsome good looks and my authoritative Aussie accent. The other managers step backwards, scowls on their faces willing me to fail.

I decide to take an entirely different approach. I quickly empty the bin and fill it again from scratch. But instead of placing the bottom row of tops flat, like they've been doing, I stand the coils on their side, thoroughly conscious that I have five sets of eyes waiting to laugh out loud at me. I'm guessing at what I'm attempting, yet somehow I'm able to get ten coils on the bottom, although standing higher in the bin than the managers' bottom row. I repeat the configuration with the second layer. It still leaves me with sufficient space on top to place another six tops, lying flat. Twenty-six tops. A new world record. Yippee! The lead manager inserts the hose, wraps the spare plastic around it and flicks a switch to set the vacuum going. The end result is a small shrunken block of tops probably sixty per cent of its original size. The lead manager tells me they're destined for Dublin.

But I'm still on life's learning curve. Instead of receiving praise, three of the managers snarl at me for achieving what they couldn't and saunter off in disgust without a word. The fourth forces a smile, but then he too walks away. The leader of the group is clearly a cut above the others. He smiles and thanks me.

Again, I'm struck by man's need to be so competitive, rather than gracious. It's like bulls facing off in a paddock: these men clearly felt threatened by someone else's success.

Upon returning to Melbourne in December 1968, I find things have changed drastically in the year I've been away. Unbeknown

to me, the directors of the firm in the UK have decided it's time my
grandfather retired. Obviously, no one felt compelled to mention
it to me. The same bosses have also decided to amalgamate the
Australian operations with a leading, Sydney-based wool-buying
firm, Frederick H Booth & Sons. The new firm is called Booth Hill
& Sons. What's more, it's run from Sydney.

It turns out I will be the last remaining Australian employee
with Hill in his name (it's my middle name). After just six weeks
I'm hauled into the Melbourne manager's office and told it's been
decided I'm to learn to be a wool buyer under the supervision of the
new regime in Sydney.

And so, for the tenth year in a row, I pack my suitcase, and this
time I head north.

They give my grandfather a pretend office in Melbourne. For
a while he continues to drive out to the woolstores at six o'clock
each day, yet eventually he realises his time is up. He takes to
delivering meals-on-wheels in his Mercedes. Three months later,
he suffers two massive strokes and remains a vegetable for two
years before he dies.

So I never do get to learn from him how to be a wool buyer.
Or about life.

I do my best in Sydney to become interested in becoming a wool
buyer, valuing wool in the woolstores early in the morning, and
then, after a quick sandwich, spending the afternoons in the city
auction rooms learning to bid for lots of wool, which the firm needs
to fill its overseas clients' orders. The Sydney office is responsible for
wool sales in Sydney, Brisbane and Newcastle–Goulburn, and we
work a week in each in constant rotation during the selling season.
Melbourne buyers likewise rotate between Melbourne, Geelong and
Albury–Portland. Adelaide and Perth have their own offices.

As hard as I try to embrace the plan mapped out for me, I just
can't get excited about spending the rest of my life as a wool buyer.

I find the wool-valuing process as captivating as rowing. True, bidding in the auction rooms is exhilarating, the speed at which each lot is sold verging on electric; organised chaos. Yet I yearn to be back on the land, back in the saddle mustering cattle, back on Charlie.

One afternoon in June, I bite the bullet and knock on the managing director's door.

'Come in, Michael,' he says. He motions with a hand for me to take a seat.

'Mr Trebeck,' I begin, 'as much as I enjoy working with everyone here, I've decided to make my career on the land.' There, I've said it. He remains quiet, so I continue. 'After my year of jackarooing the year before last, I find city life stifling. I want to be back on a horse. I know a lot of people will be disappointed in me, but it's how I feel.'

The managing director then speaks the words I've been expecting – and dreading.

'You do realise you're throwing the silver spoon out of your mouth, don't you?'

I shiver in front of him. My mind leaps straight to my mother – I can hear her explode. Which is exactly what she does when I phone her later in the day to tell her. Mr Trebeck is right. I'm throwing the silver spoon out of my mouth, recklessly. Does Mum go berserk, or what.

I don't need to be Einstein to work out that, if I remain in the firm, by the time I'm thirty I'll probably make junior director, like the Booth twins did by that age. And while being a wool buyer won't make me rich, I guess I won't starve either. But the life isn't for me.

The next morning, I get in my car and begin the dreaded drive down the Hume Highway to face my mother's wrath. I don't even want to think about what I'll get from my dragon of a grandmother.

14

Shedhand

Before leaving Sydney and the world of wool-buying, I phone Mr Webb to ask if he'll have me back at Habbies Howe to be a second-year jackaroo. But I haven't figured on the five-year waiting list, have I?

I take his rejection as genuine, yet it puts me in no man's land. To be honest, I'm scared witless. The only world I know and love, the only world I want to know and love, is up in the hills to my left as I drive along the Hume Highway towards Melbourne through Euroa.

I think about the boy who replaced me at Habbies, whoever he is. He'll be riding Charlie – and he'd better be treating him good, otherwise he'll be ripe for a nuggeting. He'd also better not be a weakling. I can't bear that in a person.

When I get home, all hell breaks loose. Mum totally loses it.

'I just don't understand you, Michael,' she cries the minute I set foot in the house. She must have been rehearsing it for hours. 'In my father's day men kept one job for life. If your grandfather wasn't lying there in the nursing home like a zombie he'd be furious with you.' Then comes the blackmail. 'As for your grandmother, she's been giving me a dreadful time over it. She's taken to her bed and is threatening to put you out of her will.'

Who gives two shits about my grandmother? The dragon hates me. She's always favoured Penny over me. Mum says it's because she only had a daughter that she doesn't understand boys. What utter bullshit. The woman is mean and miserable, and those are her strong points. At last, I'm getting my own back at her for the way she's treated me all my life.

Mum saves the most cutting remark for last. 'After all your grandparents and I have done for you . . .' she says, now sobbing uncontrollably. Things aren't going very well.

On the night my mother booted my father out – when I was five – he drove off and took the gatepost with him, and then returned the next day and handed Mum a twelve-page letter saying that if he couldn't drink, he'd leave forever. She told him to get out. I'm determined to make my departure more dignified. Calmly, I reach for the Yellow Pages and look up 'Stock & Station Agents'.

The AML&F agency has always been good to Mr Webb, so I begin with them. I don't want finance, I just want a job. I'm put through to the personnel department.

'My name's Michael Thornton, I'm nineteen, I've been a jackaroo for Dick Webb at Habbies Howe, I've just spent a year learning about wool in Bradford, England, and I'm ringing to ask if you have any shedhand vacancies while I look for another jackaroo position.' (I could have asked for a jackaroo position, but working as a shedhand for a month will give me better wages while I work out what to do.)

It turns out I've called on just the right day.

'How soon can you get to Hay?' asks the pleasant-sounding woman at the other end.

'It would probably work out best if I leave straight away,' I reply, glancing at Mum, who's sitting over by the window staring aimlessly out, hanky in hand.

'What's today? Tuesday . . . The shed at Tupra starts on Thursday.'

'Which side of Hay is Tupra?'

'West. About seventy kilometres.'

'How long will the shed last?'

'A month. When you get there, report to John Bell, the contractor. I'll tell him you'll arrive tomorrow. All right?'

A month as a shedhand in the Tupra woolshed will give me time to plan my future – to get the right position as a jackaroo. Plus, working in a shearing team will let me relive the wonderful month I spent in the Habbies Howe woolshed.

And it will give Mum time to calm down. I can't get to Hay fast enough.

For the next four weeks I'm back working in a place I love, this time as a full member of the contractor's team. I pretend it's the Habbies Howe shed and it makes me as happy as a pig in mud. I'm working on the famous barren Riverina salt plain in New South Wales, in a twelve-stand woolshed.

The pecking order sees young, less-experienced boys pick up fleeces as they come off the sheep, throw them onto the wool table, and then quickly sweep clean the shearer's area on the board before he re-emerges from his pen with his next sheep. Older shedhands stand along the sides of the wool tables taking rough and soiled wool off the edges of the fleece before it goes on to the wool classer.

When the wool classer hears I've just spent a year learning wool qualities in Bradford, he promptly puts me on one of the two wool tables, which basically means I'm given a gentleman's role for the month. The task suits me just fine. I'm not only reliving the Habbies Howe woolshed and the buzz it gave me twenty months ago, I'm being paid award wages for doing the easiest task in the woolshed.

Tupra is owned by Sir Alec Creswick, who owns more than one pastoral holding in the Riverina district. He later becomes chairman of the Victoria Amateur Turf Club. More than likely, he knows my grandfather. He would definitely know Dick Webb, yet in this environment I'm sure not about to name-drop. I'm just an out-of-work, humble and anonymous jackaroo, and very happy to remain that way.

Two weeks into the shed, early one morning and with the shearing in full swing, Sir Alec arrives, unannounced. He parks his Bentley by the woolshed door, enters the shed and perches on a spare wool table, inches away from the first shearer. The man looks a real grump. Yet, after experiencing Uncle Sir James Hill, Bt in Bradford last year, he doesn't scare me. Nonetheless, to be safe, we keep our heads down while he's around. I decide that if having a knighthood means you have to live life as a miseryguts then I'll forego one, thanks very much.

Sir Alec sits on the table for the entire run, observing the shearer's work, watching to see if he makes any wasteful second cuts in the wool or, worse, cuts holes in his sheep.

At the end of the run, he goes up to the shearer and asks, 'How'd you be?'

The shearer, furious that he's had his work scrutinised for nearly ninety minutes, replies, 'I'd be a lot fuckin' better if I had your money.'

Sir Alec promptly departs the shed. For this year's shearing, at any rate.

I'm so pleased I didn't waltz up to Sir Alec and introduce myself, and tell him who my grandfather is, or that I've worked for Dick Webb.

Or ask him, *How'd you be?*

Much of the wool I sorted last year in Bradford came from the Riverina. Tupra takes up 64000 hectares of the Hay Plain, making

it no small spread. Despite its hellishly low stocking rate – one
sheep to less than two hectares, compared with four sheep to one
hectare at Habbies Howe, making Habbies' pastures eight times
more productive – this country is excellent for Merinos. Indeed, the
harsher the environment, the better the Merino will do. Australia
is rich in such ironies.

To put stocking rates in perspective, at Rawlinna Station on
the Nullarbor Plain between Adelaide and Perth, each Merino
needs twenty hectares to survive – that's eighty times more land
required per sheep than at Habbies Howe. Makes you wonder why
they bother.

Tupra is close to Booligal, a place made famous by A B (Banjo)
Paterson in one of his best known poems, 'Hay and Hell and
Booligal':

> *And people have an awful down*
> *Upon the district and the town –*
> *Which worse than hell itself the call;*
> *In fact, the saying far and wide*
> *Along the Riverina side*
> *Is 'Hay and Hell and Booligal'.*
>
> *The big mosquitoes frighten some –*
> *You'll lie awake to hear 'em hum –*
> *And snakes about the township crawl;*
> *But shearers, when they get their cheque,*
> *The never come along and wreck*
> *The blessed town of Booligal.*

(Many Australians assume that Banjo Paterson lived his entire
life in the bush. In fact, he was a Sydney lawyer who lived in the
posh suburbs of Edgecliff and Woollahra. He spent only twelve of

his seventy-seven years living outside Sydney, yet he was a prolific writer who left us with many magnificent poems and prose.)

The Hay Plain is truly desolate. Apart from the lines of trees warning you of a creek or river bed, if you get out of your car and stand on a road or salt plain, you'll be the tallest thing around for as far your eye can see.

You know you're passing through another property when you drive over a cattle grid.

Tupra runs 40 000 Merinos, its annual rainfall being closer to three inches than twenty-three. The woolshed is huge, with fifty shearing stands, although it's been many years since all were used. Yet even the team of twelve shearers requires thirty men and boys to make it click. The cook, far madder than the one at Habbies Howe, has two offsiders. And it's here where the cook, whose food I have to admit isn't a patch on what I sampled at Habbies, is replaced one morning between breakfast and smoko – as quickly as that. Another cook has been staying at nearby Maude, just waiting to get the call.

When sheep are declared 'wet' by shearers, the latter down tools. At such times shedhands continue to get paid, but the shearers don't. When rain tumbles down at Tupra, the contractor looks for menial chores for us to do, but eventually he gives up and allows us free time. And what better way to spend it than to shoot rabbits?

I've always been reluctant to hold a gun in my hands, ever since a tragedy that occurred when I was in Year Seven at school. Two brothers – the younger of them in my class – were home on school holidays and were cleaning their rifles in front of TV when the older boy's rifle discharged, killing his brother. It caused me to have a lifelong fear of guns. In cadets, I did everything I could to avoid being near one; I achieved my goal by joining the band. Not only was I not required to touch a gun, I also didn't have to stand in boiling-hot sun for hours on parade, like other boys were made to do, or to go on long marches at cadet camp at Puckapunyal. Instead, the band marched the foot soldiers out each morning about a kilometre for their day's forty-kilometre march. We then returned to camp and practised music all day in the shade of a big tent, before going out again late in the afternoon to march the exhausted cadets back into camp. On Anzac Day, while the soldiers stood at attention on the school oval in often sweltering heat, the band again sat in the shade playing music, watching on as one by one the foot soldiers collapsed – still at attention.

One wet day, two rouseabouts and one other shedhand in our group take their guns and we head out on our afternoon shoot. I'm happy just to tag along. Halfway along the main drive into Tupra between the front entrance and the woolshed, there's a swamp which the driving track bisects.

'Great spot for ducks,' says Brian, in a loud voice. Brian, twenty, thinks he's the leader of our small group, but he's an idiot. The ducks, upon hearing his loud voice, as one rise out of the swamp and make their escape across the tops of the trees either side of us.

'Look out!' yells Stewart, the youngest in the group and somewhat of a loser. The kid ought to be still in school. He raises his shotgun – fortunately above our heads – and blasts away. Of course, he misses each and every bird. He lowers his gun and continues to mope ahead of us along the track.

The other two keep their eyes peeled and their guns raised, hoping more ducks will rise out of the water. But of course they don't because stupid Brian scared them all away.

'Hey, Stew,' I say, half loudly.

'What?' he calls back, without turning.

'What are you going to do about the phone line?' I ask.

This time he turns to look at me.

'What phone line?' he asks, mild panic developing in his squeaky voice.

He hasn't noticed, and neither have the others, that his shot sliced through the telephone line that hitherto drooped between old wooden poles along the edge of the track we're on.

'What do you mean?' he asks, his voice now shrill.

No one has seen the coils of wire lying on the ground near the two poles some twenty metres either side of us.

Stew looks one way, then the other. 'Shit,' he says, his brain now working overtime. 'Is it important?' He's trying to get a measure of how much trouble he'll be in when we front the contractor.

Brian is the first to speak. 'Don't worry, Stew,' he says, 'it's only the main power line for New South Wales.'

Stewart, the poor bastard, immediately drops his gun and begins to cry. 'What should I do?' he asks, looking up at me as he continues to blubber.

'Got any ammo left?' replies Brian.

'Shut up, Brian,' I tell him and turn to Stewart. 'Don't worry, it's not the power line. It's just the phone line to the woolshed and shearers' quarters. We can strain it up in a jiff. Brian's just being a prick.'

I glare at Brian. I've been the victim of bullying for too long to let the poor kid take any more. Like all bullies, as soon as I challenge Brian, he capitulates.

Stewart wipes his eyes and we go back and tell the contractor what happened. Of course he's pissed off at us, but says he's grateful of my offer to fix the job if I can just borrow a set of fence strainers, a pair of pliers and a ladder. He loosens up, but says it's all right, he'll get the job done himself.

'Thank you,' Stewart says after we leave the office.

'Don't take any notice of Brian,' I tell him. 'He's a prick.'

The down side to the incident is that I now have Stewart

hanging around me like a lap dog. That he thinks I'm good for his protection is his silliest mistake.

Shearers play this amazing game called Bull Ring.

Here, it's played in the pub at the tiny hamlet of Oxley, just down the road from Tupra, and it's the attraction on Friday and Saturday nights.

The game requires four simple components: an eye screw, a piece of string, a metal hat peg and a hollow, metal ring about eight centimetres in diameter, like those you find on a saddle girth, or the kind they put through a bull's nose. Hence the game's name.

The eye screw is placed in the ceiling about two metres out from a wall, with the string tied to the screw. The bull ring is initially tied loosely onto the hanging string and then carried through its pendulum to the wall, so it fits neatly over the hat peg, positioned roughly chin-high. The string is then tied off on the ring at that length.

The player takes the bull ring and carries it to the far end of its pendulum, furthest away from the wall. If the ceiling screw is two metres from the wall, the far end of the pendulum naturally will be four metres out from the wall. Holding the bull ring with his thumb and first two fingers, the player executes not a throw but a confident downward swing left or right through the pendulum. The swing to the left or right is critical – it can't be directly down and up to the peg on the wall, because if you do that, the ring will hit the peg and simply bounce off it. The ring needs to be going past the peg, so to speak, so it latches on as it goes by.

Such a simple game – and just five dollars to set up – yet shearers and rouseabouts wager as much as a week's pay on ten 'throws'.

One Saturday night, Robert, a quiet, red-headed, slightly built rouseabout has the temerity to challenge the most physical of the shearers – to ten throws. The bet: one hundred dollars. The immediate area is cleared and the crowd goes quiet so everyone can take in the action.

Why would a timid, seventeen-year-old rouseabout want to lose a week's pay to a tough shearer? And if by some extraordinary fluke he were to beat the bruiser, what will his life be worth afterwards? For a moment I wonder if Robert has had too much to drunk. But the kid is stone cold sober.

As the pub hushes, the shearer calls to the boy, dismissively, 'So, who goes first, kid?'

'You can,' replies the rouseabout, coolly.

The shearer turns back to face the bar and skulls his glass. He walks casually to the dangling ring and takes hold of it. One of his mates stands by the wall beside the hat peg, so each time the shearer gets the ring on the peg, his mate can release and send it back to him without the player losing his stance. Standing at just the right spot is part of the knack of the game, much of the skill being about getting yourself in position and not moving throughout your turn.

With the pub silent, the shearer sends the ring down for his first throw. Clunk.

He's good – he gets eight out of ten throws on. He then saunters back to the bar to receive slaps on his back from several shearer mates, all of them men you'd want to have as friends.

Young Robert takes up his position, holding the ring in his outstretched right hand. Again, the bar goes silent. The kid takes an inordinate amount of time to get his stance right.

I glance across at the shearer. His smirk is gone; he now wears a puzzled expression.

'Come on, kid,' calls out one of the shearers. 'Get a move on.'

But Robert isn't about to be rushed. If anything, he takes even longer to steady himself. This kid is as cool as a Riverina cucumber, if there is such a thing.

Clunk. His first throw goes on. The boy's stare is ice-cold, his concentration deadly.

Clunk. Clunk. Clunk. The kid gets ten out of ten on the peg, without getting a sweat up.

'Keep going,' someone shouts, and the boy stands still. Steely faced, he beckons to his minder at the wall to send back the ring for another throw – his eleventh.

The kid gets nineteen on in a row – but misses the twentieth.

'Jim got beat good,' someone says, the only person in the pub silly enough to state the obvious out loud. The only other sound in the entire building is the pub's fridge humming.

I look over at the shearer. He isn't happy. He pulls out his wallet and slaps a hundred dollars on the bar. After collecting his money, and without a word spoken between the pair, Robert returns to the far end of the bar and his group of young friends.

My eyes stay on the shearer and his cohorts. None of them is smiling, or talking. The air is thick, the mood icy, as if all hell is about to break loose.

A few moments later, the oldest of the shedhands, a man in his sixties who works with me on the main wool table, sidles over to the group of boys and whispers something to them. For a moment I'm distracted, but when I look across again to Robert and his friends, they've gone. They must have slipped out the back door.

Someone calls out loudly, 'Anyone for Bull Ring?' Clearly, it's a distraction.

Later, I hear that the older shedhand told Robert's friends to get him out of the place, quick smart. They did – they drove him back to Tupra to get his gear, then took him into Hay so he could find another shed to work in. It wouldn't have been worth his life to have stayed at Tupra, the old guy told the group. It all seemed a hell of a lot of upset just to win a hundred-dollar bet.

On my next trip to Oxley, I use the public telephone box across from the pub to call Rob Hooper, the brother of my sister's best friend. Rob was born on a farm at Camperdown in the Western District and he now has a farm in north-east Victoria. I ask him if he knows anyone good wanting a jackaroo.

By chance, Rob does know of a place. The younger brother of one of his old school friends has just left the family farm at Mortlake to spend a year as a jackaroo in the Riverina, and the family is looking to hire a jackaroo to replace him for the year. Rob is even able to give me the Allens' phone number.

Again, God is looking after me, and the following Saturday, the day after the Tupra shed ends, I leave early and drive south-west through the depth of Victoria to Mortlake, the very epicentre of the hallowed Western District. I've secured an interview with Mr Ron Allen, at Dornoch. Mr Allen, so Rob told me on the phone, is one of the best commercial cattle breeders going around and I'll learn heaps working for him. It's a good thing I took my sports coat, tie and slacks with me to Tupra (not that I wore them there – no way). I praise God that Mum wasn't my valet in the Riverina woolshed.

At Mortlake, I veer south towards a hamlet called The Sisters. Several kilometres on, past my destination, the road leads on to Warrnambool. I'm on the verge of Victoria's rich, dairying country. Further south, towards Portland, they grow potatoes.

Unlike the bare Riverina plains I just left, this country enjoys high rainfall and it's green, albeit with short grass due to the dormant winter growing season. Also, unlike at Tupra, rainwater lies everywhere.

Plus, it's cold enough to freeze your balls off, as Dougie would say.

Five kilometres south of Mortlake I come to the entrance, the name DORNOCH on the front fence next to the cattle grid. Only prosperous farms have a cattle grid, which makes coming and going so much less of a hassle. No gates to open (or to run up to).

Well-nourished, well-bred and exceptionally quiet Hereford cows and calves loll about on the raised driveway – it being the driest part of the paddock. For a moment I wonder if these cattle might live in the front paddock to impress a visitor. I squeeze my way past the cows and calves, which barely move out of the way for me. Neat rows of mature cypress trees line all sides of the paddock, making the whole scene picture-perfect.

All in all, I have the feeling I'm entering a pretty swish operation. What's more, I'm almost back on the land as a jackaroo.

15

Mortlake

Most graziers prefer their jackaroos to be farm-raised. It makes sense. Why employ a boy from the city with little or no experience when there are lads off farms who have a lifetime of experience, and who, on the face of it at least, are more likely to want to make a career on the land? One would expect them to make for a more committed jackaroo.

Yet Mr Allen takes me on. From the moment I shake hands with the man, he draws me in as a member of his family. Never once do the Allens make me feel as if I'm just a hired hand.

Two incidents best sum up my new boss. The first involves me; the second, shearers.

Mr Allen tells me he and I will be mucking out the silage pit in readiness for the new season's hay. The pit, which measures some forty metres long by ten metres wide, consists of a huge concrete apron with reinforced concrete side walls. Both ends are left open to enable freshly cut hay to be brought in using the front-end loader, whereupon the hay is jammed tight, covered, and allowed to cook for several months before the sweet result is fed to the cattle in winter.

To clean the pit prior to filling it with the new season's hay, Mr Allen and I take with us the big, green John Deere tractor with its front-end loader bucket, and a shovel. My immediate inclination is to grab the shovel and to get to work clearing out the difficult-to-get-at corners of the pit, which Mr Allen won't be able to get to with his tractor.

'Michael,' Mr Allen says, holding out his hand for me to pass him the shovel, 'give me that and you hop on the tractor.'

'But, Mr Allen,' I insist, 'you're the boss and I'm the jackaroo. It's meant to be me with the shovel.'

He won't hear of it, and for the next two hours on what is an ice-cold morning I enjoy the comfort and warmth of the tractor seat, working the front-end bucket, while Mr Allen slaves away with the shovel to get cow shit and old silage out of corners. What a great lesson for me in setting an example to your worker, and in selflessness.

Mr Allen also teaches me never to ask someone to do something you can't do yourself.

Later, during shearing, he finds it necessary to tick off a shearer for making too many cuts in a sheep's skin, which is obvious to everyone because there's blood everywhere. The issue really is about taking pride in one's workmanship.

The shearer is indignant. 'If you're so fucking clever,' he says, 'do it yourself.'

Whereupon Mr Allen walks into the shearer's pen, grabs the first sheep he comes to, and shears it as cleanly as you'll find anywhere, and in two-thirds the time it took the shearer.

Rather than say anything contentious to the shearer – which lesser property owners might be tempted to do – Mr Allen gives him back the handpiece and goes about his business.

No words are necessary.

Or, to paraphrase St Francis of Assisi: speak in love; use words if necessary.

The Allens own three properties on different sides of Mortlake. At Dornoch, the property on which Mr and Mrs Allen live, they run six hundred Hereford cows and calves. Thirty kilometres to the west at Denholm Green, just past the town of Hexham, their elder son, Will, has 3000 Merinos. Twenty kilometres to the north and equidistant from both other properties, close to the hamlet of Woorndoo, a third property without a home on it is used as grazing country for dry sheep (wethers) and for growing crops.

I spend half my time working with Mr Allen at Dornoch, and the other half with Will, four years my senior, at the Hexham and Woorndoo properties. We have beds at both houses. Will, who like his father is brilliant with sheep, admits to being no academic. We have that in common, at least. Will was a boarder at his school in Melbourne, where he says one of his teachers said to him in his final year, 'So, William, what are your plans after school?' Cheerfully, says Will, he looked at the teacher and replied, 'Going back on the land, sir.' To which the teacher said, 'What as, fertiliser?'

You might ask why the Allens' other son, nineteen-year-old Bruce, who is away as a jackaroo in the Riverina, didn't just stay home and learn about sheep and cattle from his clever father and brother. Fair question.

Apart from the obvious benefit of learning the business of farming from another top farmer – and being able later to apply new practices at home – the truth is one's children often don't make the best employees. If they don't like a job their parent gives them, they can ignore the instruction, or just plain refuse to carry it out. The trouble often begins when a son gets his driver's licence and he's itching to go to a party late on a Saturday, while there's work still to be done. (Not that the Allens' jackarooing son is necessarily like that – I've not met him.) A jackaroo, on the other hand, will stay back to complete the task, without questioning it.

Parent–children relationships and succession planning, about which I will learn much a lot later, are two of the most difficult issues facing farmers – or any family business, I guess.

Mr Allen also must figure that the cost of my wages for a year is worth it over having Bruce remain at home.

Again, I'm working for one of the best graziers going around. While studs produce bulls for other studs and commercial breeders, so too commercial breeders sell bulls. Ron Allen is regarded as a legend among commercial cattlemen. And while many graziers buy their bulls from a recognised beef-cattle stud, many others buy from him, a leading commercial producer.

But now it's time for Mr Allen's herd to have a new bull. There's a Hereford stud at Heyfield in Gippsland, he says, which has just the bloodline he wants. So he takes me along with him to the sale. It's the kind of thing I would never have been given time off work to do at Habbies Howe, where the idea of such an outing would have been unthinkable.

The stud in question is holding its annual, on-farm sale. We take the Bedford truck with the stock crate on the back in the expectation we'll find a bull suitable for the Dornoch herd.

The moment we arrive, Mr Allen tells me to go off and inspect the fifty young bulls on offer, each one broken in and tethered to the freshly painted white fence which surrounds a neatly mown grass area about the size of two tennis courts. Five metres behind the white fence on all sides is a row of cypress trees, all neatly trimmed for sale day.

Mr Allen says to come back at lunchtime and tell him which bull he should buy.

Hundreds of people are at the sale, everyone dressed in their finest: men in white moleskin trousers, sports jackets and stockman's hats; women in slacks, jackets and brightly coloured scarves. It's all designed to conjure a carnival atmosphere – and big spending at the auction. Plus, there's a free grog tent to lubricate bidders' inclinations to bid up high.

Stud cattle sales still operate very much on eye appraisal alone, even though sale catalogues are starting to include objective measurement criteria such as the average birth weight and growth rates of calves each young bull's father has sired, as well as things like the incidence of twinning and percentage of problem births the parent bull might have caused his 'wives' to go through. Agro-scientists continually come up with new things to measure, like the size of a bull's testicles, believing the bigger the balls, the higher quality his offspring will be. Hmm.

Putting a degree of science into the job of selecting stock isn't a bad idea, given what happens in the judging rings at royal shows. Years later, as a journalist on *The Weekly Times*, I will be required to record comments made by international judges – men and women flown from Europe and the Americas at great expense. Awarding first place, these overseas judges will make statements like: 'I awarded first place to this bull . . . because he walked across the ground on four legs.' How many legs did the judge expect the bloody thing to walk across the ground on?

At lunchtime, as instructed, I find Mr Allen and I tell him which one I think is best.

Everyone wants to know which bull Ron Allen plans to buy, such is his reputation. He inclines his head towards me so no one hears, and I whisper, 'Number thirty-eight.'

'Nah,' he replies, almost too loudly for my thinking. 'Narrow shoulders.'

I feel stupid. Obviously, I have heaps still to learn about judg-ing cattle. Yet, I can't understand the 'narrow shoulders' bit (that would, of course, mean less chunky and therefore less of a meat-producing sire). In my humble opinion the shoulders on number thirty-eight are as broad if not broader than all of the other young bulls up for sale. And anyway, we all know that shoulders mustn't be too wide, given they can be the part of a calf that often gets stuck during the birthing process.

I leave the lunch tent and head back to take another look at bull number thirty-eight, feeling I've let down both my boss and myself. Pretending not to look directly at him in case someone sees me, I cast an eye in his general direction. Suddenly, a grazier appears next to me from nowhere. He must know I work for Mr Allen because he immediately asks me which bull my boss likes best. I sense straight away I'm being pumped for information – and so brazenly.

'I wouldn't have a clue,' I reply, looking elsewhere. 'Certainly not the one I like.'

Clearly, the man thinks he's found an easy way to buy the best bull on offer. Everyone here today will want whichever bull Ron Allen thinks is best.

Like many beef-cattle studs of the day, which now have on-farm annual sales, this stud has built its own circular, roofed-in sale ring. Surrounding the sale ring, tiered seating stretches to the roof, which provides welcome shade for everyone present. Stock agents conducting the auction stand in an open booth just outside the circular ring, near ground level, while agents' spotters are spread throughout the crowd on all levels – they take bids wherever a hand goes up or a half-secret nod is given. Grown men do look silly when they rub the side of their nose just before a bid is announced.

Starting smack on two o'clock, the first bull is led around the ring through ankle-high straw. All very posh. Mr Allen has me sitting on his left. We're seven rows up, while the stock agent Mr Allen has briefed sits directly opposite at the same level, twenty metres away. The agent's bidding instructions are unknown to me, but that isn't unusual, given a jackaroo exists on a need-to-know basis.

Forty-nine of the fifty bulls sell for $2000 or less.

Number thirty-eight causes the most interest, before the

auctioneer finally bangs his gavel on his benchtop, declaring, 'Sold, for $3500, to R G Allen, Mortlake.'

Mr Allen, clearly pleased with his afternoon's work, leans towards me and asks, 'So, Michael, what do you think?'

I lean in and reply, 'Not bad for narrow shoulders.'

He laughs. 'I'm sorry. I didn't want you put under pressure in case someone asked you which bull I had my eye on.'

'They did.'

We take number thirty-eight back to Mortlake – and to the four-legged treats that await him.

Farming has many vicissitudes, one of which is long hours spent preparing paddocks for crops or new pasture. When it's that time of year and your machinery is working beautifully – plough, seeder or scarifier – and the weather is kind to you, and your tractor has headlights, there's no excuse not to work through the night. Will and I frequently take it in turns to do just that, and I have to say how exceptional it is to know that while you're out driving a tractor all night long, everyone else you know is tucked up in bed with a good book, or with someone who's read one.

Ploughs have round disks set at an angle facing slightly across the ground which, when towed behind the tractor, dig deeply and turn the soil to put air into it. A seeder has web feet with rubber hoses behind that drop grain or grass-and-clover seeds and fertiliser a few inches down into the soil. A scarifier also has web-shaped feet, but they just disturb the soil – making for a lighter, less invasive 'ploughing' process.

On one night-time shift, well after midnight, I'm driving the scarifier round and round a paddock at Woorndoo, when suddenly ahead of me I see an object. In the dark, I can't make out what it is. Getting closer, a cold sweat suddenly comes over me.

It's my scarifier – it's fallen off the back of my tractor during my last round, and I've just done an entire lap without looking behind me and noticing it missing. Thank God no one saw me do that.

My mistake is bettered only by Will himself, who in the middle of another night dozes off altogether while towing the seeder. He awakes to find his tractor heading diagonally across the paddock towards a rocky outcrop on the far side. He has to complete sowing the entire paddock before someone arrives and sees the embarrassing evidence.

Will and I decide we'll embark on a poultry enterprise. It has its beginnings one night after dinner while we're watching TV. Will is reading *The Weekly Times*. 'Hey, Mike,' he says, 'listen to this: "Day-old pullets. Four dollars a hundred." Can you believe it? Chook on the table for four cents each.'

'Cheap on any account,' I reply, more interested in what Bill Peach is saying on the TV.

A week later, we get a call from the Mortlake railway station to say our order has arrived. We drive into town and take delivery of four hundred cute little fluffy yellow things.

Fortunately, Denholm Green has a set of poultry yards, though they haven't been used in years – certainly not in the time that Will and his family have owned the property. The pens are perfect for our new enterprise. We also have heaps of seconds wheat; again, ideal for feed.

What we haven't figured on, of course, is the space required for four hundred chooks once they turn big and white. It isn't long before the blighters have to take it in turns to land.

The other downside to this otherwise brilliant scheme is the killing and cleaning of the birds. Even after slicing off their heads with an axe, as sensitively and as caringly as one can – which we do at Dornoch because there's a big old copper boiler there for scalding the feathers off – for a moment the amazing critters continue to run around the ground headless, squirting blood all over Mrs Allen's fresh washing on the clothesline.

One especially warm lunchtime while ploughing and sowing at the Woorndoo property, Will and I are sitting on the ground, each of us using a tractor wheel as a backrest, eating our respective chooks with both hands, when Will tastes something strange. He draws the carcass away from his mouth, examines it and watches as clumps of maggots fall onto the ground. Clearly, we hadn't been refrigerating the birds as well as we should have.

Regrettably, the whole enterprise comes to a sad and grubby end one Sunday afternoon when we return to Denholm Green to find a sea of feathers starting at the highway and continuing all the way up the drive to the homestead. There are enough feathers to fill doonas for a small army. At the chook pens, it's a whole lot worse: feathers are stuck in the wire netting well above head height, even high up in nearby trees.

It turns out that overnight the sheepdogs have slipped their chains and found a way into the chook pens. They must have opted for takeaway DGFC (Denholm Green Fried Chicken).

Still, we rejoice in having enjoyed many a good meal – with or without maggots – at just four cents a chook. Cheap on any account.

I'm a jackaroo in Victoria's Western District in an era when my generation – we will become known as 'baby boomers' – exhibits an unashamed born-to-rule attitude. I preclude from this broad-brush accusation my employer's family. But many young people my age here have everything they will ever want, let alone need, yet zilch by way of social conscience. Apart from farming, their lives appear confined to sex, grog and union-bashing. I may as well throw in football as a fourth reason for living. These are true red-necks, Young Liberals with a capital Y and L. The only way to beat the socialists, I hear them say often enough to be downright scary, is for you to get them before they get you.

Most of these graziers' sons and daughters have been brought up to know that with privilege comes responsibility, yet very few, it seems, put principle into practice.

One night, the Victorian Premier, Sir Henry Bolte, comes to Mortlake to address the Young Liberals. During question time, a leading member rises and asks a question regarding a political agitator at the time: 'Sir Henry, what are you going to do about this Albert Langer fellow? If I had my way, I'd hang him.' To which Sir Henry is said to have jumped to his feet and, with considerable animation, replied, 'Now you're talkin' my sort of language, sonny.'

If these young people's politics weren't terrifying – not to mention the Premier's dangerous encouragement of such thinking – they'd be mildly funny.

I guess being an outsider makes me see things differently. The young blue bloods truly believe it's their birthright to run the world, and that whatever they need to do to advance their own economic gain is justified. The truth, of course, is that many of their forebears simply squatted on the land their families now occupy. They paid hardly a cent for what represents a veritable fortune, and today they see it as their life's duty to protect and defend the land from the socialists. The more financially incompetent of them sell off back paddocks every second year to enable them to maintain their ultra-extravagant and selfish lifestyles, and to pay their children's enormous private-school boarding and tuition fees.

Derek's family farms nearby. One polling day his sister and her city-bred boyfriend are visiting from Melbourne. They vote absentee at the local polling booth. It turns out the boyfriend's vote is the only one cast there all day for Labor.

'We don't need the likes of you around here,' says Derek's uncle, a scrutineer for the National Party, to the boy.

So much for a fair and free vote in Australia.

Fire is a farmer's worst nightmare, along with drought and flood, of course. A lifetime's work of breeding and growing quality stock and pasture – and constructing good fences – can be destroyed while a test cricketer puts on fifty runs between lunch and the tea break.

Which is very nearly what happens at Dornoch one Sunday afternoon in January 1970.

It's a stinking hot day with a fierce, hot northerly wind; a day of Total Fire Ban. We're inside watching the test cricket, each of us with one eye on the window in case we see smoke, and an ear cocked towards the telephone in case news of a fire comes to us that way.

The phone rings. It's the neighbour on our north-west boundary. A grass fire has started on the property next to theirs and is heading towards Dornoch's boundary fence.

Throwing on our jeans and long-sleeved shirts, we run to the eight-tonne Bedford truck, which throughout the summer carries a water tank filled with 2500 litres, a pump and two fire hoses. The truck also is kept full of fuel, as if inviting fire to try it on.

Within seconds, Will is at the wheel and driving at speed along Dornoch's central laneway towards the rear of the property, where smoke and occasional flame are visible in the distance. I stand on the back, one hand firmly on the Bedford's back rail, the other ready to start the pump. I don't mind admitting my adrenalin is racing several metres ahead of where Will is driving. At each gate, I jump off and run to open it (with good reason this time). I leave the gates open for Mr Allen to drive through after us in his small tray truck, on the back of which he has his own small water tank and fire unit.

The fire hasn't yet reached Dornoch, but it's close. Seconds later, we get to the back boundary gate that leads onto the lane-way dividing Dornoch from the neighbouring farm, across which the fire is rapidly spreading. The flames are less than fifty metres from us.

There's no gate into the neighbouring property where we need it, but that doesn't fuss us one bit. Will stops the Bedford, I jump off and with a pair of wire cutters slice through eight strands – faster than I've ever cut through wire before. I quickly drag the wires to one side and Will drives on through. As he does, I jump back on board, dropping the wire cutters safely by my feet on the tray. This time I don't care about hanging on. Instead, I pull the starter cord and the pump bursts into life. Immediately, both lengths of two-inch fire hose wriggle into life and become stiff – signalling they're full of water – and confirming their state of readiness to fight the fire.

What strikes me straight away about my first-ever fire, apart from the sheer scariness of the flames coming at us, is its symmetry: the two-metre-high wall of flame is running east–west per-fectly evenly and advancing methodically across our neighbour's paddock, in a southerly direction. It's being fanned by the strong north wind. What's also scary is that there are no other fire trucks in sight – including Mortlake's CFA trucks. We're the first here, unless the other trucks are working on other arms of the fire some-where else, and I can't see them due to flames and smoke.

The paddock we're in is surprisingly lacking in grass, unlike the Allens' pastures which are never overstocked to this extent, never eaten this bare, and for a moment I think how battling farmers must live so close to the edge in terms of what resources they have. And yet right now the lack of combustible fuel is a blessing. It's the

burning cow shit lying everywhere that causes a lot of the smoke.
I try hard to avoid breathing it in.

There's no time to waste; we have to snuff out the wall of flame
running beside us. Will now has the truck at the eastern edge of
the fire, in the flames' path. He starts to drive across the paddock
in a westerly direction across the fire's front, two metres out from
the flames. I open the nozzle and point the jet of water at the base
of the advancing fire, and in an instant begin to extinguish flames.

'Okay?' Will calls out from the inside the cabin.

'Go for it!' I shout back at him, scared totally witless, but not
about to tell Will that.

He plants his foot on the accelerator but the truck moves too
quickly for me and I miss a bit of flame. 'Whoa!' I yell out. He
slows the truck a touch, even though we both know he needs to
keep moving. I realise I'm trying to put too much water on the one
spot. I need to keep up with Will and shoot water directly at the
seat of the fire – and not even think of playing mop-ups.

We quickly get ourselves into a working rhythm. Then I do
something really stupid: I glance back along the line of the fire, to
see if what I've already sprayed is still out. In doing so, my spray
drifts off the flame. I miss a bit.

'Whoa!' I yell again. Will brakes to let me shoot water backwards. He has his window down, and because he's forward of me
and directly beside flames I'm yet to extinguish, he has to shield his
face from the intense heat. I realise I need to bring the spray forward, to down below his window, to get myself forward of where
I'm working. But in doing so, I miss another bit of flame. Fortunately, this time Will sees it.

'Hang on,' he shouts. He swings his steering wheel hard left,
away from the flames, and accelerates. I hang with one hand
gripped to the rail behind the cabin. Will does a full circle, coming
back onto the line of flame further back. I squirt fresh flame. This

time I keep my eyes firmly on the flames directly beside me.

We come to a fence – not that fire cares a jot about fences – and Will pulls up sharply. This time it's he who dives out of the truck and, with a second pair of wire cutters in hand, chomps his way through the wire netting and four strands of plain wire. The flames are almost on him and I realise my job is to blast the fire around him – on him – where he's cutting, plus keep the flames off the Bedford and me.

Save Will first, I think, *then the truck*. Without meaning to, I drench him. I have to.

'Holy shit, Mike,' he calls out, as he runs back to the cabin. 'Steady.'

He jumps back in the truck and throws his wire cutters over on the passenger seat. Now, however, we're on the black side of the fire – it seems the north wind has pushed the flames under the truck, somehow without harming Will, the truck or me.

'Going through,' he shouts, as he performs another sharp circle and crashes back through the flames.

'Fuck, Will!' I yell at him. My body spins with the momentum and slams itself into the truck's backboard. I feel my left wrist, which is gripping the rail, twist in a way I'm sure it's not meant to. Despite the pain, I again get my hose onto the seat of the flames, resuming where I left off before the fence interrupted us. I have no idea whether we're winning or losing. But then, I'm not the lieutenant of the Mortlake Fire Brigade; it's not my place to worry about such matters. I'm merely a jackaroo fire fighter – and a pretty bloody good one at that.

What I haven't noticed – and I get the fright of my life when I do – is that suddenly, from nowhere, there's a kid standing on the truck, gripping the rail on the other side of the water tank to me. He must have jumped on board while Will was cutting the fence.

Recovering from the shock of discovering him, but with my eyes glued firmly on the seat of the flames, I yell across to him, 'Where did you come from?'

'We live over there,' he replies. Fourteen, I guess, going by his height and squeaky voice. He's most likely pointing somewhere, but I have no idea where. I have my back to him, fighting the fire, and nothing will make me take my eyes off the flames.

And yet, curiosity getting the better of me, I glance across. The idiot boy is wearing shorts and thongs – precisely what you don't wear to a fire. For a moment, I wonder if he's a hundred cents in the dollar. I suspect not, which means I'll need to look after him. My mind races. Should I tell him to grab the other hose, or will he just waste precious water? He'll probably drink it, I think, unkindly. Anyway, I'm doing the only thing that needs doing.

'Just hang on to that rail,' I yell at him over my left shoulder. Then, as an afterthought, I add, 'And don't touch anything.'

I decide I should tell Will about the boy. 'You know we've got a kid on board?' I shout down to him, leaning my head towards the cabin window, but with my eyes fixed on the seat of the flames.

'Yeah, I saw him,' Will yells back. 'Tell him to hang on.'

An hour later – it's still not yet tea in the cricket – we, together with six other fire trucks, including two CFA units, get the fire out. Everything around us is black. The only things still smouldering are clumps of cow shit and a burnt-out hayshed. Sadly, Will and I weren't among the trucks battling the haystack, which would've been fun.

The pain in my wrist has subsided. Probably numb. No one is hurt, no home is burnt to the ground and no stock have been lost, although seeing how close the fire came to the farmer's home makes me realise how lucky he is.

The seven fire trucks gather in the shade of a tall, unharmed gum tree, their drivers and crews taking it in turns to drink from shared water sacks. The kid who was on our truck has disappeared. I can only assume he's okay.

Everyone is of course eager to hear gossip of how the fire started. The whisper is that the farmer whose property we're on was using his old Fordson tractor – on a day of Total Fire Ban. Totally illegal. Totally stupid.

The farmer isn't among us. Someone says he's in the house, too scared to come out.

It's Friday night. I've had far too much to drink in the Bottom Pub and I decide to head home.

About five kilometres from Mortlake, heading west along the highway and driving more slowly than usual due to my state, I sense I'm being followed. It has to be so – I'm driving so slowly the car behind should have easily overtaken me. For a moment I worry it's the cops, and a cold sweat comes over me at the thought of losing my licence – and the embarrassment it will cause the Allens. Such fears soon abate because if it is the police, then why aren't they pulling me over and booking me?

The car comes up close behind, puts on its left indicator and slows to a stop.

Another cold sweat develops as, suddenly, I fear it might be town hoons out to get me.

Ignoring even that danger, I put on my left indicator and pull over. I must be mental.

The car takes off again, drives around me and stops several metres in front. As it slides past, I look inside. It isn't a cop and it isn't hoons.

It's a girl.

I feel my heart leap a thousand beats. Before I can think another thought, the girl jumps out of her vehicle, runs back to mine and pushes interesting parts of herself through my window – which I've already unwound, just to be helpful. You never know, she might be lost and in need of directions.

'Hi,' she says, slightly out of breath. I can't tell in the dark if she's eighteen or twenty-eight. 'Followed youse out of town.' Her eyes drill into mine. She has light brown hair and is partially wearing a white blouse. She looks pretty, but then I have just spent three hours in the Bottom Pub.

'Jenny's me name,' she continues, her eyes now penetrating my inner being.

'John's mine,' I reply, feeling my face turn scarlet and my nose grow ruler-length.

'No it's not, stupid,' she says, with a forgiving smile. 'Your name's Michael. You're a jackaroo or something at Denholm Green.'

'Jackaroo,' I say, preferring it to 'something'. I've been sprung, but it's okay.

'Do youse want me to follow youse back to your place?' she asks, casually adjusting her upper extremities so I don't lose focus.

Should I? I think to myself. Well, to be honest, I don't think that at all. Certainly, one thing I'm not thinking is how Jenny is torturing the English language. But then, at this moment who cares about words? It's actions that count, given I've just died and taken the express route to heaven – without interview.

Can Jenny follow me back to my place? Of course she can. I'm twenty, a virgin, and I've just spent three hours in the Bottom Pub. Isn't that the perfect recipe for . . . happiness? Plus, I'm miles away from anyone even remotely likely to advise me to act responsibly.

Of course Jenny can follow me back home. After all, no one else will be there, and she'll make pleasant company for the evening. We might even play some records. And I can work on getting the 'se' off her 'youse'.

Suddenly, my thoughts turn to my mouth, which I realise is open wide enough to give birth to a small calf.

'I'll follow youse,' she says, with a smile, as if she really does like me. 'Okay?'

Without waiting for my reply, Jenny withdraws her equipment

from the window and begins to trot back to her car. I feel my dry throat try to mumble *Okay* and wonder, just briefly, if we'll be able to develop better conversation skills. I watch her run back to her car.

She lets me go first and we continue on to Denholm Green, one car behind the other, for twenty-five of the longest kilometres of my life. It gives me time to think how this really isn't the right thing to be doing; time to think of possible consequences; time to think responsibly; time to think in a mature and sensible and moral way . . . and time to convince myself how this is the mother of all my lucky days, and the heck with doing the right thing, with responsibility and consequences, and mature and sensible and moral ways.

The house is dark and quiet. After turning on the lights we make ourselves comfortable. It doesn't take long for me to figure out that of the two of us, I'm the only one for whom this is a brand-new experience. I suggest a drink but Jenny says to forget the drink. I stop myself short of suggesting we play a record. Jenny asks instead where my bedroom is.

Moments later, she's sitting on my bed, drawing circles on the cover with her right index finger. I stand at the door, watching as the circles grow bigger.

'What's stopping you?' she asks, her hand now patting the bed, her head on the side.

Still, I remain standing at the door, hesitating.

'It's your first time, isn't it?' Jenny asks in a softer voice.

I don't answer. I turn my face away and raise my eyes, as if wanting to say *Get real*, but stopping myself because I know she knows. And because I've never been a good liar.

'It's true, isn't it?'

'Yes,' I hear my voice answer, without my permission.

'Come on,' she urges, reverting to drawing small circles. 'I'll show you.'

Nervously, I move to the bed, but sit right on the edge. Jenny leans in, throws her arms around my neck and pulls me sideways towards her. We fall together in a heap. She forces her mouth hard onto mine, plunging her tongue deep inside my mouth.

I'm gone.

And when I wake up in the morning, so is Jenny.

Maybe it was all a dream. After all, I did spend three hours in the Bottom Pub.

Before I can blink, it's August, and Will's brother Bruce returns home from his time away as a jackaroo in the Riverina. My wonderful year with the Allens of Mortlake is over. When we shake hands to say goodbye, I'm sure Mr Allen wants to say how, if he could, he'd have me stay on. But, with Bruce home, he can't afford wages for both of us.

It's not yet the go for men to give hugs. After a polite handshake I drive off.

Much of Australia's farming still occurs on family-run farms, as opposed to corporate outfits. Some folk go as far as to say the family farm still forms the backbone of our nation, although numbers of family farming units have dwindled to make that unlikely. Yet, the family farm also makes for community. And what a wonderful thing a rural community is. Unlike in the city, where people put their heads down as you pass in the street, where neighbours often only speak to one another to fight over loud music or a new fence, in the bush life demands that you get along. People drop in without appointment for coffee or to borrow something, always with a jar of something homemade or home-grown in hand. And when danger is imminent, like fire, everyone closes ranks. They pull together.

It's a special and wonderful thing, the land.

Oh, for the country life.

16

Interview

They say the only way onto the land is to marry onto it or inherit it. With little prospect of either, my next option is to become a station manager. And the states to do that in, I'm reliably informed, are New South Wales, Queensland or Western Australia.

I apply to Linkletter's Place in Esperance, owned by American children's TV host Art Linkletter. As a child of the '50s, I loved to watch Linkletter's show. A real character, he describes in his book *Linkletter Down Under* how his first wheat crop at Esperance failed to germinate because, he believes, 'the seed was sown upside down'. The American friend who introduced him to Esperance then got him excited about another land purchase, this time on WA's north-west coast. Writes Linkletter: 'Beachfront in California costs $1000 a square foot, so at four cents a square mile it has to be a bargain.' He buys in.

Sadly, Linkletter's manager replies by saying there are no jackaroo positions available.

What next? One of the Allens' close neighbours at Mortlake is the nephew of Sir James Balderstone, who is not only chairman of BHP, but chairman also of Squatting Investments, a pastoral company with a number of sheep and cattle holdings in New South Wales and Queensland.

Working unashamedly on the principle of who you know rather than what you know – even if it is a long bow citing the chairman's nephew as the neighbour to a place where previously I've been a humble jackaroo – somehow I secure an interview with the company's pastoral inspector, a fellow called Mr Miles, in Melbourne. Of course, the clincher that gets me the interview is that I've been a jackaroo for Dick Webb at Habbies Howe. It always will be the thing to get me over the line, for a job on the land at any rate.

Squatting Investments' headquarters are in William Street in the heart of Melbourne's business precinct. The rooms are dark – really dark – and Mr Miles himself looks particularly dark and threatening as he motions me with a wave of his hand into his grim office.

Some people have the knack of making you feel totally at ease the moment you meet them, exuding natural friendliness and warmth. Mr Miles isn't one of them. His heavily cracked, whiskey-induced red face and enormous red nose make him appear positively ferocious, as well as dreadfully worn. It's probably the result of a career as a station manager, or from having spent the past twenty years firing them.

Suddenly I think to myself, What am I doing here? Why would I want to end up like this joker? What a monster! What a grump!

'Sit there,' he says, curtly, looking me over from head to toe and then pointing to a single chair without arms on my side of an enormous desk. His voice is scarier than his looks.

As threatening as the pastoral inspector appears, what is far more imposing is a huge map of Australia that covers the entire wall behind him. What I find especially amazing is how my home state of Victoria ends at knee height – just how small it is compared to the rest of Australia. I take it for granted that each of the numerous red dots stuck to the map signifies a Squatting Investments cattle or sheep holding.

I'm asked the mandatory, mundane questions, including why I want to work for Squatting Investments, which I'm not all that sure I do now that I've met this guy. Each of my brief answers is followed by a period of silence from the other side of the massive desk. I assume the pauses are to give the man thinking time – either that or I'm boring him witless. He takes another hard look at me before drawing in a massive breath, probably to give him strength to throw me out, then pushes back his chair and drags himself to his feet.

Things turn sour. He reaches to his left and takes hold of a metre-long cane, like the one my housemaster at school used to belt the crap out of me after I called a teacher by his nickname. It was back in Year Eight – the only time in my entire schooling I tried to be brave, and I failed miserably. And got caned for it. The worst part was waiting all Sunday – nine hours – for the caning, which I knew was coming the moment my housemaster got home from his pleasant, family outing.

Swinging his stick, I duck as the ferocious-looking grump turns to face the big map and begins to tap the lowest red dot, the one just above knee height.

Tap, tap, tap.

Where he's tapping is just north of Corowa, across the border into New South Wales. Then, as if he can't be bothered lifting the cane any further up the wall, he declares, 'You can stop here the first night.'

Tap, tap, tap.

Without asking my opinion, the old goat lets out enough breath to propel a small yacht. He takes in another lungful of air before he forces the stick up the wall in search of another dot.

'You can stop here the second night,' he says, tapping his cane at Brewarrina in northern New South Wales. We're about one hundred kilometres east of Bourke. My eyes start a journey of their own – they race on north to see if there are any red dots on Papua New Guinea.

Tap, tap, tap.

'The property is called Quantambone,' he splutters all over the map, still smacking his cane on the red dot, before adding, 'It's raining there at the minute, thank Christ.'

Somehow, I don't think the Lord Jesus plays a huge part in this man's world.

Again, without further comment, he continues the stick's journey to a spot level with his chest – halfway to the ceiling. It has now crept across the border into Queensland. He stops at Augathella, an inch or so north of Charleville. Glancing quickly from right to left on the map, I figure Augathella is halfway between Brisbane and Birdsville in the Simpson Desert.

Tap, tap, tap.

What am I doing in this office? I ask myself, yet again. Sometimes I'm such an idiot!

'You can work here,' he says, letting go of yet another carton of air, as if he's been keeping it there in reserve. He turns to face me and then slumps back in his chair. 'The place is called Burenda,' he says, shoving the cane back where it belongs. 'It's our Merino stud. Thirty thousand sheep and a few hundred head of cattle.' He seems proud of the number, as if he personally sired each one of them. I detect the faintest of smiles emerge on his fully florid cheeks at the prospect.

Slouching back in his chair, he asks, 'So what do you think about that, young fella?'

The name's Michael, you stupid old fart.

'Looks good to me,' I reply, shitting myself, even though I have no one else to blame, because I'm the idiot who asked for the interview. All I can hope for is that the pastoral inspector doesn't make too many visits to Burenda. What a bundle of laughs that would be.

What am I getting myself into here? Then again, I take pause and think maybe, just maybe, this could be the making of me. I tell myself to think positively. And I do just that, especially when I get home and Mum asks me how the interview went. Mum is still as mad as all hell that I quit the family wool firm.

'It was a breeze,' I tell her. 'I'm off to manage western Queensland.'

Before heading north, I drive up to Habbies Howe, to get Mr Webb's advice.

'W-whatever you d-d-do,' my mentor says, 'd-don't become a g-gin j-j-jockey.'

I don't reply. Of all the fatherly advice Mr Webb could give me, he chooses to make it about sexual behaviour. That he should think my one aim in life is to bed Aboriginal women comes to me as a dreadful shock (and no doubt would to the poor women as well). I find it embarrassing, demeaning and surprising. The man, I realise, doesn't know me well at all.

I drive back to Melbourne feeling hurt and disillusioned. Maybe I was just a servant-jackaroo at Habbies Howe after all.

I arrive at Squatting Investment's southernmost station at Corowa, in the Riverina, late in the afternoon. The manager, Geoff Parkes, and his wife Janet greet me as I climb out of my ute. A couple with no children of their own, I take them to be in their mid-thirties. Geoff's pride and joy are his kelpie sheepdogs, which he makes a point of showing me the moment I arrive. The dogs see us approach and strain at their chains, barking madly, bursting to be set free. Geoff unclips the chains and the dogs promptly go crazy, running back and forth, the males among them lifting their legs on everything in sight, including the wheels of my precious ute. Thanks very much.

It's funny how people who can't have children, or decide not to, often substitute animals. Perhaps they think that breeding dogs is a whole lot easier than kids. Maybe they're right.

Over dinner, the couple want to know where I've worked. And I'm keen to know how they find being managers for Squatting Investments. It turns out they've only been in the job a few weeks and naturally they want to defer judgement for a while longer.

'How do you find Mr Miles?' I ask, hoping we'll enjoy a laugh at the buffoon's expense.

'He knows his stuff,' replies Geoff, dryly. It's obvious these folk don't share my weird sense of humour – or my opinion of Miles.

I decide on a more serious tack. I tell the couple how it's my goal to do what they're doing: become a station manager for Squatting Investments.

'In that case you'd better get yourself a wife,' says Geoff. I file his comment in my brain, but I don't reply. I'm unsure if he means a wife is necessary to counter the loneliness of station life, or that it's a formal prerequisite for employment as a manager for the company. Maybe it's both. I look for an easier topic.

'How long will it take me to get to Quantambone?'

'To Brewarrina?' Geoff scratches his forehead. 'I'd allow eight hours, counting stops.' He looks at his wife for confirmation. Janet is on her feet taking dishes from the table. 'What do you think, honey?'

'Yes,' she agrees, now at the sink. 'I'd give it eight hours.'

At eight o'clock the next morning we say our goodbyes and I head north. It turns out to be not an eight-hour drive, but nine – nine hundred kilometres. As I drive, I think more about the Parkes and how, if they do want kids, they ought to adopt a bucket-load. They seem to me like they'd make great parents. The other issue – the one about needing to get myself a wife – also plays on my mind. I think about it while I try to find a radio station that doesn't fart back at me.

A wife wouldn't be bad – perhaps I could do with one of them. But where to get one? Definitely not Jenny at Mortlake, or Sharleen

back in Yorkshire. Anyway, by now Sharleen probably has a tribe
of kids to one of those horny wool sorters up on the top floor.

Goodness knows what will become of Jenny. If indeed she
exists.

Quantambone is big and bleak, and it's stocked with a thousand
Shorthorn steers. Well, that's the number they estimated in last
year's annual return. Who knows how many cattle there are on
these vast and desolate stations? It's like trying to count the pig or
kangaroo population: nigh on impossible.

The district is half flooded for my arrival, as the charming
Mr Miles warned me. When I leave the more solid gravel road
and head up the soft driveway to the Quantambone homestead,
I not only hear but feel mud squelch off my tyres as it builds up
inside the wheel hubs. The vehicle begins to groan until, finally,
it grinds to a halt just as I reach the house, all four wheel hubs
and wheels caked in red mud. Were it not for the fancy wide tyres
I splashed out on at Mortlake – to make both ute and driver look
super tough – I wouldn't have got this far.

'Yep, you sure won't be goin' nowhere in a hurry,' says Jason
Ramsay, the overseer, coming out to greet me. Jason is in his late
twenties and built like a stick. We shake hands as he observes my
ute. 'The road goin' north will be hopeless for any amount of days
yet,' he adds.

Number of days, *amount* of chaff, I think to myself. Not that
I'm about to correct the man.

Quantambone, Jason tells me, is between managers, which
places him in charge. He supervises two young jackaroos – the sum
total of the staff – but the boys are out on their horses checking for
cattle stranded by the floods.

I'm struck immediately by the shocking state of the vast

homestead. The rambling weatherboard home has an enclosed veranda all the way around, which of course makes the house look far bigger than it really is. But the veranda's wire windows are full of holes, which renders them useless in terms of their primary purpose – to keep out flies and mosquitoes.

For a moment Jason leaves me on my own, so I explore the building. Some of the rooms I can tell haven't been used or indeed cleaned in years. One end of the house is ghost-like. It's all quite sad, really. Jason and the two boys live in four rooms at the other end, near the kitchen. It's a stark existence and I say a quick prayer to thank God this isn't my final destination. I can put up with it until the ground dries out sufficiently to enable me to make my escape to Queensland. Then I realise this is the first time I've set foot in a farmhouse – any house – where there isn't a female present. The place looks as if it might be twenty years since it felt a cleaning touch. But what worries me a heck of a lot more is how as a virile, twenty-year-old man (okay, boy) desperate to make his mark in the world as a man, I should notice the state of the house. Aren't I supposed to be besotted with manly things, like cars, smokes and booze – and raunchy women?

Quantambone's normally dry creeks, ravines and low-lying plains are awash with flooding waters. Where the water has receded, a green tinge rises as you watch it. I spend the week with Jason in his Nissan Patrol checking the station's vast paddocks for cattle stranded by the floods. Even with its four-wheel drive constantly engaged, the Nissan slips and slides all over the joint; we hardly ever stay on the track. But that doesn't bother either of us because there's nothing out here to hit even if we do slide off. Anyway, tracks out here are for direction only, not for driving on.

Jason is ecstatic because already wherever we look there's new growth starting to shoot, thanks to the flooding rains. He promptly declares the sight better than sex. And sex, he assures me several times during our week together in the Nissan, is something he knows heaps about. Where in this bleak existence he finds human partners for the enterprise, I daren't ask. I decide to take his word for it.

'This rain is fucking fantastic,' Jason declares for the millionth time as the vehicle again slides sideways. 'It means we can turn the steers off earlier and restock the station with young calves,' he adds, in an ever-quickening voice. His excitement is just a bit over the top, but then, current climatic conditions are probably the biggest news around these parts in decades.

During my long week at Quantambone, I seldom see the two jackaroos, except at mealtimes. Even then I say little in their presence. They're just kids, probably sixteen and fifteen, their worlds and conversations limited to horses, beer and sex – only two of which I dare say they have any practical experience in. I can just imagine – when I'm not around – Jason enthralling the boys with stories of his sexual exploits, real or fantasy. The whole idea makes me grateful to be moving on.

Like me and my year at Habbies Howe, these jackaroos spend almost all of their days on horseback, constantly checking for beasts that might be bogged or stranded on temporary knolls, which leave the cattle without feed. Where they find beasts in such a predicament, they need to bully them across the wet area to higher, drier ground, just like I had to force my cows and calves across the swollen Hughes Creek at Habbies Howe.

Finally, using a shovel, I'm able to clear sufficient mud from around my ute's wheels to get them to turn, which allows me to escape from Jason and his less-than-believable yarns.

It's Saturday, and I spend most of the seven-hour drive to Augathella wondering when a kangaroo is going to write off my ute. There is nothing romantic about kangaroos in the real Australia. They eat

valuable pasture, they destroy fences and they dart out of the scrub
beside the road – in this case the Mitchell Highway – at enormous
speed, always aimed specifically at the softest and most expensive-
to-replace panel on a moving vehicle. The best kangaroo (read also
pig, fox, rabbit, wombat, snake) is a dead one. Stuff misguided,
moronic animal-lovers who don't have to deal with the economic
havoc these pests cause in the real Australia. Sure, it's great to
save a wombat, but what about the $800 steer that falls down the
wombat hole, breaks its leg or hip and becomes a black hole in the
farm budget?

Keeping one's eyes peeled along the highway's edges for 'roos
is tiresome, but it's better than getting wiped out.

I arrive at Charleville mid-afternoon, and with Augathella less
than an hour's drive away, I take my time to cruise around the
town, taking it all in. The centrepiece of Charleville is the magnificent Hotel Corones. It was built by a Greek, Harry Corones,
over six years and finally completed in 1929. Photos on the walls
show the squattocracy living it up in grand style, one photo caption
reading: 'Guests dressed in Paris gowns, dancing to the strains of
imported orchestras and savouring international cuisines prepared
by the finest chefs.' The hotel has accommodated everyone from
Johnny O'Keefe to royalty. Every upstairs bedroom has double
doors opening onto a massive balcony.

I also find the Anglican church. Like a kangaroo drawn to the
most expensive panel on a moving vehicle, wherever I go my sub-
conscious always delivers me to church. I'm convinced God wants
me to feel safe, knowing home base is within easy reach.

I'm proud of my smart-looking ute, with its lowered chassis,
wide tyres and the fancy 'roo bar I made and welded to the front
in the Allens' workshop at Mortlake. The bar got well and truly
tested the time we went to the snow and a grader driver whacked
a huge metal clamp on it to drag us out of a bog. No one was

more surprised than me that it survived that ordeal. Then there are mandatory car stickers on the back window, ones which any half self-respecting jackaroo needs to have to ensure the vehicle complies with the required image: they feature classy and intelligent sayings like 'I got laid at the Hamilton B&S' and 'A jackaroo eats roots and leaves'. Everything about my treasured vehicle makes me feel as tough as any jackaroo can get; as tough as I can get. This is the life, I tell myself, as I cruise around Charleville, losing count of the pubs – any amount of them!

Still, Augathella is more to my liking because it's small and looks especially peaceful nestled on the banks of the Warrego River. But the tranquillity quickly ends at the town's single hotel. What impresses me at first sight about the pub is the pair of swinging front doors – like those you see in Western movies, through which some unfortunate cowboy gets hurled to land in the water trough before the camera pans back to the doors, which remain swinging for a few seconds as a kind of epitaph, as the cowboy heaves himself out of the water, his red neck-scarf still bone-dry.

I head east out of town along a third-class road towards my final destination. I cross another cattle grid and realise I'm probably already driving through part of Burenda.

Sure enough, fourteen kilometres on I come to the entrance to a station. It isn't a gateway as such – as I am used to – but two scrawny wooden poles with a bar across the top, from which hangs a sign that tells me I've arrived at BURENDA MERINO STUD.

Another adventure is about to begin.

17

Burenda Merino Stud

The unimpressive entrance to the stud tells me straight away that I'm entering a different world to the prosperous, privately owned and run properties I'm used to – a totally foreign socio-economic environment. The depressingly bare ground I saw at Brewarrina and now here (the rains haven't happened at Augathella) are so unlike the lush green pastures I experienced in Victoria's Western District and Habbies Howe. Again I ask myself, can't I do better than this? It makes me feel as if by coming here I've gone down a few of life's notches, not up.

Ahead of me, a hundred metres down a slight incline, sits a huge Queenslander, with a wide veranda all the way round. I can see straight through underneath – the only parts touching the ground are the stilts it sits on and a set of stairs at either end. It will turn out to be the stockmen's mess and the kitchen, where the homestead meals also are cooked, but a place which otherwise remains the domain of the station hands and stockmen.

Way off to the right I see a set of horse yards, and next to them a long, narrow shed which I guess must be the workshop and tack room. Between both facilities, further down the incline, lies the homestead. It gives itself away as the main building because of the tall green trees that surround it. I drive on down.

There's not a sign of life. Admittedly, it's Saturday afternoon and stinking hot, but even so. I get out of the ute and I walk through a small wire gate and along a short path towards what looks to be an office entrance. I knock.

Moments later a short man with dark, wavy hair, probably in his mid-forties, comes to the door. He introduces himself as Robert Lawson, manager. And for a moment I wonder if I've struck Henry's great-grandson, given I'm now in what might be considered the 'real' outback where the famous bush poets wrote their stuff. 'Henry' leads me through the office to the homestead proper, and introduces me to his scantily clad, drop-dead stunning wife, Caroline. I also catch sight of their two boys, Cameron, aged eleven, and Billy, eight. It takes me a nanosecond to realise the offspring are totally feral, obvious victims of massive doses of red cordial and other substances designed to push children over the edge. I pray it's a 'long weekend' from boarding school and that the little monsters will soon return to where they belong.

Caroline offers me coffee or tea, and I happily accepted the latter. Dick Webb taught me to love tea: he drank enough of the stuff to finance Ceylon.

Henry is quiet and neatly dressed, as if he's about to go out. Yet something about him seems out of place. He doesn't give me the impression he's much of an outdoorsman, the rugged stockman type I was expecting to find as the station manager here. Certainly, he's nothing like the Other Mr Webb at Habbies Howe, who was wiry and muscle-bound. There is nothing like that about this joker – he looks to me to be more of a bean counter than a man who sits easily in a saddle. Maybe he's related to the dreaded pastoral inspector back in Melbourne, and that's how he got the job.

Henry drinks coffee and seems quite at home sitting in a deep canvas chair on the veranda. Caroline knows she's hot, what with her bottle-blonde hair and a blouse that does half the job for which it was made. It causes my mind to leap to places it oughtn't, although it isn't long before I'm brought back to earth with a thud, again distracted by the boys. The younger one seems to spend his time running about the house screaming at nothing, like he has rabies. The older one punches walls. Both of them, I quickly conclude, need an appointment with Mr Miles's cane. I can't believe the way both parents ignore their behaviour, acting almost as if neither child exists. They give no admonishment whatsoever, not a skerrick of discipline.

After the drinks, Henry takes me to the jackaroos' bedroom. It's on the north-west corner of the homestead, with a bathroom accessed via the veranda. Lying on his bed in the far corner, propped up against the wall with a magazine in his hands, sits my fellow jackaroo. I can tell straight away from the magazine's cover that the guy is seriously into horses.

Henry Lawson introduces me to Tony Lewis, and then leaves us alone.

There's another bed, diagonally opposite Tony's, next to where I'm standing. It has to be mine. And here I am, aged twenty and back sharing a bedroom. I sense immediately that Tony isn't happy; he seems to have a huge chip on his shoulder. And yet he comes across as far too angry for someone just eighteen years of age. I promptly place him as someone from 'the other side of the fence'. He's no silver-spooner like me: his demeanour, his mannerisms and, it soon turns out, his language make that clear. That he's different to me doesn't faze me; I've always felt like an opposite in the 'class' into which I was born. I felt totally out of place as a private-school boy, living alongside wealthy graziers' sons, whose parents sported false English accents and lived a life pretty much full of pretence.

But why the chip on Tony's shoulder? I wonder. I sense he's far stronger than me (which wouldn't be hard) – he has a fit, nuggety build – and I promptly decide to be on my guard. His dark, curly hair makes me wonder if he's part-Aboriginal. He's quite good-looking when he smiles – not that he smiles much.

'So,' I ask, 'how long have you been at Burenda, Tony?'

'Three months,' he replies, from behind the magazine, which he then lowers. 'And I can't wait to get the fuck out of the place,' he adds, now glaring at me.

My heart sinks. Why am I always lumbered with the misery boots?

I try to get on with people. If I were to do one of those personality tests, I'm sure even at twenty I'd come across as a peacemaker. 'For blessed are they . . .' I like to get on, and to see other people get on as well. I believe everyone is equal, that we're all put on God's earth to battle life's vicissitudes together. I like to mix with people, all people. Conflict appals me. My Jesus side wants to make friends with Tony, but then you need two eggs to make a half-decent omelette.

For some reason, Tony makes me think back to Freckles at Mr Donnet's swimming pool. He was from a public high school yet our love of swimming cut through any ethnic, social or religious barrier. Our backgrounds, our families' means, our schooling, were irrelevant. Swimming connected us; it made us soul mates.

I sense I'm not about to become Tony's soul mate. Anyway, there's nowhere to swim.

Tony ignores me and resumes reading his horsey magazine. I decide to go for a walk.

I venture up through the kitchen and the stockmen's mess. The dining area is pretty basic, with trestle tables and bench seats – not a comfortable chair in the room. I notice another, much newer Queenslander-type building two hundred metres north-west of the homestead. It turns out to be the stud sheep shed: a huge, elevated, modern facility with open walls to let air in and numerous small pens inside. Around the outside there are eight small grass yards – four down either side – with a healthy crop of lucerne growing in each one thanks to an abundant water supply, which must come via the hoses and sprinklers scattered about. I notice the hoses aren't rolled up, which suggests their continual use. Only the homestead garden and these lucerne pens sport green grass – definitely a sign of priority and status.

The shed houses just a handful of stud rams and ewes. Judging by the whiteness of their fleeces, I guess sheep must spend all of their life inside the shed, except when they're allowed out onto the lucerne. That the shed is nine-tenths empty seems such a waste and begs questions – such as whether Burenda does in fact do much trade – even if the few heavily woolled sheep which live in it do look dreadfully pampered.

Dinner is an experience. The stockmen and station hands, of course, eat in their mess, while we jackaroos dine in the homestead dining room with the Lawsons.

Apart from being amused by the way Tony gathers peas on the face of his fork – he wouldn't score too highly at the Frasers' dining table – I'm distracted by the out-of-control behaviour of Cameron and Billy.

'Cut that out,' Henry orders his elder son, who sings at the table. Cameron takes absolutely no notice. For his part, Billy climbs up on the table and tries to swing from the rotating fan above. I can't believe that the parents do absolutely nothing to curtail them. And apart from the constant distraction caused by the feral boys, all through the meal my eyes keep wandering to Caroline's poor attempt at wearing her blouse.

After dinner, while the boys run off to murder someone (hopefully each other), the four of us repair to the veranda for coffee. The night temperature still is in the high twenties, yet a pleasant cool breeze blows through the wire screens on the veranda, which mercifully here are intact and keep the mosquitoes at bay. I later discover that down at the creek the mozzies could bring down a horse.

Tony downs his coffee and promptly leaves us, which seems far too soon for good manners. Neither Lawson comments. Henry tells me how, what with my background in wool – a fact the pastoral inspector in Melbourne must have passed on – henceforth I will be in charge of the stud sheep shed. It will mean feeding and watering the sheep morning and night, letting the rams and then the ewes out onto the lucerne for half an hour each night after work, and watering the outside pens to keep the lucerne alive.

I leave the manager to concentrate on his wife's bewitching cleavage and walk up to the mess hoping to meet some of the men. And who is sitting among them playing 500? Tony. He ignores me completely, even though a modicum of decency would see him introduce me to the others in the room.

While I'm tired after my long drive, I'm determined not to let Tony beat me at whatever game he's playing. I introduce myself in turn to each man and shake his hand, brushing past Tony, trying to digest and remember each name as I move around the table. Tony throws in his hand of cards and promptly gets up and leaves the room without a word of goodbye to anyone.

'Want to join us?' asks Don, the head stockman, offering me Tony's place. I grab it.

For a few moments the talk revolves around the cards before Don says, obviously for my benefit, 'His father's a copper in Charleville, you know. Word has it a few weeks ago he and one of his sidekicks went down to Cunnamulla and they beat up some graziers.'

'Why?' I ask, worrying about the potential threat in my bedroom.

No one answers my question. Maybe I shouldn't have asked it. The need-to-know mentality must work here in Queensland, too.

Or maybe I'm delving into dangerous waters. Maybe bashing folk is normal behaviour for Queensland police.

Silence. It's as if no one dares comment, fearing for his safety.

'Anyway,' continues Don, finally, without answering my question, 'the kid says if Lawson or anyone here gives him a hard time, his old man will come out here with his mates and sort us out.'

And I have to share a bedroom – and my working days – with this guy?

A stockman calls, 'Six No Trumps.'

Later, Tony's father becomes Commissioner.

Burenda has a 'night' horse, an old nag kept overnight in the yards so that before dawn each morning one of the stockmen can ride him out to the horse paddock and bring in the full complement of station horses for the day's work. If I thought for one moment that seeing the nine horses at Habbies Howe come galloping into the yards was a spectacle, it's nothing compared to the stampede of fifty or more rough stockhorses that come bounding in at Burenda. The dust storm these horses kick up is enough to give Brisbane an eclipse. I remind myself never to get in their way.

Henry Lawson doesn't appear at morning orders. In fact, he never appears for anything. In all my time at Burenda, only once do I see him outdoors – he never does anything approaching a day's physical work. I think of the manager at Habbies Howe, and Mr Allen at Mortlake, even Jason at Quantambone, and their work ethic, their example. Henry is stone motherless idle.

But then, maybe he's employed as nothing more than a bookkeeper, and the 'manager' bit is just a fancy title. One day, I catch him sitting at his office desk, feet on the table, reading *Playboy*. This single act shatters whatever regard I have for him or the office he holds. In fact, it's a defining moment for me, a turning point; my dream of becoming a station manager for Squatting Investments suddenly souring, especially when the man sees me and does nothing to conceal the magazine. I turn and walk away, wondering why the rest of us bother to work our butts off in the heat when our boss is such a slack-arse. Lawson becomes a lasting, memorable lesson for me in mediocrity.

The one time I do see him outdoors is when Mr Miles makes one of his twice-yearly visits. Henry actually breaks into a slow jog to fetch the station wagon to take the pastoral inspector on a tour of the place. I'm surprised the man knows where to drive. But when the pastoral inspector visits, everyone runs. Even Tony quickens his step.

By comparison, the overseer, Phil O'Loughlin, is a champion. He's a real worker and I take well to him once we get a regrettable initiation out of the way.

Phil tells Tony and me to saddle up and move a flock of sheep some five kilometres from the homestead. The instruction isn't the problem; it's what happens next that hurts. Tony, with a conniving nod I notice he gets from Phil, points to the horse they think I should ride. I should be twigging it's a set-up, but of course I don't.

'Try this one,' says Tony, cornering a mangy-looking brown nag.

Catching the horse and fitting the bridle and saddle is the easy part, and soon we're heading out – at walking pace – to begin the job at hand.

'Better get going,' Tony says, after we've walked our horses maybe three hundred metres from the yards. He gives his smart-looking chestnut a slight kick with his spurs and straight away his horse breaks into a beautiful, graceful canter. I can see immediately that if there is one thing at which Tony excels, it's riding a horse. What's more, he knows that he knows how to ride. I also notice how he has all the right gear, which he isn't slow to tell me he owns.

Things happen vastly differently for me. The moment I give my motley nag a gentle kick in his flanks, I find myself lying on the red dirt, winded excruciatingly. I can't move a limb. Tony stops cantering ahead, turns his horse and comes back to where I'm lying. It takes me ages to get my breath back before I can even try to stand up.

'You okay?' he asks, without emotion, as he watches me lie motionless. As if he cares.

Aching all over, completely without breath, I need to wait thirty seconds before I can squeeze out, 'I'm okay', and only then on the back of a huge heave of a breath. My chest feels like it's got a steamroller on it. Meanwhile, my prick of a horse stands just metres away, grinning, with the reins dangling to the ground.

Tony watches as slowly I get to my feet, collect the reins and climb back on my horse. I hope the expert horseman is awarding me something out of ten for being gutsy enough to try again. Back in the saddle, I kick the shit out of my bastard horse, to get back at him for the pain he just caused me. In an instant, I'm eating the same piece of red dirt I was just moments ago. This time I'm winded a whole lot worse. I lie motionless, stunned.

Tony climbs off his horse.

'Here,' he says, after I finally manage to get to my feet, even though I'm still bent double. He offers me his reins. 'You take my horse while I sort yours out.'

I climb onto the chestnut, my ribs aching terribly. I can't believe how comfortable Tony's saddle is – fifty times more so than mine. And the softness of his well-oiled reins. And the horse is as quiet as a mouse; a beautiful animal, so smooth.

For the next five minutes I watch the best rodeo exhibition you'll see anywhere in the bush, close-up and for free, a private viewing. Tony literally pounds my horse's flanks with his spurs. Apart from terrifying me, it makes my horse as cranky as all hell. Each time Tony launches into it with his spurs, it arches its back, puts its head and tail down, and leaps about the place in small circles, as if performing a sacred dance for royalty.

Tony clearly is in his element, showing off and loving every minute of it. I can tell he's done this many times before. Indeed, the more the horse tries to buck him off, the more Tony sinks his spurs into it. It's his way of getting control over the animal. From the safety and comfort of his horse's saddle, I lap it up. Revenge. That's what Tony is doing on my behalf. I love it.

Eventually, horse and rider come to a standstill, as if the meter on a kids' rocking horse in the local shopping centre has run out of coins.

With my horse now quiet and the show in expert horsemanship over, Tony climbs off and hands me back my reins. I get back on my horse – for the third time – and in the moment Tony has his back turned, I sink my heels into its ribs as hard as I can. Who says a Christian can't take revenge? The mongrel horse lets out a shrill shriek, but he doesn't ever try to buck me off again.

'Thanks for doing that,' I say to Tony. He doesn't answer me. So much for us bonding.

Water is the lifeblood of any farm. Without it, life on the land is hopeless.

South-west Queensland is in severe drought, one of the worst in memory. There's not been a drop of rain on Burenda in years. Drought doesn't take hostages, it just kills. Sheep die in search of water, and, just as sadly, even when they find it, ironically sometimes the windmill or water trough is faulty and the entire surroundings nothing more than a boggy mess. Sheep will get bogged trying to get to the water. They'll 'drown' without even tasting the stuff. Finding water can be the biggest curse.

One of my main tasks at Burenda, apart from feeding out

bought-in and expensive hay to sheep and looking after the ram shed, is repairing broken and leaking water troughs and bores.

Often stock will bother the working parts of a watering point until it collapses, causing water to escape and form bogs. Cattle are worse than sheep: they have a determination to break every piece of apparatus ever invented by man. They'll kick and head-butt, chew and gnaw anything made of wood or metal. Sheep too will bother a water trough until they find and break the ball float (a copper ball on a rod that floats on the water to trigger a cut-off value when the trough's full), which normally will be hidden under a concrete cover. Somehow, given time, they'll find a way to wreck it. Another way watering-point mechanisms can be disabled is the old standby: time. Over time, equipment just disintegrates, and when that happens an unending flow of water will spill onto the ground and cause massive flooding – and mud – which always seems to entice sheep to get bogged and die a slow death.

Replacing the internal mechanism on a windmill is a big deal. The inside rod rises and falls within a metal casing, lifting water as it goes. At the bottom of the rod is a foot valve with a rubber ring, which captures water when it slides downwards, then closes before it draws back upwards. It's the rubber ring at the bottom that needs replacing every so often. The operation is known as 'pulling' a bore. A foot valve is normally a long way down, maybe fifty metres or more. Each section of internal rod needs to be raised, secured and detached before the next piece of rod is brought up, until finally the foot valve appears – collectively a heavy load.

To raise the rod's sections we use the Nissan Patrol and a rope-and-pulley mechanism, with the pulley attached to the top of the windmill. One end of the rope is tied to the top of the leading piece of rod, and the other end is passed through the pulley at the top of the windmill. It then runs down to the front towing hook on the Nissan. By reversing the truck away from the windmill, the rod is pulled up to the top of the windmill and tied off. That piece of rod is then detached and the process repeated up to a dozen times. A team of men can spend hours raising rods, section by section, until the foot valve appears. Once the rubber ring is replaced, the operation is repeated in reverse.

I find huge satisfaction repairing water points. The mournful looks on sheep's faces are suddenly replaced with expressions of glee when once again they can get a drink.

It's time I got myself a working sheepdog. Without one, I'm only half a jackaroo, half a shepherd. Yet, with a dog, I'll be able to do any amount of sheep work – on my own.

Because I can't decide between a kelpie and a border collie, I buy one of each – two pups I name Pip and Snip. Pip, the kelpie, has short brown hair, while Snip's a long-haired, black border collie. Unlike Skye at Habbies Howe, Snip is black all over; he doesn't have a white muzzle or white socks or white on his neck creeping onto his shoulders. Both dogs, which are less than a year old when I get them, are gorgeous. Both have at least one ear that is yet to stand up.

The downside to buying dogs so young is you have no idea if they'll turn out to be good workers. I also need to learn how to train them – a task I obviously fail at miserably, because neither dog will ever shift sheep in any direction remotely resembling that of going forward.

Never mind. I will keep Pip and Snip for their pat-ability, if for no other reason.

Saturdays are for going into Augathella. One Saturday, Harry, one of the station hands, asks if I'll give him a lift into town. In what amounts to another act of stupidity on my part, I decide to wear my jacket and tie. Clothes are always getting me into trouble. It's all Mum's fault – she brought me up to be a snob, like herself. Here's what happens (maybe it's Lawson's namesake on my brain, but I'm moved to try some verse):

THE LOCUM DOCTOR

I've arrived at Augathella and I've done a month of work,
And I think the time is right to go to town and drink some
    squirt.
So with Tussie Jumper Harry and the ute filled up with juice,
I give the rams a final eye to check no gates are loose.
Now the town is close to empty, though the bowling club is
    packed,
The betting shop is busy too, with many a horse there backed;
Yet the place to be on Saturday down Augathella way,
Is the Ellangown pub – quite the coolest place to stay.
The familiar sign is missing: the famous CUB,
But in its place, the Fourex sign is a pleasant sight to see.
On entering the premises, the boss is introduced,
A tall and dark and bulky man called William Braddock-Bruce.
Now Bill B-B is a jovial cove, he likes a bit of fun,
He drinks his beer in pints all right, then follows them with rum.
A publican of great respect, his job is never done,
He likes to play a prank or two on any raw, new chum.
So in I fall, take hook and all, as Bill declares me name,
'Michael Briggs from Bendigo; best doctor in the game.'
It gives me quite a start, of course; I'm not expecting that,
The locals form a clinic, and line up for a chat.
A locum doctor, don't you see, in open surgery,
What can I do but accept the role, less me doctor's fee.

Well, up they came in ones and twos, some with wonky dicks,
And broken bones, and drovers' moans, and things for me to fix.
Consultations sure to heal get handed out galore,
God knows what I am doing here, yet up they come for more.
A stockman holds his leg up high, and says, 'Doc, it hurts right
    here.
It's been this way for a week or two, since I had this fight with
    a steer.'
I diagnose a breakage and I send him home to bed,
But the bugger disregards my call and drinks more beer instead.
I continue on 'til after dark, until they all are done,
I've satisfied some half of them, and drunk my share of rum.
Finally the room is bare, Old Harry has managed well,
He didn't blab to no one, though I thought that he would tell.
Then I think of what will happen, I think of the mighty blue,
When they hear in Augathella, I'm only a jackaroo.

Medicine isn't the only unlikely profession I end up with by visiting
the Ellangown Hotel. Another Saturday morning, I decide to call in
for a cool ale, only to see Bill B-B running up and down behind the
bar like a madman, trying to serve too many customers on his own.

'Do you want a hand?' I ask, casually, as he rushes past me to
serve another drinker.

'Can you pull a beer?' he shouts out, now some distance away
along the bar.

'Nope, but I can soon bloody well learn.'

'Then get over this side,' he calls back, nodding to his right at
the hatch.

I pull my first-ever beer, ninety per cent of which is useless
white froth. Hopeless. My second attempt is better: you can see
a centimetre of brown ale at the bottom of the glass.

Squatting Investments is noted for a reason other than its stud sheep. More than a decade ago, the company's directors had a massive fight with the Australian Taxation Office. The fracas is especially memorable because the company, convinced it was on solid ground, took the dispute all the way to the Privy Council in London. At huge cost. And it lost.

Many years after the Second World War, Squatting Investments, like other woolgrowers, finally received a payment – in its case, £23 000 – from the Australian Wool Realization Committee, for the wool compulsorily acquired by the government during the war. The company argued that the payment amounted to the return of capital, not income. As capital, it would not have been taxable. The tax office said the payment was taxable income, albeit delayed; Squatting Investments should have been happy with the interest it had earned on the money it was waiting on. Their Lordships at the Privy Council sided with the Australian Taxation Office. Hardly surprising, by my reckoning.

And here's the sting in the tail. My grandfather was second-in-charge of the acquiring body, which would have made him somewhat a key player in the dispute. I wonder if the charming Mr Miles, with his big waddy and map on the wall, would have been quite so quick to hire me if he knew of my grandfather's role in his company's costly legal fiasco.

Things get worse between Tony and me. One day we're told by Phil, the overseer, to feed out our millionth truck-load of hay to the desperate, dying sheep. With the expensive hay loaded, Tony declares, as usual, that he will drive the truck while I feed out the hay on the back.

For me, I lose either way. If I stand my ground and say, *No, you arsehole, this time I'll drive*, Tony will lazily throw off half or even whole bales at a time, often with the bale still wrapped with its twine. If sheep get bale twine in their gut, they die. Sheep need hay fed to them in small 'biscuits'. Goodness knows they're having enough trouble just surviving in this decade-long drought without us making life even more difficult for them. Yet if I agree to unload the hay, Tony gets to slack off – again. Either sheep die, or I lose.

Tony's way of driving is to engage the truck's manual throttle, then lie down across the cabin's bench seat and doze. The problem isn't that we'll hit something, because there's nothing on the barren, red plain to hit other than the occasional salt bush. No, it has to do with the work ethic, the principle of the thing.

Mercifully, the following week Tony tells Henry Lawson he's quitting. His announcement makes my day – my year. And as if to celebrate Tony's departure, it rains cats and dogs.

Once again, God does have the most amazing sense of humour.

This is the place where they invented the saying 'It never rains but it pours'. Pour it does, and pour and pour and pour. Days later when it stops raining and we can finally drive a vehicle, we witness the carnage. In low-lying places, sheep that previously couldn't find grass to eat on the ground are now dangling, dead, three metres up a boab tree, as if they were looking up there for food. It's a thoroughly depressing sight.

The homestead area is safe. As usual for a station's hub, it's on a high piece of ground. Other folk in the district aren't so lucky. Some families leave their homesteads by boat, others by rescue helicopter. Most in tears.

A city person cannot comprehend the range of conditions farmers face. Occasionally, just occasionally, they might experience a good year. More often, however, it's catastrophe.

It's lamb-marking season, although at Burenda, Phil uses rubber rings to place over lambs' scrotums, not his teeth. After dinner each night I excuse myself from coffee on the veranda and drive into Augathella to help Bill behind the bar. As the clock strikes midnight I can be found counting the till, returning to Burenda for a few hours' sleep before rising at four o'clock to resume lamb marking. I know the crazy regime can't last.

Bill B-B wants me to return to Melbourne and to put our names down jointly on Carlton & United Brewery's waiting list for a pub in Melbourne, to go into business together. That really would be the last straw for Mum – it would give her total heart failure.

I try to explain to Bill how it never would work, but he doesn't understand about snobs. I decide instead to return to Victoria to advance my career on the land in my own state.

Before leaving Burenda, I phone through an advertisement to the *Stock & Land* newspaper in Melbourne, advertising myself as a Senior Jackaroo. Then I begin the long drive home, via the coast to remind myself of a different Australia, one inhabited by two-legged beasts. Pip and Snip lap up the half-naked girls on the beach at Surfers Paradise.

I call Mum from a payphone to ask if there have been any replies to my ad. Yes, she says: three. One of them, she adds, will impress me.

It's the Honourable Malcolm Fraser, MP.

18

Nareen Pastoral Company

It must be because Mr Fraser hired me personally that he didn't give his manager, Don Mellor, a say in my appointment. Because just one week into my time at Nareen, the moment the manager returns from his annual summer holidays, he takes an instant dislike to me. Which is unfortunate because he gets to say what I do each day.

Apart from the hostile manager, life as a jackaroo at Nareen is great. Certainly, Mr Fraser is good to us. Our quarters are cosy; our weatherboard bungalow is set smack in the centre of the working precinct of Nareen. We each have a small bedroom – another pleasant change. Between our bedrooms is a shared sitting room, and behind that, a bathroom and laundry. We also have a television in our quarters, another first for me.

The other jackaroo, seventeen-year-old Andrew Walker, is a likeable local lad. His father manages a small soldier-settler's farm for an absentee owner about twenty kilometres north-east of Coleraine – about thirty kilometres away from us as the crow flies. Andy also has visions of becoming a farm manager, like his dad. After Tony at Augathella, he's a breath of fresh air; cheerful, good-natured and chirpy. His parents are lovely too.

We eat our meals in the homestead but in a small room off the kitchen, not in the main dining room where I had my interview/test on Christmas Eve.

Mr Fraser proves to be a genuinely fair employer. I'm on station-hand wages, normally unheard of for a jackaroo. What's more, as I will discover, Mr Fraser pays overtime. Indeed, my only gripe is that I'm required to mow the homestead lawns on a regular basis. But at least we get to take it in turns using a ride-on mower.

Directly behind our quarters sits a small cottage, home to Nareen's chief character, Jack Willoughby. Jack is Nareen's head stockman. Well, he isn't really *head* stockman because there isn't another one. But he likes the title – and everyone here bar the manager plays along with the idea. Jack, and his wife Dot, quickly become legends in my new life at Nareen.

Jack is well into his sixties. He still has a thick mop of grey hair, and a set of false teeth that he jiggles up and down whenever he speaks. Initially, the jiggling is disconcerting, like he's falling apart in front of my eyes, but I soon get used to it. His use of the English language is best described as quaint. He talks about driving on the 'bitimin', going to see a 'fillum', and the 'Veetnam' war. But I wouldn't have him any other way. He's the true definition of a family retainer: he taught the four Fraser kids to ride a horse, and he's sure Mr Fraser will let Dot and him stay in their cottage until they kick the bucket.

Jack tells me about his interview at Nareen. It was twelve years ago, with Mr Fraser's late father, who walked him around the garden. 'And if you hear a noise coming from that small room over there,' Mr Fraser senior informed him, pointing to a toilet on the corner of the veranda, 'it's my son practising for parliament.'

Jack has a heart of gold and I have no hesitation addressing him as 'head stockman', as a mark of respect. What Jack doesn't know about stock isn't worth knowing. Plus, he's as funny as a stand-up comic on fire.

Like me, Jack doesn't click with the manager. One night while we're sitting on his veranda, each with a beer in hand, he tells me how their relationship soured. It happened on the manager's first day.

'I could tell it wasn't gunna work from the start,' Jack begins, his teeth bobbing up and down.

'How could you tell?'

'Dunno. I could tell just lookin' at 'im. That was enough.' Jack sniffs a big sniff, leans to his left, and with a finger blocking his right nostril, he blows something ugly out the left side.

'What happened?'

'We was standin' in the Quonset for mornin' orders on his first day, and he says to me, "Jack, is it?"' I imagine Jack standing there, lifting his tired hat and scratching his head as if to ask himself whether indeed his name was Jack. 'Then he says to me, "You can fetch the ewes and lambs in Little Nareen and bring them up to the yards for drenchin'." So I says to him, "Yeah, and what do I take?"'

Jack expected the answer to be his horse, as usual, or, as a second option, the Toyota HiAce truck. 'You can take one of the bikes,' replied the manager. It was a reference to one of the new, gutless Honda 90 motorbikes that had recently arrived at Nareen. '"Be fucked," I told him. "I'll take the truck."'

It became the start of what is a lasting battle – let's be honest, a war – between the pair.

When it comes to politics, Jack isn't a Liberal like his employer. Another night after work Jack and I are again sitting on his porch, having a cup of tea this time, and he asks, 'Have I told you what I told the boss at the last election?' The front door opens. It's Dot with a plate of freshly baked scones.

'Tell me.'

He lifts his hat, scratches his head, and lets his teeth bob. 'Every time there's an election, he gives his openin' speech down at the hall in front of three graziers and their kelpies. Anyway, he comes by me house the mornin' he's to give his speech at the last election, and he calls out, "Coming down to hear me speak tonight, Jack?"' With this, Jack lets out a quiet chuckle. 'I told him, "Nup. Won't be goin' nowhere near the joint. You know who I vote for . . . and it ain't you."'

Jack wasn't being impertinent. He's told Mr Fraser more than once, direct to his face, how he hopes he'll lose his seat in parliament because it will bring the family home to Nareen to live, allowing Jack to work for Mr Fraser direct, instead of reporting to the manager. Indeed, there'd be no need for a manager.

Every day for two weeks the manager has been sending Jack and me out to the cattle yards, which are located towards the middle of Nareen. Our task: to paint the wooden railings with a substance called creosote. When mixed with sump oil, creosote works to prevent the wooden railings from deteriorating in the weather. Yet, the potent brew is lethal for mankind to inhale. Even the warning on the can tells a bloke not to go within fifty metres of the foul stuff.

Jack is concerned about the risk to our health – his and mine – and at morning orders yesterday he produced an article from *The Weekly Times* that lists the dangers to life and limb from handling creosote, and the need for workers to use protective clothing. Jack handed the article to the manager, telling him we shouldn't be working with creosote unless we're given full, protective gear – including goggles. We all laughed, because we knew Jack made up the bit about goggles.

Jack of course knew he was on a slow road to nowhere. The manager said he'd look into it, and in the meantime Jack and I could resume working with the creosote. He just didn't get it.

And so today at morning orders in front of all the men, and Andy and me, the manager again tells Jack and me to resume creosoting the yards.

'What about the fuckin' cancer it causes?' protests Jack.

To everyone's surprise, from behind his back and hitherto hidden, the manager produces a small jar containing, of all things, barrier cream.

'Here,' he says, handing the jar to Jack. 'Rub some of this on you.'

Jack takes it and, holding it out in front of him, begins to examine the label, rotating the jar in his outstretched hand, scrutinising it top and bottom in a slow, exaggerated way. 'What do you want me to do with this?' he finally says. 'Take two fuckin' tablespoons?'

Andy and I don't dare laugh, but it doesn't stop the station hands, who can't contain themselves. Bruce, the mechanic, is almost in tears.

Apart from his frequent use of the f-word, about the bawdiest Jack ever gets is when he tells his favourite joke (it must be his favourite because he's told it to me three times), about the two bulls, one young, one old, looking down the hill at a mob of young heifers.

Says the young bull to the older one, 'Let's run down and do a couple.'

To which the old bull replies, 'Nah, let's walk down and do the lot.'

Tuesday, 8 March 1971 is a day famous in Australian politics. It's the day Malcolm Fraser makes a speech in federal parliament in which he explains why he abruptly resigned two days earlier as Minister for Defence in Prime Minister John Gorton's Cabinet.

Not that he knows he's doing me a huge favour, but the manager kindly sends me to kill Nareen's ration sheep, which allows me to listen in to the parliamentary broadcast.

After bringing the mob of 'killers' into the yards, I let them settle while I hang my transistor radio on a nail on the killing shed wall. Just as I tune in, the ABC commentator drones, 'We cross now live to Parliament House in Canberra.' I work in silence.

For a second, I feel mixed emotions. Mr Fraser is my boss – he pays my wages – yet all through my school years we had John Gorton held up to us as a war hero, and now Prime Minister: the perfect role model for any aspiring schoolboy. Yet, my boss has called Mr Gorton disloyal, and I'm forced to choose between them.

In the end it's not a hard decision; I decide to go with my boss. He pays my wages.

The Speaker calls the House to order and begins the Lord's Prayer. I exit the killing shed, pounce on my first victim, and drag it inside, as it bleats loudly.

'Amen,' reply the politicians.

I reach for the long, sharp knife, which hangs on the wall in its sheath next to my radio.

'The Honourable Member for Wannon seeks leave to make a personal statement,' announces the Speaker, amid hissing and jeering from the Opposition benches.

It's time. I stretch the sheep's neck back around my left leg just below knee height and, with the blade hard against the wether's neck, slice through the wool and skin and cut through its windpipe. Blood gushes onto my killing floor.

'Mr Speaker . . .' begins Mr Fraser.

The wether hardly kicks as pulsating blood spurts onto the concrete. The sheep is now limp in my hands, and I rest its head on the floor gently as a mark of respect.

'He has a dangerous reluctance to consult Cabinet and an obstinate determination to get his own way . . .'

I hope the Frasers enjoy the loin lamb chops I'm preparing for them. I kneel and with my clenched fist begin to pummel skin away from the carcass. I then lift the sheep by its hind legs onto the hook that hangs from the ceiling.

'He ridicules the advice of a great public service unless it supports his view . . .'

I make a long clean cut down the length of the stomach. As my knife reaches the breastbone, cream-coloured guts cascade onto the floor where, upon impact, the stomach sack splits open, green slime oozing out to mingle with the now-congealed blood from the neck wound.

'He is not fit to hold the great office of Prime Minister.'

Reaching for a clean sheet on a handrail, I wrap the body, which I then lift off the hook and carry on my shoulder out through the killing shed door. I place the wrapped carcass on the tray of Mr Fraser's Toyota HiAce. After completing the ritual thrice more, I flick off the radio and drive up to the homestead, the day's slaughtering on Nareen – and in Canberra – complete.

It's Friday and the Frasers are due home for the weekend, Mr Fraser now but a humble backbencher for the first time in fifteen years. After work, I take my rod and reel down to the Little Nareen dam, where I catch a magnificent rainbow trout. I bring it up to the kitchen and give it to Barbara, the cook, for the Frasers' dinner, as a commiseration gift.

Of course, the happiest man in Australia – apart from Mr McMahon, who becomes the new Prime Minister out of all the kerfuffle – is Nareen's head stockman, Mr Jack Willoughby.

With the prospect that the Frasers will spend more time at home, Jack is hoping for a different kind of regime change here at Nareen.

Nareen is seriously into modern breeding practices, including what's known as performance recording. The program includes switching from British Herefords to German Simmentals. (Surely there's something treasonable in that.) Inherent in the new program comes the need to identify each calf with its mother, to enable vital statistics to be recorded – things like calving history of cows, frequency of twins, birthing problems, the calf's sex – anything that will give the cattle breeder objective criteria by which to improve his or her herd.

The first stage in the process involves placing an identification tag in each calf's ear the moment it's born. To try to do it any later is pointless as by then the calf is able to run faster than Andy and me, and we'll never catch it. To tag calves as they are born, we ride our bikes around the birthing paddocks morning and night during the calving season.

All of this may sound like fun, even romantic – scooting around Nareen's beautiful, green, undulating hills on a motorbike – yet I can think of four reasons why the twice-daily routine during the calving season is far from joyful: the first is hitting something and being thrown off the bike, the second is rain, the third is Nareen's gutless Honda 90 motorbikes, and the fourth is the large number of seriously demented Hereford mothers that want to kill us while we insert the tag into their screaming offspring's ear.

Nareen's calving and lambing occurs in late autumn–early winter, by which time it's getting cold. Bloody cold. And given Nareen's location in the south-west corner of Victoria, it's likely to be raining. Riding a farm motorbike invites rain, and even wearing a thick Drizabone coat and broad-brimmed hat, the biting rain still will find its way to your skin.

When it comes to the bike, we jackaroos are not allowed anywhere near Mr Fraser's powerful Bultaco motorbike or the manager's gutsy Suzuki. Andy and I must make do with the Honda 90s, pathetic little jobbies that posties use to deliver mail in quiet and leafy suburban streets. Comparing management's bikes with

Honda 90s is like pitting a V8 Holden against a Goggomobil. Still, beggars can't be choosers.

Finding newborn calves often isn't easy. Cows have an amazing knack of hiding their newborn in long grass or tussocks – to hide them from foxes and mean jackaroos. Many times, it's simply a case of stopping the bike in the middle of a mob, and just watching and waiting for that moment when a mother, still with the telltale sign of afterbirth protruding from her rear end, can't resist the urge to go and check on her precious calf. She'll lead us straight to it. It's our cue to ride up, hop off the bike and pounce on the cute yet often still slimy little bugger, check its sex, and whack a numbered tag in its ear. The latter involves holding the calf firmly between the knees, fitting a tag (green this year) into the business end of the applicator, placing the applicator teeth over the ear, and squeezing hard. We then record the calf's sex, and its ear tag's number against its mother's tag number.

As with lamb marking, it's important not to put the stem of the tag through a blood vessel. Of course, by this stage the little fellow is screaming its head off, which tends to upset the mother. There's no time to waste before the mother makes her presence felt. She has two huge, spiky horns protruding from the top corners of her head, and weighs up whether to run one of them fair through my chest, or stand back and just blow snot in my face.

Seldom do I have time to record the respective ear-tag numbers before departing the scene. I hop back on my useless Honda and ride some distance downhill – to get up speed – before stopping well away to enter the numbers in my notebook.

One Saturday morning I'm checking for newly born calves just up from a creek bank when I come across one, just a few hours old, tucked away in tussocks. I glance round to see where mum is before getting off the bike to tag the calf, tools in hand. The calf lets out a huge cry as I grab it. I look up to see a cow, obviously its mother, running towards us down the hill on the far side of the creek – maybe a hundred metres off – to save its baby from this nasty jackaroo. The cow, which I recognise straight away as one with which I've had ugly dealings in the cattle yards previously, has horns long enough to be confused with rowing oars.

I figure I have maybe thirty seconds to get the tag into the calf's ear and escape the scene. Even though my time is limited, I know to panic will only slow me down.

First, I lift the calf's top back leg to see what sex it is: a bull (later to be made a steer). Next, I take an ear tag and the applicator from the bag. I mentally note the number: sixty-nine. Methodically, I insert the tag into the applicator's arms, place them over the ear, and position the arms far enough down to imbed the tag sufficiently. Then I squeeze. The calf lets out its loudest scream yet. Who can blame it?

As I loosen my grip and withdraw the applicator, I hear thunderous galloping coming from the higher ground behind me. I've completely misread the situation. The cow crossing the creek and now heading uphill to come and skewer me is only the auntie; mum is coming at me from behind, at full throttle, running like she wants to claim first prize in lotto.

I drop the applicator, jump to my feet and dive at the bike. I pull it off its stand and push it down the hill towards auntie – who's heading straight for me on her way up. I hop on. With one hand on the handlebar, I use my other to flick on the key. With my riding boot I kick the gear lever into third gear – the easiest in which to effect a running start. I'm heading right at auntie, basically because I don't have any choice: I've not yet got power from the engine to turn and go up the hill, or even sideways across it. I'm gambling that I need to escape the far more cranky, snorting mother and that auntie, however angry she might appear, in the end will get out of my way – which she does. She sees the bike (and me) coming straight for her, with the bike's wimpy horn screeching. She jumps clear just as I'm about to hit her.

Fortunately, mother cow, still snorting madly, stops to inspect her precious calf and I'm able to turn the bike enough to traverse the hill, ride a hundred metres, stop and get my breath back.

I look across to the mother, who now stands over her calf, shaking and snorting loads of snot in my direction, throwing her head around in the air like a mad woman. Then, for probably five minutes, she smells the tag in her baby's ear, before licking the calf all over. Finally, when it's had enough of being licked, the calf gets to its feet and both mother and son walk away, the calf gingerly on its less than day-old legs, to find a new hiding spot.

I ride back and retrieve my bag of tags and the applicator. Only four hundred and thirty-one calves to go.

We ride the birthing paddocks morning and night, rain or sunshine, cows happy or cranky, our Honda 90s giving us little assistance. But I guess it's better than walking. How might this activity be viewed by a future Department of Occupational Health and Safety? Not very well, I'd guess.

As well as tagging, we spend a lot of cold, wet autumn and winter days and evenings checking all is well with the first-time calvers (maiden heifers) and lambers (maiden ewes). But it always needs to be raining before we go out to check on them. If an animal is about to struggle to give birth – breach birth or even just a lamb or calf stuck or with its head tucked backwards – it will always happen in the rain.

Nothing ever goes wrong with an animal if it isn't raining.

A heifer or a cow in strife needs to be walked slowly to the nearest set of yards to have her head locked in the crush and her calf pulled out using chains and fence strainers. If the calf's head is turned back, first we need to slide our hand inside her to pull the head forward. It's amazing how this can be done and both cow and calf (and jackaroo) survive to tell the tale.

Corriedale sheep are different. Not only do stricken ewes always choose to be in their sorry predicament in teeming rain, they also choose the wettest part of their paddock in which to attempt to give birth. It proves once again God's fantastic sense of humour.

Late one evening I come across one such mother sheep, lying prone in part of a half-flooded paddock. Of course, the ewe is in the half that's underwater. My only course of action, I quickly decide (she's far too heavy to pick up and carry, and no way will my pathetic motorbike drag her anywhere), is to lie down beside her in the water, lock my riding boots around her neck so she won't slide backwards, and pull the lamb out. But with my arms bent at the elbows, even though I'm tall, I haven't enough leverage to drag the lamb's two protruding front legs and head out of her rear end. A fully stretched Corriedale, from neck to birthing department, must be six feet long.

I have a thought to bend the upper half of my body backwards, away from the sheep, to give myself more leverage with my arms. It works, and the lamb and all of the gooey afterbirth comes cascading out all over me.

Unfortunately, the lamb has been stuck half out of its mother for too long, and it's dead.

The groaning ewe still isn't happy. I wonder if she has another lamb inside her, given that certain sheep breeds will deliver twins more often than cattle. Pinning her down again with my feet around her neck, I stick my right hand way up inside her. Sure enough, my fingers touch something hard: it's the head of a second, well-cooked lamb. With the passageway already swollen from the first lamb, the second little fellow needs only a tug. He comes out with a rush. He's alive, and I pride myself on having saved two out of three lives.

Does Mr Fraser know we do these things for him in the name of sheer loyalty?

Who was it who said 'Life wasn't meant to be easy'?

One winter's day Jack nearly kills himself. He's feeding hay to cattle using the old John Deere tractor with its front-end loader spikes on which to carry hay bales. While traversing a steep hill – which he knows he shouldn't be doing with or without a load of hay on the front, because it's dangerous, but it's cold and he wants to get home – he rolls the tractor.

Tractors are the single biggest cause of farm fatalities.

Dot is visiting a relative overnight, and no one notices Jack hasn't returned home after work. Around nine o'clock, just as Andy and I are turning in, there's a bang at our door. I get up and go to see, but no one's there. Then a voice on the ground calls out a strained, 'Down 'ere.' It's Jack, lying in the foetal position on our doormat, covered in mud.

He's crawled four kilometres on his hands and knees, dragging himself across wet paddocks and under live electric fence wires. The sad part – aside from the pain he's suffering from his bunch of broken ribs – is that to get to our quarters, he crawled right past the manager's home and refused to go to the door, just metres away. It meant an extra two hundred and fifty metres of crawling.

I hope no one ever hates me enough to go to such lengths to crawl past my house.

Three months later, Jack returns to work, and on his first day back, guess what job the manager gives him . . . He tells him to hand-fill bags with wheat and then feed the sheep from the bags. It requires lifting and manhandling seriously heavy bags of grain onto a truck. The man is still recovering from broken ribs, for goodness sake. He should be given light duties – for several weeks at least – while he eases his way back into more physical farm work.

I'm sure Mr Fraser never hears about it, and I will forever kick myself for not having the guts to tell him. Shame on me.

Almost all of Nareen's fences are electrified. In this, Mr Fraser is well ahead of his time.

As well as the permanent fences that include at least one electrified wire, a series of portable electric fences are used to subdivide paddocks, temporarily confining grazing stock to one portion of a paddock. It's called 'strip grazing', and it forces cattle to eat out a section of a paddock more efficiently and fully for a fortnight before allowing them onto a fresh section.

Every few days in winter Andy and I are dispatched to move one or more sections of a portable electric fence a hundred metres across a paddock. It isn't a difficult task, it just becomes another of farming's necessary duties. The few metal 'star' droppers that are required to keep the fence upright come out of the wet winter ground easily enough – these fences aren't about physical strength, they rely on the powerful current running through the wire to contain cattle. A young calf will test a live wire with its wet nose, but it will only do so once.

After first disconnecting the portable wire from the permanent fence, we remove the uprights and tow the lot behind the HiAce to the next location further across the paddock, where we set it up and give it 2000 volts again. Often the manager will sit on his motorbike on a nearby hill and watch us, as if conducting a time and motion study. And if there's one thing human nature – *my* human nature – cannot abide, it's being watched while at work. But the manager can't help himself.

'He's watching us again,' says Andy.

'Go slow,' I say.

So, for several minutes we exaggerate our every action, like taking half a minute to lift the sledgehammer and knock in the next post. Eventually, we piss him off so much that he gives up and rides away. Serves him right – you just don't spy on your workers like that.

Mr Fraser's way of checking the voltage in an electric fence is to grab the live wire tightly in his fist and let the current pulsate through him. It's not a pretty sight, seeing such a tall man rise off the ground as each pulse pumps through his body. Yet Mr Fraser seems to enjoy it.

I can't help thinking what a good thing it is our one-time Minister for Defence can withstand torture.

One day when we're out in a paddock together, I hold a blade of dry grass and tap a live wire with its tip, to check for a telltale spark.

He looks at me and says, 'Michael, why don't you do it like I do?'

I turn to my employer and reply, 'With respect, Mr Fraser, you don't pay me anywhere near enough money to do it your way.' I'm allergic to electricity pumping through my frame.

Another time, Mr Fraser and I are sorting sheep in the yards when I come across a stray lamb that's missed being castrated.

'What have you got there?' he calls out from a couple of pens away, then climbs over two sets of low railings to get to me.

'It's a lamb that needs castrating, Mr Fraser. Do you want to bite them out, or shall I?'

He replies, 'Either you can bite them out or we'll use the rings.'

So while he holds the lamb, I take out my pocket-knife, slice open the lamb's scrotum and remove his testicles using my teeth. Like at Habbies. Then I slice off the tail.

While I perform the operation, Mr Fraser tells me about a local grazier who lost a gold tooth doing what I'm doing, but how the man successfully claimed on his insurance policy for a new one. He lets out a chuckle and I'm pleased I've brightened his day momentarily.

If only I had a camera and could somehow persuade him to castrate the lamb using his teeth. Surely that would be the political photo of the century.

Artificial insemination, or AI, proves another whole new education for me. The way it's done is to 'catch' semen from the bulls, sufficient to later impregnate hundreds of cows – in other words, make the semen go much further than it otherwise would if cows were inseminated using nature's proven method. A bull standing in a paddock will service some forty cows a year. With AI, one dose of semen can be used to impregnate hundreds of cows.

At Nareen, the aim is to introduce Simmental blood to the Herefords – to bring hybrid vigour to the breeding program. The term 'hybrid vigour' describes taking the best genes of two breeds and joining them to make a new, superior beast – although you don't always get the gene split you want. But the theory's good. It's a bit like an Aussie test cricketer marrying a champion Swiss netballer: the result could make for a world champion golfer or a right sporting dunderhead, if you get my drift.

But with not enough Simmental bulls to 'cover' Nareen's herd of Hereford cows, artificial insemination provides the solution. (And if much of this is about matters below the belt, I'm sorry, but that's what this farming caper is all about: reproduction to clothe and feed us.)

Collecting semen begins by placing a cow – not necessarily one in season – in the cattle crush and allowing the bull to mount her.

But instead of letting the bull insert his penis in the cow, the operator catches the organ in a very long, softly padded aluminium cylinder, which the operator endeavours to hold steady while the bull thrusts until it ejaculates a jug-load of semen. To help encourage a lazy or slow bull to do his thing (having a large human audience, one might have thought, would be somewhat of a distraction), the operator's assistant places a battery-charged lead into the bull's anus and holds it up against his prostate gland, such that when a small switch is flicked, the bull goes gangbusters – and ejaculates.

Of course, for me, working as the operator's assistant and being close to the action brings a million lines to mind. Yet I quickly notice how everyone keeps a stern face throughout the morning's work – no jokes permitted. I also find it mildly amusing that so many people deem it necessary to work in and around the cattle yards today, watching on. As if they don't have better things to do.

Having removed the semen-filled plastic bag from the pretend vagina, I place it in a metal container full of dry ice. The precious commodity will be sent to a lab for testing, then decanted into hundreds of 'straws' which will be used, one by one – when each cow comes into season – to inseminate her. She'll be marched into the yards where she will receive her straw. Nine-and-a-half times out of ten, conception will follow.

Notwithstanding the cow's loss of pleasure in missing out on her bull (females on heat will jump fences to get to a bull, so don't think it's only the male of the species that's randy), one has to feel some sympathy for the bull. He has no idea that by having sex with a piece of aluminium pipe, he's just denied himself a good time with a couple of hundred cows.

Come November, not only is Mr Fraser back in Cabinet as Mr McMahon's Minister for Education, but Nareen's oat crop is ready to be harvested. Mr Fraser promptly instructs Colin, the overseer, to teach me to operate the big self-propelled John Deere header. *Yes!*

Colin is none too happy about being made to share 'his' baby with me. It's always been his toy, exclusively. Yet Mr Fraser wants to avoid the down time while Colin sits under a gum tree for an hour and slowly eats his lunch. I'm stoked.

Across its front the big green machine has a seven-metre-wide catching mouth (called a comb), into which grain stalks and seed heads enter as the machine glides seamlessly across the paddock. The comb can be raised or lowered hydraulically to allow as little or as much of the stalk, but always the seed head, to enter its mouth. Cutting teeth whiz back and forth at the bottom of the comb along its full length – like a hundred sets of barber's hair clippers joined side by side. The seed heads enter the machine proper and get threshed over a series of metal trays, which act as sieves – they have holes just big enough to allow only a particular-sized variety of grain to pass through, while pieces of stalk and weeds or other bits and pieces are shaken through to the back of the header, where they fall to the ground. The grain is then sent up an internal auger to a bin behind the operator's platform. And when the bin is full of oats (in our case), a warning light flickers and a truck and trailer (normally my job) appears and the bin is dispatched via yet another auger into the truck and trailer.

The header mostly only breaks down when you try to feed rocks or tree branches through it.

As I say, my job is normally to drive the truck back and forth between the paddock and the silo back at the homestead, while Colin continues to do laps of the paddock on the header.

On the day Mr Fraser tells his overseer to teach me to drive the contraption, Colin reluctantly gets me to stand next to him on the driver's platform while he does several laps of the paddock.

There is just enough room for us both to be here. He begins the lesson by showing me what each lever and pedal does, and how to start and stop the cutting and threshing mechanism, as well as how to drive the vehicle itself.

After a final lap with me driving and him standing, Colin at last allows me to drive the big girl on my own. All I have to do is to keep the left side of the comb in line with the leading edge of the crop and at the right height, and watch out for rocks and tree branches lying on the ground. I also need to avoid massive gum trees standing in the way, and to watch that the grain bin up above me doesn't overload. Piece of cake.

Driving the header is awesome. First, there's the sensation of sitting two metres off the ground and lording over hectare upon hectare of crop, perched much higher than one would be in any other vehicle. It's as if I'm floating across the paddock – riding on a mat – stalks swaying back and forth under me in the sweet-smelling, hot spring-cum-summer northerly breeze.

I'm on top of the world. And what a beautiful, glorious and picturesque world Nareen is.

The next mesmerising experience is the array of controls for both hands and feet: things that make the machine go forward and back, and which raise and lower the huge comb below me, as well as levers that make the cutters race back and forth inside the comb, and then even more levers to operate the thresher.

Finally, there's the motion of spinning the entire machine left or right, which with turning wheels at the rear and power steering makes for another special sensation.

Add a touch of speed as I skirt Nareen's massive gum trees, and oh, what fun this is.

Colin, meanwhile, watches me like a hawk as he eats, all the while stewing over the fact that someone other than him has control of his baby. I'm having a ball, swinging the big machine about, lifting and lowering the power-assisted wide comb – just because I can – feeling power like I've never had before, right here at my fingertips.

Suddenly, having become almost too casual about the whole thing, I come face-to-face with a massive gum tree. To avoid it, I spin the power steering far too sharply and, in doing so, I under-estimate its quick response. I very nearly tip the big bugger over. In an instant, Colin is on his feet, waving madly for me to come back to him. He's furious, and when I get back he says that if I ever drive the header like that again, he'll tell the manager. It will then get back to Mr Fraser, which wouldn't be a good look. It would probably lead to a lecture on small things like trust and responsibility.

But I was only being a jackaroo, Mr Fraser. A jackaroo who, as Dick Webb used to say, costs him on average $5000 a year in breakages. But I haven't broken anything here – yet.

I love being at Nareen. It's December already and I'm given the job of making econ fodder rolls. Thousands of them. I use the same old John Deere tractor that Jack tipped over and nearly killed himself on back in winter. This time the tractor tows a relatively small and harmless piece of machinery, which takes in windrowed grass and spits it out the back as small round bales of hay. The tractor needs to be driven at walking pace, something not ideally suited to the state of mind of your average jackaroo. Nevertheless, I'm happy in the knowledge that I'm turning out hundreds upon hundreds of useful hay bales.

Mr Fraser pays overtime, and because of daylight saving I get paid even more. It makes the typical Queensland farmer's ration-ale for objecting to daylight legitimate and fully understandable; it has to do with money. Instead of the grass drying off from the morning dew by ten o'clock, and thus rendering it ready for cutting, with daylight saving, the grass doesn't dry off until eleven o'clock. Normal knock-off time is five-thirty p.m., although harvesting continues until dark – around three hours of paid overtime. But with daylight saving, it gets dark at nine-thirty p.m., meaning an extra hour of work: four hours of overtime instead of three. Over a seven-day week during harvesting this amounts to an extra day's pay.

I can't wait for Christmas Day, because I'll earn triple time through to nine-thirty p.m. I phone Mum and tell her to forget the Christmas turkey. I'm staying at Nareen to make serious money.

Christmas morning comes, but just as I'm fuelling up the tractor to head out to the paddock to begin making hay bales, Mr Fraser appears. Bugger.

'Merry Christmas, Michael,' he says.

'Merry Christmas, Mr Fraser,' I reply, wishing I'd been quicker to get going.

'What are your plans for today?'

I think I know what's about to happen next. 'Making hay, Mr Fraser.'

'No you're not,' he says, in his inimitable way that's impossible to argue with. 'Put the tractor away, and come over to the house at midday and have Christmas lunch with the family.'

Bugger again. So much for triple time.

Of course, Mr Fraser's kindness in including me in his family's Christmas lunch goes straight over this dopey 22-year-old's head. I'm miffed at not being allowed to earn triple pay, when I should feel honoured to be invited to join the family for Christmas – a special and private moment in any family's life. It turns out to be great: wonderful food, along with paper hats, even the ridiculous jokes that come in the crackers.

Mr Fraser doesn't want me to leave Nareen, which again is a compliment that goes straight over my head. He wants me to stay and do an accounting course at night. But Andy has enrolled at a new agricultural college, down near Warrnambool, and I'm tempted to go for an interview too.

What tips the balance in favour of college has nothing to do with Mr Fraser, it has to do with the manager. He takes me aside to tell me the overseer is leaving and asks if I want the job. I go away and I think hard about the offer. It will require making a commitment to stay at Nareen for a few years. Am I up to it? But then, I think, the manager has as good as offered the role to me – he must have confidence in my abilities. So, the following morning I tell him that, after giving it much thought, I will accept.

He says he was only joking.

So Andy and I will go to Glenormiston College, and we will go there together. Fuck him.

Although the college principal frowns at my school results, I think on my feet. 'What if I can get the Federal Minister for Education to visit the college?' I say, in what amounts to nothing short of a straight-out bribe. He lets me in.

My final task at Nareen, which I'm sure the manager takes great delight in giving me, is to take a bag, a motorbike and a pair of secateurs to Little Nareen, and cut seed heads off thistles – millions of them. What a prick. (Pun intended.)

I stand in the paddock, bag in hand, looking out upon hectares of thistles: the result of poor management. Every thistle is taller than me, and I ask myself what kind of mind, what kind of manager, would allow thistles to get like this, when it's obvious it would be better to have sprayed them a lot earlier in their growing cycle.

And then who would have someone do a task like this?

But it's time to forgive, if not forget. Time to move on. I snip away until knock-off time, then return to the jackaroos' quarters, pack my bags, and say goodbye to the Frasers.

Unlike me, Andrew struggles at college. Four years my junior, he joins up with a younger group and I don't see a lot of him. I know he finds studying hard; still, I encourage him to stick at it. I even help him with homework from time to time. But he chucks it in and returns to Coleraine, where he gets a job as an overseer on a farm not far from where his father manages a place. Andy marries and has a child, but soon afterwards develops a brain tumour and dies – just three short years after we spent a very happy year together at Nareen Pastoral Co.

Not long after I complete agricultural college, in the early autumn of 1974, I receive a phone call from the manager, asking me if I'll look after Nareen for a fortnight while he takes part in a study tour to New Zealand. It turns out another overseer has left. He needs my help.

Will I manage Nareen for the two weeks? Of course I will, given he won't be there.

Even being back on a gutless Honda 90 motorbike is fun. Together with Robert, the lone jackaroo, I spend the fortnight mostly tagging newborn calves, just like old times. I'm happy to report that I don't get skewered by a cranky mother or auntie cow.

On the first of my two Sundays back at Nareen, Robert and I agree to check for newborn calves in different paddocks. We arrange to meet in the huge back paddock known as Bijantic, and to let the other person know if we are there already, by placing a rock on the gatepost.

When I arrive at Bijantic, not only is the rock on the post, but the delinquent Robert has left a rude message for me in the gravel in front of the gate.

I set about rubbing out the message with my riding boot. Suddenly, Mr Fraser appears on his Bultaco bike, with Mrs Fraser riding on the back.

'What's that you're doing, Michael?' asks Her Majesty's Opposition Leader.

'Just Robert telling me he's here already,' I reply, still with MIKE GET F . . . to rub out.

Three years later, my editor at *The Weekly Times*, John Balfour Brown, sends me to Nareen to cover what now has become the Frasers' annual, on-farm weaner cattle sale. Why send the calves to Hamilton when you can hold your own on-farm shindig?

'See if you can get an interview with the Prime Minister,' he instructs. He isn't joking.

The prospects of my getting to talk to Mr Fraser aren't good. Now PM, he always leaves commenting on agriculture to his Minister for Primary Industry, Mr Ian Sinclair. Still, I wait until the sale concludes and approach my old boss.

'Sure,' says the PM. 'Come up to the house at four.'

I'm stoked, but scared witless. He must know he's doing me a huge favour. While I wait, I go up to the homestead and ask Barbara – still the cook – if I can use the phone. I ring my editor to tell him the interview is on. He says he'll hold the front page and page three for my story, which means I'll have to go straight to the office and write the piece the minute I return to Melbourne, well after ten p.m.

I have an hour to swat up on matters agro-political, which isn't my normal round (my brief is to write articles on farm management). *The Weekly Times* already has a political writer in Canberra, whose nose I'll be putting well and truly out of joint. Still, I'm hardly about to pass up my chance for a front cover story on Australia's largest-selling rural newspaper, the famous weekly with the orange cover.

I write ten questions on the wheat situation, live sheep trade, subsidies and tariffs, not forgetting to ask about the price of wool. And wait nervously for four o'clock.

We meet in Mr Fraser's study and I launch into my questions. Is he happy with the prices he received for his cattle today?

'I think the prices were good, especially for the Herefords,' he replies. 'The Simmentals might have been a little disappointing. But they're new and people have to use them and see their value first before buyers are going to pay any sort of a price for them. When you start something new, I think you've got to operate as a low-priced seller for some time to create a market.'

I continue. 'Australia provides sixty-four per cent of the funds for the International Wool Secretariat,' I put to him, 'yet it seems grower confidence in the organisation may be slipping. Do you think this is simply a communication problem?'

'Well, it might be. I think by and large the IWS has done a good job. I've sometimes thought we ought to promote Australian wool a bit more than we do, instead of just promoting wool. I notice some IWS funds or mechanisms were being used to promote Scottish wool. If they can promote that, why can't they promote Australian wool?'

At one point in the interview Mr Fraser stops and asks, 'Michael, why do you keep looking at the tape recorder?'

I explain that when I worked at *The Pastoral Review*, the editor interviewed a VIP, only to find when he got home to begin transcribing that his teenage daughter had removed the batteries from his recorder – to use them in her ghetto blaster. 'I want to make sure I get your every word, Mr Fraser,' I tell my former boss.

My story appears on the front cover of *The Weekly Times* the next day.

Like I say, Mr Fraser is good to his jackaroos.

Epilogue

My journalistic career started at Glenormiston College. While I had still harboured dreams of being a station manager and living my life outdoors, college taught me that you need a lot of capital behind you to be a successful farmer, and that was something I didn't have. Maybe it was something to do with Mum's and my letters to each other all through my boarding school years, but I decided I wanted to write. I began to write articles for the local newspaper, *The Terang Express*, and after having further farming stories published in the graziers' magazine *The Pastoral Review*, its editor invited me to join the staff as a journalist. The following year I moved on to *The Weekly Times*.

I've no doubt my time as a jackaroo shaped me as an adult with a degree of confidence about him. My transformation from a sorrowful and timid teenage choirboy was surely down to the discipline and training I got at Habbies Howe and elsewhere. While both Mr Webbs at Habbies were as tough as nails, they did have our best interests at heart and I remain forever grateful to them that they sorted me out. I still see the Other Mr Webb's widow, Mrs Libby Webb, and always we share a laugh about my 'resignation'.

Mum eventually got over what she considered the shame of my leaving the family wool-buying business. The combination of working for Mr Fraser at Nareen and completing ag-college, I think, finally convinced her that I could – and would – make my way in the world.

As for my half-brother, even using the Salvation Army's family tracing service I never was able to find him.

Advice to would-be jackaroos

Being a jackaroo or jillaroo can be a wonderfully rewarding experience. I was fortunate that I was able to work for some of the best farmer-graziers around.

Yet, from time to time we hear of bad things happening. At Rockhampton some years ago, I met a recruitment agent who specialised in placing jackaroos. She told me horrific stories of young boys, swept up by romantic and idealistic dreams, being treated dreadfully. In some cases – I stress *some* cases – appalling owners and managers sent young boys out for lengthy periods alone at remote out-stations, desolate places consisting of nothing more than a hut in the desert. Some poor kids became lost and went mad. One boy left his job as a jackaroo confused and disillusioned. He cried his eyes out in front of the recruitment person as he related his experience. When he later took his own life, the agent removed the station from her books, vowing to scrutinise potential managers far more carefully in future. Hopefully, things have improved.

To a young person thinking of spending a year as a jackaroo or jillaroo, my advice is to check carefully that the potential employer is reputable. Ask around; talk to a reliable stock and station agent, read the written job description – make sure there *is* a job description. Its contents will show whether the property takes having jackaroos seriously. Make sure there are responsible women on the property. Women are more likely to care about a boy or girl's welfare. Check too to ensure there are safety structures in place, including rules about wearing helmets on horses and motorbikes. Occupational health and safety issues should be taken seriously.

Some larger pastoral companies offer agricultural college course credits as part of their training. Contact an agricultural college to see if it has a list of recommended stations for jackaroos or jillaroos.

Check out advertisements in magazines, such as R. M. Williams Publishing's *Outback*. The magazine carries numerous ads for jackaroos. If you do get a job on one of the stations advertised in the press, write to the editor and tell them about your experiences.

Remember the interview process is a two-way thing. You are perfectly entitled to believe that you are interviewing the employer, just as much as he or she is interviewing you – even if sometimes the interview is more about common sense and table manners, rather than boring questions about past farming experience. Just be careful when they offer you a beer or serve spaghetti for lunch. Ask whatever questions you like. Do your homework and be careful.

Don't thrash vehicles or machinery. Well, be careful while you have sensible fun.

Keep a diary: you will never regret having done it when you are older.

More than anything, enjoy the experience. You'll have great memories to look back on.

Good luck. Maybe, just maybe, one day someone might put a hand on your shoulder and say, 'Well done, son. That's my boy.'

Acknowledgements

First and sincere thanks go to Ben Ball, publisher, and Michael Nolan, editor, at Penguin. I will remain grateful and indebted to you both forever.

Those who provided invaluable feedback include my wife Elaine Furniss, daughter-in-law Jessie Thornton, friends Di Appleby, Lyn Groves, Barry Heard, Robyn Walton and Grahame Whyte, as well as members of the Writers' Group in Hanoi. I thank our many dinner guests who urged me to put my jackarooing anecdotes into writing. I mention particularly a former work colleague, the late Ron Sampson, who, after reading my book on fundraising said I should write a real story.

I especially thank Mr and Mrs Fraser. My memoir would be incomplete without including my wonderful year at Nareen. Of the four Mr and Mrs Webbs at Habbies Howe, only the Other Mr Webb's widow, Mrs Libby Webb, remains alive. This Mrs Webb was always kind and gentle towards us jackaroos.

Finally, I acknowledge my late mother, Beverley. While I've been a bit hard on her – she was hard on me, too – Mum wrote to me at boarding school often twice a week for seven years, in every letter telling me to stand up straight. I wrote back weekly, sometimes more often, telling her I was standing up straight. Mum gave me a love for writing.

Some names and characters have been altered to protect individuals.

I'd love to hear about your jackarooing and jillarooing experiences.
Write to me at **jackaroobook@gmail.com** and check out my website at
www.michaelthorntonbooks.com.